Choose Results!

Choose Results!

Make a Measurable Difference Through Aligned Action

Raj Chawla, The OCL Group

Foreword by Michael McAfee

FIRST PERSON PRODUCTIONS ⚓ MADISON, WISCONSIN

Choose Results! Make a Measurable Difference Through Aligned Action. First Edition

Copyright ©2018 Raj Chawla. All rights reserved.

Published by First Person Productions and printed in the United States of America. Except as permitted under the United States Copyright Act of 1976, no part of this publication may be reproduced or distributed in any form or by any means, or stored in a database or retrieval system, without the prior written permission of the publisher.

This book is designed to provide information and motivation. It is sold with the understanding that the publisher is not engaged in rendering psychological, legal, or any other kind of professional advice. No warranties or guarantees are expressed or implied by the publisher's choice to include any of the content in this volume. Neither the publisher nor the author shall be liable for any physical, psychological, emotional, financial, or commercial damages, including, but not limited to, special, incidental, consequential or other damages. Our views and rights are the same: You are responsible for your own choices, actions, and results.

Cover and Interior design by Sarah White

978-0-9990538-5-0

This book is available at special quantity discounts. The author is available for consulting or speaking engagements.

www.chooseresultsbook.com
Linkedin: https://www.linkedin.com/in/raj-chawla-3a55b95/
Twitter: https://twitter.com/RajChawla

Raj Chawla
815 Gist Avenue
Silver Spring MD 20910
raj@the-oclgroup.com

CONTENTS

Foreword ix
Call to Action xi
Preface xiii
    What is Results Leadership? xiv
Introduction xvii
    Practice: The Pathway to Greater Knowing xx
    How to Use this Book xxi

PART ONE: From Fragmentation to Shared Results 1

Chapter 1: The Kinds of Problems Results Leaders Face 3
    The Nature of the Problem: A Language for Results Leadership .. 7
    Multiple Stakeholders: Multiple Interests 16
    The Dynamics of Working to Address Complex Public Problems:
        Power and Conflict 17
    Back to Indianola 20
    Chapter 1 Summary 22

Chapter 2: Aligned Contributions—From Fragmentation to
    Shared Accountability 23
    The Theory of Aligned Contributions: The Conceptual
        Underpinning of Shared Accountability 25
    Results Leader: Jolie Bain Pillsbury 27
    Results Leader: Jim Czarniak 29
    Moving Toward Urgency and Accountability 34
    Working in High Action and High Alignment 41
    Working Toward Results: Impact of Low Action/
        Low Alignment 49
    Chapter 2 Summary 51
    Apps/Tools for Chapter 2 53

Chapter 3: Moving Toward Execution—The Results Action Plan ... 67
    Commit to Using Data 69
    How Results Leaders Do Data Analysis 75
    Executing the Results Action Plan in Indianola 87
    Results Leaders: Josh Davis, Karin Scott, Carolyn Willis and
        Deborah Moore 95
    Chapter 3 Summary 98
    Apps/Tools for Chapter 3 99

Choose Results!

PART TWO: Executing to Scope and Scale 111

Chapter 4: "Me"—Leader Readiness and Working on the Self 115
    The Leader's Foundation: Intent, Values, and Purpose 117
    Results Leader: Dr. Deborah Moore 118
    Mental Models: A Gateway for Understanding Yourself and
        Working With Others 120
    Becoming a Learner: The Way To Manage Cognitive Biases . . 128
    Jenny's Learning Cycle: An In-Depth Example 133
    The Leader as Learner 135
    Chapter 4 Summary 139
    Apps/Tools for Chapter 4 141

Chapter 5: "Me with You"—Work Group Readiness 149
    Honoring Your Word: Requests, Offers, Promises 151
    Honoring Your Role 159
    Results Leader: Austin Dickson 162
    Honoring Relationships: Creating Resilience 163
    Chapter 5 Summary 170
    Apps/Tools for Chapter 5 171

Chapter 6: "Us"—Creating a Results Culture 183
    Collaborative Work Cycle 185
    Work v. Survival: What is the Primary Task? 187
    Creating a Robust Results Culture 194
    Engaging in Intentional Conversations: How the
        Results Culture Comes to Life 200
    Results Leader: David Newell 202
    How a Robust Results Culture Supports Aligned Action 208
    Results Leader: Dreama Gentry 209
    Chapter 6 Summary 214
    Apps/Tools for Chapter 6 215

Chapter 7: "Us in the World"—Working Toward Scope and Scale . . . 237
    Ex-Offenders Successfully Reintegrate Into Their Community . . . 237
    Working Toward Scope and Scale 243
    Executing at a Systems Level 246
    Shared Performance Measures: The Pathway to Scope
        and Scale 256
    Rapid-cycle Quality Improvement: Making Adjustments
        as You Go! 260
    Chapter 7 Summary 268
    Apps/Tools for Chapter 7 269

Call to Action: Choose Results........................279

Acknowledgements *283*
Next Steps... *285*
Bibliography *287*
Notes.. *291*

DEDICATION

To Rajender and Sunita for bringing forth the wisdom of the past
To Leena and Keva for holding the possibility of the future
To Patton for the here and now

Foreword

Michael McAfee

I met Raj around 2010 when I was accepted into the Annie E. Casey Foundation Children and Family Fellowship, a development opportunity for small cohorts of senior executives with leadership responsibilities in large public sector service systems, major community-based service organizations, or advocacy initiatives aimed at improving outcomes for children, families and communities.

At the time I was a Senior Community Planning and Development Representative with the U.S. Department of Housing and Urban Development. Today I am the president of PolicyLink, a research and advocacy organization that works to advance racial and economic equity. We define *equity* as justice and inclusion into a society in which all can participate, prosper, and reach their full potential.

When I met Raj, he was one of the lead coaches of our Fellowship. At that time, I was struggling to find my own voice as a leader, trying to master the discipline of what the Annie E. Casey Foundation termed Results Based Leadership. Raj became a mentor, an advisor, a coach—and sometimes even a loving critic—which was crucial for my development as a leader.

What resonates for me in *Choose Results! Make a Measurable Difference Through Aligned Action* is Raj's powerful call to action. No matter where we sit in our organizations, no matter what we think of ourselves, no matter what our inadequacies may be, we can step into our power. Because Raj has written *Choose Results!*, you don't have to step into your power uninformed or with limited capability. Raj offers a suite of proven tools, techniques, and frameworks that offer a disciplined path forward that will get results bigger than you could achieve on your own. When you begin to practice them, when you begin to integrate them into how you show up in your role, and into how you interface with systems, powerful things happen. You have a bigger impact in the world, starting today.

Only a handful of people could have written this book, and Raj is one of the best to put these tools and techniques into words, because he has done the work. He has a national purview, having worked with leaders in all sorts of different systems and contexts. His insight is not confined to one particular frame, nor is it one-dimensional. Raj has seen it all.

I love that Raj is a practicing scholar. There's something powerful about staying in the world, struggling to get results yourself, stepping back momentarily to learn from your efforts and then re-engaging with the work. I see *Choose Results!* as Raj making time to reflect and share some of his wisdom gained on his own journey, even as he continues to lead and learn.

This book matters in the world because this work matters. I truly believe that today, we must get results that are commensurate with the scale of our complex public problems. If we are going to advance equity, population-level impact is the work for our generation. Nothing less will do.

Call to Action

Jolie Bain Pillsbury

There are tens of thousands of books on leadership. You might legitimately ask, why should I pick this one up—what can it do for me that all the others can't? What is its value-add? For me, the answer to that question lies with the author.

When I met Raj Chawla, he was a very successful leadership development consultant, working globally with World Bank and United Nations leaders on issues of great importance. And yet, he told me later, during that time he felt something was missing from his approach. Raj's breakthrough came in the Spring of 2006 at the Lansdowne Conference Center outside Washington DC. There, Raj saw something he had not seen before: sixty leaders taking action together on the largest preventable cause of death in the United States—smoking.

These leaders chose to focus on the most addicted population of smokers, who light up at rates 25 percent higher the whole population—individuals with mental or behavioral health problems and substance-abuse conditions. Even after conquering their addiction to alcohol or other substances, even after receiving effective treatment for mental or behavioral health issues, these people lose ten or more years of life expectancy due to smoking. And yet, for the sixty leaders at that conference, it was not general practice to offer smoking cessation support. In fact, such support was controversial, as cigarette smoking was seen as a right and a helpful anodyne by not only patient advocacy groups but most healthcare providers.

The new "something" Raj observed at the Lansdowne Center was results leadership. He saw those leaders, in a day and a half, move from conflict to agreement on a common result, a common measure, a target, and a date for accomplishing the target. He saw the leaders make commitments to implement the strategies they developed and move immediately to action. He saw methods being used that helped leaders make decisions, figure out how to align their contributions, and take action together to achieve a meaningful and important results for people.

Raj realized that the many of the leaders he worked with lacked the capacity to take effective collection action, robbing them of the opportunity to find purpose and feel the satisfaction of making a difference for the people and communities they care about.

In the decade and a half since that meeting about addicted smokers, Raj has continued to use this results leadership approach to solve complex pubic problems. He works with leaders across the country to reduce disparities and improve success rates in areas such as babies born healthy, children entering school ready to learn, high school graduation, and ex-offender recidivism.

The leadership practices and methods Raj shares in this book, when applied with fidelity, predictably move groups to successful action. This book is a distillation of what you need to know and do to stand for a result, join with others to do the hard work that is so necessary and so important—contributing to making a measurable difference. Simply, the value-add of this book is that you will not only be able to know better, you will be able to do better—to the benefit of those you care about who could have longer, healthier, and better lives, starting now.

Preface

Human beings are natural problem solvers and have a keen ability to address tough challenges. Our collective capacity to solve complex problems has created many breakthroughs that allow us to have lives that were unimaginable just a few generations ago. If you go to the website *Our World in Data* (http://ourworldindata.org), for example, you'll notice that this is perhaps the most peaceful, most educated, and healthiest time in human history.

And yet, problems persist and are seemingly becoming more intractable and complex. How can it be that, while things may have never been better for humanity, we seem to be facing such daunting challenges? One answer may be that the success and progress we have witnessed in many areas enables us to see disparities and fault lines more clearly. In other words, we are more alert to those areas where things are not going so well. Because of our evolution, we see in a clearer light how specific communities or subsets of people are not benefiting from the broader advances in society around most of the world.

Another answer may be that each generation's solutions contribute to the next generation's problems. For example, pesticides contribute to increasing crop yields and, therefore, to more food for more people. However, the continued use of pesticides impacts the environment in unintended ways. The task, then, is to sustain ample food production to keep feeding people in a way that limits the impact of pesticides on the environment. This cycle of problems, solutions, new problems, and new solutions creates an increasing level of complexity that must be addressed.

It is with this clarity of understanding that today's leaders are being asked to confront present-day problems. Jeffrey Luke, in his book *Catalytic Leadership: Strategies for an Interconnected World*, defines these problems as public problems—problems that are interconnected—crossing organizational and jurisdictional boundaries, and which are, in fact, inter-organizational. No single agency, organization, jurisdiction, or sector has enough authority, influence, or resources to dictate solutions. He then asks the following question: *"What type of leadership works in addressing these difficult public problems?"*[1]

I love this question for two reasons. First, his focus is on *public* problems—problems such as quality education for children, safe communities, a clean environment, good health care—that all citizens have a stake in confronting and addressing. These are the kinds of problems that leaders focused on making a difference choose not to ignore.

Second, he is raising a fundamental question not about leadership in general, but specifically about what "type of leadership" we need today. Research on human problem-solving has shown that human beings tend not to perform an exhaustive search of the "problem space," defined as the multiple aspects of the problem itself.[2] Much like the parable of the blind men and an elephant, we will often default to what we are able to see, touch, understand, and/or value. Today's problems, however, demand a kind of leadership that focuses on the complexity of a problem instead of its most immediate and apparent manifestation. Today's leaders must build alignment with those who can make a contribution to addressing the global nature of the problem, and they must practice discipline to execute results.

The purpose of this book is to support leaders to practice this kind of leadership, or what I call "Results Leadership." The following pages present key tools, skills, and practices that will help a wide group of leaders make progress on public problems by focusing on the results they want and by building accountability in their achievement.

What is Results Leadership?

Many conversations about leadership focus on the individual leader. The question at the center of these conversations is: How can a leader influence and lead others in order to achieve a task or goal? Results Leadership is different because its primary focus is not on the individual but on results. The question at the center of Results Leadership is: How can leaders work effectively with others to improve people's lives?

Results Leadership is:

- A point of view, a developmental model, and an organizing frame for the work of getting better results for people and communities;
- A forcing event that allows leaders from multiple sectors to work together toward an agreed-upon "population-level" result;
- An approach to collaborative work that capitalizes on the passion that many leaders have for making a difference; and
- A discipline that puts "results in the center" and uses indicators, targets, and performance measures to assess progress towards results.

Results leaders seek to work across the boundaries of organizations and systems. Their goal is to align their work with others to achieve a common result. Working in this way requires mutual accountability. If leaders are not accountable for making progress toward the result—both to themselves and to each other—their work will likely fail.

But how do leaders work with others to make shared accountability a central pillar in their results work, especially when they hold no formal authority over their partners and stakeholders? What is required so that they be accountable for results and not wedded to narrower interests such as any single organization's fundraising or individual's career goals? How do leaders create this type of accountability throughout several organizations, and how will doing so deliver better results?

This book is designed to answer these questions, but also to do more. It is designed to help leaders put into place the practices that will integrate results into the fabric of the work of their organizations and collaborative endeavors. The goal of this book is to support leaders to build the "results culture" that will help them to meet the goals they are trying to achieve. It is divided into two parts.

- Part 1 speaks to the process of moving from fragmentation to shared accountability for results.
- Part 2 speaks to the work required at the individual and collective level to get to scope and scale.

The book also includes several stories of leaders who put results and accountability at the center of their work and partnered with others to improve outcomes for children and families.

Throughout the book, readers will find certain features:

- Sidebars that include definitions of terms, reflections that provoke leaders to apply what they are learning through introspection, and inspirational Results Based Leader Profiles.
- Apps/Tools sections at the close of each chapter, with short essays and templates designed for use with your work groups.

This book and all its primary precepts are based on the fundamental stance that the primary work of leaders is to make a measurable difference toward the following result: improving a stratum of wellbeing for all people. In other words, the essential work is not about running programs or administering grants, but about creating tangible results for children and families that directly impact their wellbeing. That means looking up, working together, and sustaining a laser-like focus on the result you want to achieve.

Introduction

Human intelligence is a rich and complex amalgam of inputs, which include innate abilities; "book learning" gained in schools and elsewhere; and influences from family, mentors, coaches, and teachers. These inputs are key, and vary depending on the individual and his or her circumstances. What is even more variable among individuals—but of the utmost importance to developing one's unique intelligence—is experience. Experience allows humans to build on the various inputs they've received and to engage in the most powerful type of learning: trial and error. In many ways, this book is a call for leaders—regardless of role and position—to use their intelligence and experience to work with others to make progress toward population-level results, in other words truly significant and meaningful progress.

This book on results leadership is the manifestation of my process of building my own intelligence in just this way. I've been fortunate to encounter many frameworks and mental models that form the basis of results leadership as I know and practice it; to engage with teachers, mentors, and coaches who have helped me integrate and apply my new knowledge in various ways; and, perhaps most importantly, to have been offered numerous opportunities to implement results leadership, including my full share of trial and error, integration, and learning.

You will see that this book intentionally includes many examples of how leaders have applied results leadership through trial and error, with much integration, learning, and evolution. These scenarios are easy to spot and, I hope, bring the narrative alive in a certain way. What may not be so easy to glean—and thus are made more overt—are the frameworks that I have relied upon to build my particular way of thinking about results based leadership. There are five important frameworks that need to be highlighted. These frameworks provide the underlying foundation for this book. I have relied on them to get my bearings as I navigated many applications of—and experiments with—helping leaders create results.

I share these frameworks below both to support the readers' grasp of the material as I present it and to make attribution to the creators of each. I am grateful for their scholarship and delighted to have encountered their work as I formed my own particular amalgam and offering.

Theory of Aligned Contributions and Results Based Facilitation

The first two frameworks are the Theory of Aligned Contributions and Results Based Facilitation,[1] both developed by Jolie Bain Pillsbury. You'll see Pillsbury's work highlighted throughout this book. These two frameworks serve as a foundation for my thinking about results and leadership—specifically putting results in the center of the work and engaging in leadership practices to create aligned contributions from partners and stakeholders towards that result. One of the most powerful contributions that she offers is the way to move from talking about results to actually executing towards results. Results Based Facilitation offers the best method I know to engage groups to move from talk to action.

Chapters 2 and 3 are built on Pillsbury's Theory of Aligned Contributions, which addresses complex public problems by way of establishing a result at the center of the work and engaging in leadership practices that align contributions from partners and stakeholders towards that result. Chapters 6 and 7 use Pillsbury's work on Results Based Facilitation as a key to building a results based culture (where groups move from talking about results to actually executing results) and going to scope and scale.

Results Based Accountability

The next frame that influenced my thinking is Results Based Accountability[2] (RBA) developed by Mark Friedman. Friedman offers a powerful model for partners and stakeholders to see how their work can fit together towards a shared result. One of the most persuasive ideas that he offers is the distinction between whole and program population and what it means to be accountable to both. I always encourage the leaders I work with to go deeper into his thinking as a way to understand their contribution to results work.

Chapters 2 and 3 use Friedman's distinctions and frames of RBA as a way to support leaders in moving towards population-level results. You will also notice Friedman's work on performance measures in Chapter 7 as leaders seek to build towards scope and scale.

The Four Quadrants of Integral Thinking

The next frame I use in this book comes from Ken Wilber's Integral model.[3] The integral model is rich, deep, and robust in its attempt to capture both human thinking and human development. What I appreciate most about the Integral frame is the flexible way in which it allows leaders to move from holding what they believe is an absolute truth to recognizing that they may only have a partial truth. In other words, this model acknowledges that the best we human beings can do is to offer our perspectives and points of view (our partial truths) based on our personal and professional experiences. Happily, by coming together and connecting these partial truths by working together, there exists the possibility of being more effective as leaders.

I won't go to deep into the Integral frame but I do want to share the insight it gave me: that humans exist as individuals and collectives and that both individuals and collectives have an interior and exterior world. Therefore, an integral approach to solving problems would suggest that on every occasion these four dynamics should be taken into account.

These four dynamics are highlighted in the four quadrants of integral thinking:

The Interior of the Individual	The Exterior of the Individual
• Values, purpose, intent • Motivations • Feelings, thoughts	• Behaviors with others • Interactions with others
The Interior of the Collective	**The Exterior of the Collective**
• Shared values, ideas, beliefs • Shared world views • Shared culture	• The systems we create • Rules and policies

Each quadrant offers a perspective and partial truth. Results leaders seek to capitalize on the wisdom that exists at each quadrant. Chapters 4 through 7 are my attempts to use these quadrants in thinking about how leaders can work together to make progress towards a shared population-level result.

Ontology

The ontological frame comes from my work with Julio Olalla and the Newfield Network on ontological coaching.[4] Ontology can be understood as the study of "a way of being" or how one is in the world. According to the *Oxford Companion to Philosophy,* ontology is the "science of being, embracing such issues as the nature of existence and the structure of reality." One important frame that Olalla shared is what he calls the OAR model which states that the Observer (O) we are allows us to engage in certain Actions (A) which, in turn, allows us to create certain Results (R). I recall the coaching he gives his students: If we want to create new and different results, we would need to have new actions, and, therefore, must examine and expand the observer we are.

You will notice the distinctions that come from ontological coaching in Chapter 4 in an inquiry about learning and in Chapter 5 on resilient relationships. Many of the reflection questions that appear in this book echo a flavor of "a way of being."

Speech Acts

The final frame is that of Speech Acts, the theory of which was developed by J.L. Austin. It was in his book *How to Do Things with Words* that he pointed out that we use language to do things as well as to assess things.[5] I first learned of speech acts through working with Julio Olalla and the works of Fernando Flores—the latter's work on trust, commitments, promises, and conversations brought speech acts alive for me. It is through the awareness of language and speech acts that leaders can work effectively with others and collectively engage in systems. I build on this work in Chapter 5 in the context of how best to engage with others—by honoring their word, their role, and their relationship with others.

These five frames are robust and rich, and as in all learning models build on the thinking and wisdom of others before them. My intent is to acknowledge these specific theories and their impact on my work and to offer my interpretation of how they exist within me., I do encourage the leaders I work with to learn from these thought leaders and to incorporate them into their own interpretations and practices. I also encourage you.

Practice: The Pathway to Greater Knowing

Throughout this book, there are stories of results leaders who practiced using these tools and methods. The place where I had an opportunity to engage in my practice of results leadership was with the Annie E Casey Foundation. The foundation was a key thought leader, sponsor, and advocate for a kind of leadership that used the discipline of data as well as the passion to make a difference to create what was called *results based leadership*. Through shared learning and experience, results based leadership morphed into what the Casey Foundation now calls *Results Leadership*™.

Donna Stark, first in her role as the Director for Leadership Development and later as a Vice President for the Foundation, and

Barbara Squires, in her role as Director for Leadership Development, helped lead a group of practitioners and staff to build a leadership platform from which leaders from multiple sectors could develop competency-based leadership skills and work in aligned action with others, all to make a measurable difference in the lives of people. In fact, many of the leaders you will meet in this book I was introduced to through the work of the Foundation. The Foundation continues to be a thought leader in this work and is using its platform of Results Count™[6] to engage in a national conversation about race equity.

You are about to begin a journey of learning and practice with peers as you bring these five frames into your work as a leader. The world is teeming with complex public problems so woven into our interconnected sociopolitical systems and community cultures that we can't even agree on a definition, much less a workable solution. It is my hope that results based leadership offers a way forward.

Results leadership connects you to your own values and sense of purpose. It is a way to lead workgroups and engage in a space of High Action and High Alignment, putting aside ego, control, and the differing mental models and points of view that confound our collaborative work. As an approach to leadership, it supports teamwork, intentionality, and progress toward scope and scale.

How to Use this Book

In my work with leaders, I start with identifying the result they want to achieve. Individual leaders may want to strengthen their ability to be a results leader. An intact team may want to increase role and task clarity in order to make their aligned contributions with others. A collaborative work group may want to co-create a results action plan or create a culture of results. Once the desired result is clear, the work focuses on identifying the next step to take to meet the result. This may include exploring the individual and/or team's learning and working styles, their preferences in gathering information and making decisions, and their ability to try new practices.

So too, with this book. I invite the reader to determine what result you are looking for as you engage with this book, and consider your prefered learning and practice style. For those who prefer starting with a big picture, you may want to skim the book and the applications and tools that are offered. For those who prefer theory and frames, you may want to start with the first part of the book. If you like personal stories and experiences, you may want to skim the book for stories and examples of where results leaders have tried these tools and concepts. If you are interested in self and how best to engage with another, you may want to start with Chapters 4 and 5. If, however, you are interested in groups and how groups engage, Chapters 6 and 7 may be the jumping off place.

However, I do encourage you to end your exploration with application. This would mean taking some of the tools and worksheets offered and trying them out. These application methods are not one size fits all. You may find some work well for you and some don't. That would be ok—just start where you are and take the next step.

Conventions followed:

I use **bold** for terms that are defined in nearby boxes.

I use *italic* to emphasize key words and phrases.

Icons you'll encounter along the way:

As you read, you'll encounter three different kinds of boxes:

Reflections: Deepen your self-development with these provocative questions and suggestions.

Definitions: Build your vocabulary with these leadership terms.

Apps/Tools: Apply your learning in the groups you lead with these applications and tools, which I use in my consulting work. In the world of results leadership, "apps" aren't just for mobile devices!

Results Leader sidebars introduce you to some of the outstanding leaders I've worked with.

Please visit this book's website, ChooseResultsBook.com, where you will find more resources for results leaders.

PART ONE

From Fragmentation to Shared Results

In Part 1, readers will work with vocabulary and multiple concepts helpful to understanding the habits and habitat of leaders in the social sector.

Chapter 1, "The Kinds of Problems Results Leaders Face," gives us language to talk about the problems leaders face; explores how the kinds of problems named differ and what they have in common; and introduces the strategy behind Results Leadership, which allows stakeholders to work effectively to address even the most complex and adaptive challenges.

Chapter 2, "Aligned Contributions: From Fragmentation to Shared Accountability," introduces results leaders to the basic building blocks of shared accountability: putting results in the center; using a shared results playbook; working with the organizing frame of High Action/High Alignment; and how to create accountability through performance measures and timelines.

Chapter 3, "Moving Towards Execution: The Results Action Plan," highlights the data and analysis that is needed to transition the results playbook to a results action plan. An example of a results action plan is highlighted as well as the story of what it took for one team to make it a reality for their work.

Part 1 is followed by a four-chapter Part 2, which uses Ken Wilber's four-quadrant integral model as an organizing frame. Part 1 is necessary background to Part 2's application of the methodology of Results Leadership.

CHAPTER 1

The Kinds of Problems Results Leaders Face

> *Our future depends upon whether each of us can step outside the boxes and participate intelligently in a complex world of interconnections. Here are a few hard truths about living and working within a complex system that I hope we can learn in time: In a complex system, there is no such thing as simple cause and effect. There's no one person to blame, or to take the credit.*
>
> *– Margaret Wheatley*

Imagine you have just brought your newborn baby home for the first time. As your family starts to adjust to taking care of your new baby, you start to imagine the future—a healthy body, a good education, a safe community, a good job. You start to realize the responsibility you have as a parent to the wellbeing of your child, even though you may not know all the challenges ahead, or the ways you will have to help your child transition successfully to adulthood.

What would you do if you were told that your child would lag developmentally by age two? That your child would not be ready for kindergarten and would continue to fall behind in the academic assessments given in third grade, in junior high school, and high school? That your child would do just enough to graduate from high school but not be academically ready for college or a job that provided a livable wage? That the best your child could hope for as he or she turned twenty would be a minimum wage entry-level job? That this would be the platform that your child would have to stand on to navigate into adulthood?

You might be enraged or saddened. You might wonder who was to blame for what was to happen to your child. Indeed, there would be plenty of "blame" to go around. The systems designed to support your child (healthcare, education, housing, etc.) might be under-resourced and straining to meet the needs of their customers. These systems might be overly bureaucratic in how they work or how they engage with their customers—focusing more on the rules and not on the real needs of people. These systems might be so "siloed" that they would use different data and tracking systems, and have conflicting or confusing rules and regulations. The parents who engage with these systems, like you, require great skill to work across boundaries to get the support they need. If they are not able to, they are blamed and labeled by others as insufficient and in need of parent training.

In this scenario, you might also blame yourself for your inability to provide what your child requires to succeed. Maybe you had to work two or three jobs to provide for your family. You did not have the time or, perhaps, the ability to take advantage of available resources. Maybe another family member endured a health crisis that took precious time and resources. Perhaps all that was available were "just enough" supports to get your family by—such as a neighbor willing to provide childcare while you were working.

Perhaps you did not know the right questions to ask of the various systems. Perhaps your support network was limited. Perhaps your knowledge had gaps regarding your child's specific needs—it's very hard to know what you don't know in order to address this lack. And yes, it's natural to blame yourself.

In a very simple way there is a lot of blame to go around:

- Policies, rules, and regulations that can tilt the balance of resources and power away from families and communities who need them the most.
- Systems that can serve their own needs as opposed to the needs of their customers.
- Programs designed to meet certain needs, which do not fully address the challenges of their customers.
- Families and communities that fall short in resources, knowledge, and abilities.

Results leaders do the hard work of shifting from blame to contributions. They—we—seek to understand and address the complex nature of the problem at hand and align policies, systems, programs, and communities to make a measurable difference in the lives of people.

"We cannot have a just society that applies the principle of accountability to the poor and the principle of forgiveness to the powerful," wrote Christopher Hayes in *Twilight of the Elites*.[1] As results leaders, we work for a just society, where everyone is aligned in shared accountability to a result.

Results leaders: Leaders working to improve a condition of wellbeing for people.

Case in Point: Indianola, Mississippi

I was introduced to Indianola, Mississippi, and its unique circumstances when I started working with the Indianola Promise Community after they were awarded a Promise Neighborhoods grant[2] in 2013. Such "Promise" grants are part of a federally funded effort aimed at supporting children in public schools to succeed and attend college. Indianola sits at the center of the Mississippi Delta, one of poorest regions in the country. Indianola has a long history of implementing programs designed to support the children and families who live there. Yet, the area continues to be saddled with high levels of intergenerational poverty, poor health outcomes, and failing schools. In fact, in 2016 more than 37 percent of Indianola residents live below the poverty level, compared to almost 27 percent for Mississippi and 13 percent for the United States as a whole.[3]

Add to these challenges the legacy of racism: White families in Indianola and surrounding Sunflower County resisted efforts to desegregate the local schools in the late 1960s. The result is that Indianola developed two school systems: private schools for white students and public schools for black students. This "separate but unequal" arrangement continues to this day. The white schools—which were created throughout the South and have become known as "private academies"—are privately funded, defacto segregated academies, while the public schools have suffered because of years of disinvestment. (Remember that most public school budgets are largely funded by property taxes which voters must approve. Taxpayers with children in the public schools would be more interested in increased funding—and those sending their children elsewhere might be less inclined to pay more.)

In 2011, the average composite score on the ACT (American College Testing) college readiness exam for Indianola public school students was 15.7 out of 36, compared to the U.S. average of 21.2. At the time, the average ACT scores for students accepted into two of the higher education institutions in Mississippi—Ole Miss and the University of Southern Mississippi—were 20 and 19, respectively.

Poverty. Poor health. Racism. Inadequate education. These are the kinds of significant challenges results leaders are really up against.

Improving results for children and families in Indianola means transforming many systems and working across multiple sectors—healthcare, childcare, schools, and more. Equally important, it means changing the community's expectations of what is possible for their students to achieve.

"The fact is, we are in one of the poorest counties in one of the poorest states in the country, and yet we continue to make choices that put our children at an enormous disadvantage," said Josh Davis, former manager of the Indianola Promise Community and Vice President for External Affairs. "It is currently expected and acceptable for a significant population of children in this community not to arrive at school ready to learn, not to succeed in high school, and not to graduate and go to college. That has to change."

With the goal of creating a system of "cradle to career" support for local kids, Davis and his colleagues have taken on an enormously complex problem. There is no simple solution to improving outcomes for children and youth in Indianola. It requires multiple strategies and concerted action by many groups to address these issues. Schools need to strengthen their educational strategies. The community needs to ensure that families have the healthcare support they need to help children hit all their developmental milestones. Parents need to support their children by being active participants in their learning; for example, by reading to them every day. Moreover, there is a need for affordable and high-quality pre-school and childcare arrangements, employment opportunities with livable wages, affordable housing, and summer enrichment opportunities. And that's naming just a few of the systems that must be part of the aligned solution for Indianola's children to reach their life goals.

The example of Indianola has its own uniqueness given the history of the Mississippi region. Yet, the story of Indianola is similar to the stories of communities as diverse geographically as Appalachian Kentucky; Phoenix, Arizona; and upstate New York—challenging problems, complex and confusing systems operating in silos, and resource constraints. While the Indianola story highlights an education focus, these wider dynamics and tensions occur in other sectors that are important to citizens, such as health, housing, community, and the environment. Urban or rural, communities are confronting the challenges of working in complex environments trying to improve the people's wellbeing.

The Nature of the Problem: A Language for Results Leadership

Before leaders in Indianola or any other community can make any progress on issues like these, it is important to understand the characteristics of the problems being faced. This includes:

1. The nature of the problem itself;
2. The multiple stakeholders, opinions, and worldviews that are connected to the problem;
3. The potentially large economic and/or political burden associated with addressing the problem; and
4. The interconnected nature of this problem and other problems.

Because these types of problems are so complex and have an impact on almost everyone, they are often offloaded to policy-makers, elected officials, agency or system heads, and business leaders to solve. Alternatively, they are written off as too complex to address, or are only partially addressed. Indeed, Indianola's public schools were taken over by the state for three years starting in 2009 after years of financial and other problems.

What results leaders know is that to make progress on these social problems requires the participation and commitment of a wide mosaic of stakeholders—all with different points of view and interests—who may or may not typically work together. For this collaboration to succeed, leaders have to fully understand the kinds of problems they are addressing.

The problems that results leaders confront are complex and have no ready solution. These types of problems require experimenting and learning. They require stakeholders to confront their own contributions to the problem itself and to identify their unique contribution to the solutions. These problems have been called public problems, wicked problems, messes, and adaptive problems. A quick review of each of these terms and their origins helps to strengthen our understanding of the challenges that so many social sector leaders face. Only when we share a defined language to talk about these problems can we speak with clarity about those problems.

Part 1: From Fragmentation to Shared Results

> **Are you a social sector stakeholder?**
> If you are, I've written this book specifically for you. The act of addressing complex problems reveals the conflicts that exist within and among the stakeholders themselves, bringing them into the open where they can be addressed. Upcoming chapters explore the skills results leaders need to help multiple stakeholders form effective collaborative work groups and get past those conflicts. Take a moment now to reflect on what questions are at the top of your mind about your own leadership or participation in solving complex social sector problems. If you are the head of a community nonprofit with a defined role in, say, early childhood education, maybe you've always wondered why your programs seemed sometimes to compete (for resources, time, attention, etc.) with, rather than complement the afterschool enrichment efforts for middle schoolers and pre-employment training of high schoolers. How could every effort complement the whole toward a single goal?

Public Problems

Jeffrey Luke, in his book, *Catalytic Leadership: Strategies for an Interconnected World,* defines certain problems—such as too few children reading on grade level or graduating from high school ready for careers and/or college—as **public problems**.[4] Public problems like these are essentially about gaps between a current situation or condition and a desired situation or condition. As in the Indianola example, these problems are difficult to fully define, analyze, and solve because they are so intertwined with other related problems. Because public problems are interconnected, they cut across the boundaries of organizations, systems, and political jurisdictions. Table 1.1 describes characteristics of such public problems.

Because of the complex nature of public problems, they involve many stakeholder groups—each with its own definition of the problem and its own point of view as to the problem's causes, effects, and solutions. These points of view may be conflicting in nature or they may reflect only a partial grasp of the problem—remember those silos?—based on a stakeholder's place in the system. They may also reflect stakeholders' conscious or unconscious biases as to the problem's causes and effects.

In many communities, part of the challenge is that many people don't recognize that there is a problem. In Indianola, for example, some people in the white community may have enough resources and supports (e.g. private schools) and not feel the impact of the complex

Public Problems: Social sector problems that are interconnected, crossing organizational and jurisdictional boundaries.

8

Chapter 1: The Kinds of Problems Results Leaders Face

Table 1.1 **Characteristics of Public Problems**[5]

Public Problems Cross Traditional Boundaries	**Public Problems are Socially Constructed**	**Public Problems have no Optimal Solution**
Problems cross organizational and jurisdictional boundaries	People understand and see the problems differently, depending on cognitive and emotional biases	Problems are intractable and never entirely solved
Issues are often "cross-cutting," transcending functional boundaries	Strategies emerge from one's definition of problem and "mental model" of causes and effects	Technical remedies are ineffective; real progress requires deeper systemic changes
Problems are multi-generational		
Problems are part of an interrelated web of other problems		

nature of the problems in the way that some in the African American community do. In fact, how polices are deployed and the way systems are designed may reinforce this power and resource imbalance and contribute to the invisibility of complex problems. It becomes very easy to blame others, enabling those in power to reduce the complexities to accusatory statements, such as "if only they had better parenting skills" or "if only they worked harder."

It's also true that those who are experiencing the impact of these complex problems may place blame on themselves. They may see the power dynamics—as experienced in institutionalized racism, for example—as designed in a way to create a persistent structural imbalance. Marilyn James, a parent liaison with the Indianola Promise Community, states that some parents have come to accept the status quo. "The biggest challenge here is getting some of the parents to dream again for their kids, and getting kids to want to improve on what their parents are doing. We need to give kids more to aspire to," she says. Other stakeholders speak to larger issues such as budget and resource decisions, the lack of adequate healthcare, the lack of opportunities, or the constant barrier of rules and regulations that seem to place undue burden and responsibility on the people facing the impact of public problems. Of these, which are the central issues to address? No one is sure.

Because these public problems have no simple fix, leaders may have to seek systemic changes to make progress. Solutions, therefore, must be founded on a collective understanding of the problem itself as well as the interdependent influences of multiple organizations and systems on the problem. Everyone has to see the "bigger picture," align their efforts, and create something that is greater than the sum of the parts.

Wicked Problems

Wicked Problems: No solution exists; system is chaotic and adaptive.

According to Peter Denning, problems come in categories of difficulty. The simplest are the ones where the "solution knowledge" already exists. Complex problems are those where there is no known solution, and thus require a process of developing hypotheses and experimenting so that new knowledge is developed.[6]

The most difficult problems—known as **wicked problems** or wicked messes—are those where there is no known solution and the system where the problem exists is chaotic and adaptive. Wicked problems require focusing on a small or local part of the system, collaborating with others, creating proof of concepts as solutions are tried, and experimenting with going to scale in other parts of the systems. Examples of wicked problems include eliminating poverty, fully educating everyone, having healthy citizens, eliminating war. Characteristics and actions associated with Denning's categories are described in Table 1.2.

Table 1.2 **Categories of Problems**

Name	Characteristics	Actions
Simple Problems	Solution knowledge exists in your own domain Solution knowledge exists in another domain	Redirect attention Find an expert or become an expert and design own solution
Complex Problems	No solution exists in any domain; system is very complex but responds in a consistent manner	Develop hypotheses, design experiments, look for patterns and implement new solutions
Wicked Problems (messes)	No solution exists in any domain; thus system is chaotic and adaptive, does not repeat patterns under the same probes	Organize collaboration in a local part of system, and then spread other parts of the system

Chapter 1: The Kinds of Problems Results Leaders Face

Wicked problems tend to appear in conflicted social systems and have ramifications that make them difficult to solve. Conklin and Weil state that a wicked problem meets the following criteria:[7]

1. The problem is an evolving set of interlocking issues and constraints. Indeed, there is no definitive statement of the problem. You don't understand the problem until you have developed a solution.
2. There are many stakeholders—people who care about or have something at stake in how the problem is resolved. This makes the problem-solving process fundamentally social. Getting the right answer is not as important as having stakeholders accept whatever solution emerges.
3. The constraints on the solutions, such as limited resources and political ramifications, change over time because of larger changes in the community and the world around it. Stakeholders come and go, change their minds, fail to communicate, or otherwise change the rules by which the problem must be solved.
4. Since there is no definitive problem, there is no definitive solution. The problem-solving process ends when you run out of time, money, energy, or some other resource, not when some perfect solution emerges.

In our taxonomy of problems so far, we have Denning's schema of categories ranging from simple problem to wicked mess, and Luke's categorization of public problems: both speak to the complex challenges that leaders must face. Now, let me add another dimension: the degree to which these problems are technical or adaptive in nature.

Technical Problems or Adaptive Challenges

Ron Heifetz and Marty Linsky define the difficult problems facing social sector leaders as *adaptive* in nature as opposed to *technical*. They state that **adaptive challenges** are difficult to solve because they, typically, are grounded in the complexity of values, beliefs, and loyalties rather than technical complexity. These problems also stir up intense emotions rather than dispassionate analysis. Table 1.3 lists the characteristics of **technical problems** versus *adaptive challenges*.

Heifetz and Linsky state that the single biggest failure of leadership is to treat adaptive challenges like technical problems. Organization and community leaders are often under pressure to find quick fixes that don't require stakeholders and partners to make any sacrifices—that is,

Adaptive challenges: Cannot be easily solved, because they are connected to values, habits, beliefs, and role of stakeholders themselves.

Technical problems: Can be solved applying existing know-how and known processes.

Table 1.3 **Characteristics of Adaptive and Technical Problems**[8]

Technical Problems	Adaptive Challenges
Easy to identify	Difficult to identify (easy to deny)
Often lend themselves to quick and easy (cut-and-dried) solutions	Require changes in values, beliefs, roles, relationships, and approaches to work
Often can be solved by an authority or expert	Are counterintuitive such that those experiencing the problem have a contribution to both the problems creation as well its solution
Require change in just one or a few places; are often contained within organizational boundaries	Require change in numerous places; usually cross organizational boundaries
Often have technical solutions to which people are generally receptive	May be so divisive or seemingly intractable that people often resist even acknowledging them
Often have solutions that can be implemented quickly—even by edict	May have "solutions" that require experiments and new discoveries; thus may take a long time to implement and cannot be implemented by edict

to question, change, and perhaps modify their own behavior in relationship to the adaptive challenge at hand.

This tendency to view adaptive challenges as technical problems implies that stakeholders, voters, and partners are expecting solutions with the least amount of pain and in the shortest amount of time. This expectation puts pressure on leaders (if they want to retain their status as leaders) to provide immediate answers, solutions, and plans, rather than to lift up the hard questions or ask stakeholders to embark on new learning. As a result, there is pressure for these leaders to avoid addressing the adaptive nature of the problem and instead, offer technical solutions.

In adaptive challenges, stakeholders themselves are contributors to the problem as well the solution. (If this seems counterintuitive, just think of a town council whose members are considering tearing down a beloved old high school to make way for a new consolidated elementary school. To get to consensus, some members must give up their sentimental attachment to the hallways they walked as youngsters while others must change their thinking that "only small schools can be good schools for young kids.") Therefore the ability to identify causes for the problem and offer possible solutions lies within the stakeholders. To make this a reality, results leaders have to acknowledge that technical solutions are not enough to address the problem. They have to frame the right questions, identify the realities that need to be addressed, and challenge stakeholders to take responsibility for tackling the adaptive challenges. Results leaders have to support their stakeholders in examining how their existing values, habits, beliefs, and attitudes may have contributed to the problem and then support them in engaging in new learning and applying new practices and behaviors. This is truly the only way to make progress when facing an adaptive challenge.

The following in-depth example demonstrates a blend of technical problems and adaptive challenges.

Arizona Grade-Level Reading

The Campaign for Grade Level Reading,[9] as implemented in the state of Arizona and the city of Phoenix, offers a vivid example of the challenges present in confronting adaptive challenges. Terri Clark, Arizona Literacy Director and a key leader for the state grade-level reading campaign efforts, gives a detailed and very vivid account of the issues from many points of view across time.

> ...Initially there was disagreement on the problem itself. It had become a blame game—the parents, the teachers, the policy makers. Arizona had an early literacy crisis and we struggled to agree on the root cause and where we needed to focus first. We had this mandate to improve statewide grade-level reading scores and had to work with local communities to ensure local solutions.
>
> Our initial work was to get out of blaming and get into fixing. We had to acknowledge where we were and stop finger-pointing. That was our initial hurdle. We had to figure out how one team focused on state efforts was going to work effectively with local teams throughout the state.
>
> Our statewide efforts focused on data collection and assessment, professional development, and family engagement. Our Phoenix colleagues, for example, focused on lack of adult support for the children. This meant creating opportunities for more mentors and tutors for the children and encouraging greater parent engagement and involvement with their children and with the school.

Part 1: From Fragmentation to Shared Results

Because we had no formal authority or accountability with each other, the state and Phoenix team seemed to be working on parallel tracks. We would share information when appropriate, offer encouragement when needed, offer perspectives, and show up at each other's meetings when appropriate. Of course, we would complain about our work because nothing was changing.

Looking back, it was clear that we both had pressures to produce solutions quickly in order to show that progress was being made. For example, we were trying to work with the state Department of Education on certain policies that we thought would support grade-level reading. If we could score some policy changes, it could demonstrate some progress toward our work. Our Phoenix colleagues were also under pressure to produce something. They landed on increasing volunteers and mentors to show they were mobilizing resources at the school district level to support grade-level reading. It was clear that there was pressure to produce something and not ruffle any feathers. It was clear that we were defaulting to technical solutions—increasing mentors, making slight modifications to some rules and regulations—to what was clearly an adaptive challenge.

My big breakthrough happened when I could see clearly that what we were creating would be no different than what was created before. I could see that our work was just on the margins and—in fact—we were just hoping that something big would occur with our efforts. My mantra became, "Hope is Not a Strategy." I recall, during one meeting, challenging both the State and Phoenix teams to see that we needed to change our habits and our default ways of working and engaging. We had to stop doing what we always were doing and shift to doing what was effective.

We had to start seeing the other sectors that were involved in grade-level reading—for example, we had to start looking at the health sector. When we looked at the impact of heath, we noticed the pre-K children who were not hitting their developmental milestones at their appropriate ages were not likely to enter kindergarten ready to learn. This was going to impact their ability to be on grade-level reading by third grade.

We also noticed that the kids who were not hitting their developmental milestones were also children who were disproportionally of color. Also, they came from families that lacked adequate economic resources to support their children. We had to start factoring in race, ethnicity, and equity in our work.

It was clear that the work to get children to be on grade-level reading was more than an education problem. It was not just getting a few more volunteers and mentors—as if that, in and of itself, would change anything. It was not just having better data systems—while essential, the data needed to be used to create the urgency for additional work to occur. It was a health problem. It was an economic—and therefore an employment—problem. It was a problem that was disproportionately felt by economically disadvantaged families and families of color. We had to change the way we were thinking about the work, the way we were working together, and the risks we were willing to take to change the way large sectors currently worked. We had to risk having difficult conversations with each other, we had to challenge each other's assumptions and points of view, we had to start seeing the work as it actually was—not how we wanted it to be.

As the Arizona example illustrates, whether you call them public problems, wicked problems, wicked messes, or adaptive challenges, the problems that social-sector leaders face share a few key aspects:

- They cut across organizational and system boundaries;
- There may not be consensus on the problem itself;
- They are socially constructed by multiple stakeholders who may have different views as to the causes and effects of the problem;
- They spur conflict and tension over the work that has been done to date to address the causes of the problem and/or current state of affairs; and
- The stakeholders' values, habits, beliefs, and attitudes contribute to the problem, meaning that solutions require new learning, adapting of worldviews, and adoption of new habits and ways of working.

For this book, I use the term **complex public problems** as shorthand for the types of challenges that results leaders face: those comprised of public problems, wicked problems, wicked messes, and adaptive challenges.

> **Complex public problems:** Problems that are connected to multiple sectors and systems, involve multiple stakeholders and partners, have no ready solution, and require new learning and experimentation. Those comprised of public problems, wicked problems, and adaptive challenges that typify the challenges results leaders face.

Part 1: From Fragmentation to Shared Results

Cartoon ©2013 by John Trever, Albuquerque Journal. Reprinted by permission

Multiple Stakeholders: Multiple Interests

A common characteristic of complex public problems is that there are multiple stakeholders who have competing ways of defining the problem and, therefore, competing solutions to those problems. To make progress toward a solution requires the ability of these stakeholders to avoid blaming each other and come together to collaborate, use their collective intelligence, and then deploy their collective resources.

Jeff Conklin, President and Founder of CogNexus Group and the CogNexus Institute, calls the challenge these stakeholders face in coming together *social complexity*.[10] Conklin suggest that the more stakeholders involved in a collaborative action, the more socially complex it is. This **social complexity** emerges from different and sometimes conflicting values and beliefs, and from different points of view based on experiences and education. This social complexity can make working together—or taking advantage of collective intelligence—very difficult.

One consequence of social complexity is **fragmentation**—a condition in which the stakeholders who are deeply connected to the problem at hand see themselves as more separate than united, as competitors not allies. Stakeholders in this state of fragmentation exist in an environment where information, knowledge, and resources are

---

Social complexity: The difficulty in collaboration that increases as the number of stakeholders increases, with their diverse behaviors, understanding, processes, and tools.

muddled and scattered.[11] Fragmentation can also be a condition where accountability is limited, blame is abundant, and stakeholders get stuck in a cycle of failure. This is the landscape of social complexity.

What these stakeholders fail to see, in this space of fragmentation, is that they represent merely a piece of the "whole." To add to the challenge, the "whole" is complex, changing, and perhaps unknown. They mistake their individual perspectives, understandings, and experiences for objective reality. In our Arizona story, for example, the different perspectives, understandings, and experiences of the individual stakeholders convinced them that their versions of problem definition (i.e., a parent problem) and, therefore, their version of the solution (i.e., parent engagement, parent training) are correct or primary. Collaborative action requires these stakeholders to engage in the hard work of exploring differences, building resilient relationships, and ultimately having a shared accountability to making progress toward solving the problem at hand.

> **Fragmentation:** A condition resulting from social complexity in which stakeholders see themselves as more separate than united; more as competitors than allies.

> **Right or Effective?**
> Sometimes stakeholders' perspectives of their own righteousness can be held at an unconscious level, manifesting itself as an assumption that their understanding is complete while others who may have a different opinion or point of view are wrong. Would you rather be right or be effective?

The Dynamics of Working to Address Complex Public Problems: Power and Conflict

The first piece of hard work results leaders have to do is to assess the levels of conflict and power dynamics that currently exist among stakeholders. An understanding of both conflict and power dynamics allows leaders to know what types of actions—authoritarian, competitive, collaborative—are needed to resolve the problems that are present. Let's define those types of actions.

Authoritarian Actions

If there is a low level of conflict among the stakeholders, then the problem at hand may just be a simple or technical one. If power is not contested, then the problem at hand may best be handled using authoritarian actions. Authoritarian actions are designed to put the problem solving and power in the hands of one or a few stakeholders (also known as formal authority) and/or experts who are given the authority to define the problem and then come up with the solution. Authoritarian action has many advantages over competitive and collaborative actions including:

- Quicker decision-making process—moving to action more quickly;
- Reducing or minimizing any conflict that may be present; and
- Bringing the experience and expertise of outside experts to create a sense of objectivity.

However, an over-reliance on or misuse of authoritarian action (formal authority) can derail or compromise the hard work needed to address complex public problems. For example, relying on formal authority to deflect or minimize the conflict that may be present may compromise the work stakeholders need to do across large systems or multiple sectors. In addition, off-loading the hard work of complex public problems to experts means that the stakeholders become further removed from a personal connection to the problem and thus to solving it.

Competitive Actions

Competitive action (or competition) is deeply rooted in the work of complex public problems. In competition a zero-sum game gets played out: If my opponent wins the right to define the problem and then chooses the set of solutions, then I lose. If I win, my opponent loses. This competition gets played out daily in order for individuals to gain power, status, budgets, resources, and control. Central to competitive work is the search for power. Gaining power allows the stakeholder not only to define the problem and solution, it allows the stakeholder to contain or deflect any conflict that may be present. Gaining competitive advantage becomes the pathway to establishing authoritarian decision-making rights. Unabated, competitive decision-making narrows the focus of the complex public problem and allows only a subset of stakeholders to engage in the work. For example, defining education as only a teacher-problem eliminates other potential stakeholders more identified with community, health, family, housing, etc.

However, there is a role for competitive action. If the conflict exists not over the definition of the problem but, rather, on the set of possible solutions, then what may be required is for the stakeholders to design experiments, develop pilot projects, implement quality improvement based on learning that emerges, and build or augment solutions that can go to scope and then scale.

Collaborative Action

At the core of collaborative action and work is the central idea that no one organization, agency, or leader "owns" the problem. Rather, the very nature of the problem and the conflicts rooted within the problem require all stakeholders to work through their own interests and points of view in order to find workable solutions.

This is not an easy task. Rather, it is a most difficult endeavor. Having multiple stakeholders engaging in collaborative actions (particularly those stakeholders who are impacted the most by the problem itself) can create high "transaction" costs, such as:

- Time spent exploring the long-standing and deep structural and systemic issues that have contributed to the problem itself;
- Focused meetings to develop interconnected and interlocking strategies and solutions;
- Disciplined action rooted in data and analysis; and
- A willingness to learn, fail, and engage in quality improvement.

To be successful in collaborative actions requires results leaders who want to solve the complex public problem to acknowledge that engaging in the conflicts and difficult conversations and working across multiple sectors and systems—real power sharing—can be both uncomfortable and necessary. It also requires these leaders to know that there are benefits to both authoritarian and competitive actions and that there are appropriate times to engage in both.

The dilemma that stakeholders face is how to make headway on a mutually acceptable set of solutions if there is no agreement on the problem itself. The answer to this dilemma—and the key of effective collaboration—is in creating a shared accountability toward a result by first creating shared understanding about the problem, and shared commitment to the possible solutions. Shared understanding does not mean we necessarily agree on the problem, although that is a good thing when it happens. Shared understanding means that the stakeholders understand each other's positions well enough to have intelligent dialogue about the different interpretations of the problem, and to exercise collective intelligence to co-create the multiple solutions needed to make progress.

One initial step that results leaders take in confronting the problems they are facing is to understand the power dynamics and conflict level that are present among the interested stakeholders and potential partners. Table 1.4 offers an overview of the intersection of the power dynamics and conflict levels to the problems at hand.

Every complex public problem has multiple stakeholders who bring their diverse, conflicting, multiple interests—i.e. social complexity—to the hard work ahead. The consequence is too often fragmentation that makes collaborative action a heavy lift. Results leaders learn to recognize the types of problems their stakeholders are engaged in by assessing the conflict and power dynamics going on in the group. This allows leaders to choose the right actions—authoritarian, competitive, or collaborative—to move the group toward solutions that can be brought to scope and scale.

Back to Indianola

After a year of attempting to navigate the complex public problems in Indianola, Josh Davis and the Promise Neighborhoods team decided to change the focus of their work. During that first year, they had worked toward a specific goal: to placate the multiple interests by creating a host of programs that impacted a portion of the students in the K-12 school system. Their hope was that by creating new programs (i.e., after-school, mentoring) and strengthening existing ones (i.e., classroom teaching aides) the education system would work more effectively for a larger number of students. What they realized was that they could not "program" their way to larger results; quite simply, they could not create enough programs to meet the needs of the entire community. They encountered competition among service providers, lack of systems capacity to engage in a data-driven manner, lack of community accountability, and insufficient funding as the primary driving forces for engagement. They realized that nothing was changing and that when their funding stopped, so would any new programmatic work. They knew that the service providers in their community felt passionate about the work they did and were working hard to cultivate relationships with funders to do the work they felt was important. Additionally, as often happens, their work was tied to funding cycles and quite a bit of their energy was focused on continuing their funding streams.

It was then they decided to engage in results work and focus on becoming results leaders. They took the risk of asking partners and stakeholders to join for the sake of a result—not just for additional dollars. They took the bold step of creating a shared results action plan where everyone was accountable to progress—not just to a funding organization. They challenged each other to work more effectively together. This included a willingness to risk having difficult conversations, to use data to assess progress, and to create a results culture that could sustain the work long after the funding cycle was complete. They dedicated themselves to a results journey.

Table 1.4 **Intersection of Power Dynamics and Conflict Levels**

Type of problem	This might look like…	Problem solving actions
Technical or Simple Problem • Conflict Level: Low • Power: In the hands of one or a few	Setting up a shared calendar system, a communication protocol, a schedule for meetings, logistics, etc.	Authoritarian: • Recognize the problem • Establish routines and standard procedures to address it
Hard or Difficult Problem • Conflict Level: Moderate • Power: Competition over power • Zero-sum Game	An agreement on the problem (i.e., too many children not reading at grade-level) Disagreements may exist over proposed solutions or strategies (class-room work, parent engagement, teacher training, etc.)	Competitive: • Stakeholders work on their strategies that align with their points of view (i.e., stakeholders who hold teaching as a key issue implement strategy on teacher training)
Complex Public Problem • Conflict Level: High • Power: Shared and equally distributed • Positive-sum Game	Stakeholders champion competing/conflicting solutions Stakeholders unwilling to resolve conflicts Political restraints are present Resource restraints are present	Collaborative: • Work to understand the multiple aspects of the problem • Design the work across systems and multiple sectors • Engage in experiments and failures in order to learn

Chapter 1 Summary

Understanding that the complex public problems that many communities are facing are connected to multiple stakeholders, involve multiple systems, involve competing and complementary interests and points of view, and have embedded in them places of conflict and tension is a precursor to the journey to making progress on their solutions. Also, knowing that complex public problems have embedded in them other kinds of problems (i.e., simple or technical problems) renders the challenge to be faced that much harder. With this in mind, you have now set your feet on the path to becoming a results leader. You are on a results journey, like the good people of Indianola, Mississippi, and Phoenix, Arizona.

You should now recognize what results leaders are really up against—the inherent nature of complex public problems. I've given you some terms and definitions that I hope will enable you to think and communicate more deeply and precisely about these problems. Recognizing their nature—what differentiates a merely public problem from a complex one, or a wicked mess from a wicked problem, or a technical problem from an adaptive challenge—is essential before the search for collaborative solutions can begin. I hope you also feel inspired by examples that show that individuals can indeed make a difference when they have a playbook for working together across systems.

To make progress on these problems requires bringing the mosaic of stakeholders together (with all their multiple and often conflicting interests), despite the social complexity that swells as the number of stakeholders increases. Results leaders learn to do this by assessing the landscape of conflict and power dynamics in which those stakeholders operate. They learn to apply an appropriate type of action—authoritarian, competitive, or collaborative—based on the lay of that land.

In the next chapter, I'll show you how follow this path through the landscape of complex public problems, using my Results Playbook to move from fragmentation to shared accountability.

CHAPTER 2

Aligned Contributions— From Fragmentation to Shared Accountability

Never mistake motion for action.

– Ernest Hemingway

There are times when I engage with a group of leaders representing a variety of sectors, such as health, education, housing, philanthropy, business, etc., who are interested in collaborating using the concepts, tools, and methods of results leadership. As they start the process of working together, they bring their individual experience and passion in leading successful programs that do great work in cities, communities, and neighborhoods. I engage with them as a coach and facilitator using concepts drawn on results leadership and its associated processes to help shape their work together toward a common goal. Sometimes they bring with them the experience of leading large, national intermediary organizations and a particular expertise gained from working across multiple sectors with a large network of local organizations. Sometimes they are in the public sector and bring with them the commitment to bring support and services to those in greatest need in their community or region.

While they all may be interested in the same people or the same issue (such as healthcare, education, or community) they bring with them different ways to define a given problem, different data systems to understand the scope and impact of that problem, and different (and sometimes competing) theories of change. After a few conversations and debates about the problem, these leaders will often ask me how I intend to assemble all these pieces of the puzzle so they can work together.

I find this to be an interesting question and I understand where they are coming from. After all, some leaders have had the experience of failed collaborative efforts—where all they seem to do is share information and update each other about what they are doing on a regular basis without deep results. Some have had the experience of trying to work together—to coordinate efforts or to cooperate with each other on future action—only to have limited success or outright failure due to competition and power struggles. Often funding opportunities are the forcing event for cooperation—when the funding ends, so does their work together. As experiences of failure accumulate, some leaders grow doubtful that collaborative efforts can ever succeed.

Some leaders I've worked with have had the experience of being successful on a small or trial scale, and then been successful in receiving large grants to expand those efforts—for example, grantees of the Promise Neighborhoods sites. The influx of funding mixed with the status and authority of being recognized by a funding entity as being successful brings with it possibility, expectation, and anxiety. In talking to these leaders I find that they share their excitement about the possibility of expanding what they are doing so well. They look forward to hiring new staff, to bringing in other partners by purchasing their services, and to influencing larger systems and policy makers with their authority as a recognized organization.

However, this success also brings with it problematic expectations. Their funders and community partners may expect that they know how to solve the problems at hand. Partners—including some that may be receiving funding from them—may expect them to keep the funding going so they can do what they do. Finally, the community itself will very likely expect to see progress in the areas of concern.

These leaders then acknowledge the anxiety they feel about the work itself, the expectations of others, and their responsibility to their organization and to the community. They know the problems they are trying to solve are complex, adaptive in nature, and are inherently wicked problems. I remind them that there is no single program that can solve large, complex social problems. There is not enough money or resources for them to grow their programs enough to solve these problems. This reality is often followed by an acknowledgment that receiving a large multi-year grant has created a sense of competition with other providers, as well as suspicion from government systems trying to do the same things. Even people in successful organizations experience doubt that collaborative efforts will succeed.

The way forward in either circumstance is to create shared accountability among stakeholders and partners with the intent to define together a shared result. This is a dynamic process that involves creating a *results action plan* (detailed in Chapter 3) that allows multiple stakeholders and partners to see the work in a similar way; to bring in likely and unlikely partners who have a contribution to make; and to use data and analysis to sharpen and refine the execution of the shared work. This chapter will explore the conceptual underpinning of a results action plan, in which stakeholders and partners create shared accountability through a common Results Playbook (described later in this chapter). The next chapter explores the data and analysis needed to move from a Results Playbook to a results action plan.

The Theory of Aligned Contributions: The Conceptual Underpinning of Shared Accountability

There is nothing so practical as a good theory.

– Kurt Lewin

Being a results leader is inherently challenging. It is not easy to join with others in the spirit of **shared accountability for a result**. Nor is it easy to work in a collaborative group where peer accountability is required as opposed to hierarchical authority. However, that is what results leaders must do. This approach is different from traditional ways of leading in that the focus is on the result—not on power, control, authority, charisma, or status. For both the leader and the collaborative work group he or she leads, this runs counter to expectations.

The conceptual underpinnings of shared accountability emerge from Jolie Bain Pillsbury's Theory of Aligned Contributions described briefly below.

The Theory of Aligned Contributions attempts to articulate the necessary and sufficient conditions needed to bridge the gap between desired results and current reality in complex adaptive systems. It posits that **population-level results** are most likely to occur if a core group of multi-sector, cross-agency leaders not only responds to a call to action, but also takes aligned actions at scope and scale toward a

Shared accountability for a result: Leaders working across boundaries of an organization, system, and/or sector toward a shared result, and sharing accountability for the progress toward that result.

result. Without alignment of actions the quest for change is just business as usual.

This theory tests the hypothesis that progress toward **population-level results** occurs when leaders from multiple sectors 1) make a choice to be publicly accountable for the result and 2) work together to take aligned actions that are measurable toward the result. In order to make this a reality, the crucial elements include:

- Focusing on a single, measurable population level result;
- Creating both urgency and accountability toward the result; and
- Working together in "High Action and High Alignment" to create scope and scale toward the results.

> **Population-level result:** Improvement in a "quality-of-life" condition for a whole population of people in a specific place.

The results leaders I work with understand the inherent challenges embedded within complex social problems. They recognize the need for multiple stakeholders to work together to make progress. They know that each stakeholder has a contribution to make and that each contribution has to align with others so together they contribute to a measurable difference.

As stated in the Theory of Aligned Contributions, the first step is to define the desired result in a way that is compelling enough to attract multiple cross-sector stakeholders and motivate them to put that result at the center of all the work. The next step is to co-create a shared results playbook that supports both the urgency and accountability to the result. The final task is for stakeholders to execute their work in a fashion that demonstrates working together in both "High Action and High Alignment" (a frame I'll explain later in this chapter).

For example, I was invited to work with a statewide organization in Minnesota whose primary focus was early learning. They ran many successful programs designed to support early-learning providers with the necessary curriculum and training to support young children ages two to five. It was when they did the hard work to declare a population-level result—in their case it was "all children in Minnesota enter school ready to learn"—that they were able to join with others (such as those in the healthcare and community sectors) who held the same result.

Chapter 2: Aligned Contributions—From Fragmentation to Shared Accountability

Results Leader: Jolie Bain Pillsbury

I first met Jolie Bain Pillsbury when I was working in what appeared to all to be a very successful long-term engagement with several international clients. I very much enjoyed working with leaders in different sectors on their leadership styles so that they might produce better results. And yet I could see that my work was not having the lasting impact I sought. Leaders might have had better insights about themselves and the teams they were working with but they were not able to sustain the ability to make a measurable difference after I left. This was a source of frustration for me and left me seeking different ways to engage with those leaders.

Some while back, through an invitation from a mutual friend, I ended up having a ninety-minute phone conversation with Jolie about leadership and results, the first of many. Though her *Theory of Aligned Contributions* had not been formally written and published, it certainly was alive in our conversations. We talked about the importance of leaders holding a common results frame, using data to track performance, and the leadership skills it takes so positive results happen in communities and for those who live in them. I've had the opportunity to work with Jolie over the last 12 years or so as the *Theory of Aligned Contributions*.[1] has come to life and have witnessed the impact of having results in the center in improving attempts to work toward those results.

Jolie has offered leaders an intuitive way to hold results in the center of their work and examine how multiple sectors must align to make a measurable difference in their shared results. Her work has also allowed leaders to move from competing over problem definition and solution to creation of a result that all work joins. Her words below are a succinct and empowering overview.

> The public sector is complicated and so are residents, families, and communities. At the system level, there are all these different ways people think, talk, and understand the world… [so] for the major issues, you need to engage multiple sectors. That is demonstrated again and again. For example, schools cannot do it alone. Parents, families, business, communities all need to be involved. The public sector is crying out for a theory for people to align.
>
> People also can be blind to the fact that multiple systems have different mental models, different incentive structures, and different language. That in and of itself creates a barrier to cross-system-level collaboration.

Part 1: From Fragmentation to Shared Results

The Theory of Aligned Contribution comes alive when you implement it with the picture that puts results in the center. Before you have that revolution, leaders and systems see themselves as the center and everyone circling around them. This is radically different.[2]

The Focus on a Single Measurable Result: Results in the Center

> *Among the authorities it is generally agreed that the Earth is at rest in the middle of the universe, and they regard it as inconceivable and even ridiculous to hold the opposite opinion.*
>
> *– Nicolaus Copernicus*

> The Results in the Center Worksheet in the apps/tools section at the end of this chapter is designed to help you map who else can contribute to the result.

The big shift in thinking, acting, and working as a results based leader begins with putting the result at the center of all work, like the Sun in its proper place at the center of the universe.

The only way to navigate through the challenges of collaboration is to first frame the problem as a result so that others can join in solving it. Then, leaders put the result at the center of the work so that everyone's contributions roll up to make a measurable difference. Figure 2.1 depicts these relationships. Figure 2.2 shows this template in use.

Figure 2.1 **Theory of Aligned Contributions, as Diagrammed by Jolie Bain Pillsbury**

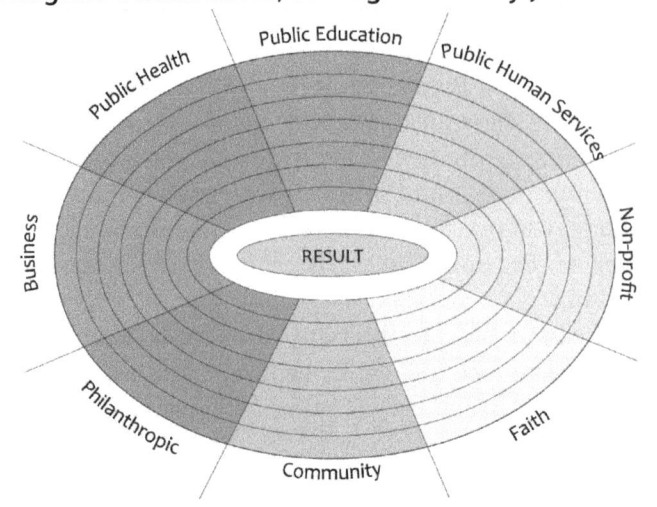

© Jolie Bain Pillsbury

Chapter 2: Aligned Contributions—From Fragmentation to Shared Accountability

Results Leader: Jim Czarniak

I want to introduce you to Jim Czarniak. Jim is currently the Deputy Commissioner for Child Welfare for Onondaga County in Upstate New York. I first met Jim when he was part of the Annie E. Casey Foundation's Applied Leadership Network—in conjunction with the Juvenile Detention Alternatives Initiative (JDAI).[3] At that time, Jim was the Director of Onondaga County's Juvenile Justice System and working to implement reforms in that system.

During some of our earlier conversations, he shared that one of his greatest frustrations was the inability to work across sectors with other key stakeholders to make sure the kids in the juvenile justice system were supported in the community. His powerful words summed up the situation.

> People were afraid of having responsibility for what they couldn't control. That was juvenile justice reform before. My first few years in the job, we changed what we could control. At the detention facility, I changed our policies—but then we hit the wall. Kids were still getting arrested. We would have a kid on probation commit a crime and there would be finger-pointing every time something happened. When they went back on street and committed a crime, the neighborhood watch group would blame the police and the courts. That was the work. The work was defending your bubble.

After his first introduction to the results work, he went home and worked hard with others to create a population-level result (shown in Figure 2.2) that would hold the contributions of multiple cross-sectional stakeholders. He knew that all the stakeholders—including those in his own system—had to realize that they could only control their own work and had to trust each other in order to address the larger issues confronting these kids and their families. He remembers his initial meetings as being all over the map, again powerfully captured in his own words below.

> We had a diverse group of stakeholders—from advocates to practitioners—and they were quite vocal as to what the problem was and what the solution should be. It was everything from things we cannot control, like poverty, to "you have to make sure that people are not poor." It was clear that we could not take on poverty but we had to make sure that every stakeholder could state their point of view and that others could understand

Part 1: From Fragmentation to Shared Results

Results Leader

their colleagues interest.... For example, judges might say, "I do not want to see violations of probation—kids need to go to school. We need to focus on school." Law enforcement was worried about unsafe kids roaming the neighborhood. They said the biggest thing was that these kids need to be held accountable. That was the undercurrent. So we said all right—placement is a way to hold accountability. So as opposed to me lecturing and telling them how smart I am and what they said at Columbia University, I was able to talk about all of us working hard to create alignment toward a shared result. I recall the word "safe" dominated half a meeting. To work through it and get to consensus—that word was important—to victims (of crime), law enforcement, and others. So we did not run away from safety. We said we would measure that.

As a result of their hard work they adopted a population-level results statement: *All youth involved in the juvenile justice system successfully transition to adulthood.*

With this result, Jim and his team used the results in the center map (shown in Figure 2.2) to identify who else might be needed and what their aligned contribution might be toward their result.

Figure 2.2 Theory of Aligned Contributions in Action, as Diagrammed by Jim Czarniak for Onondaga County Partnership for Youth Justice

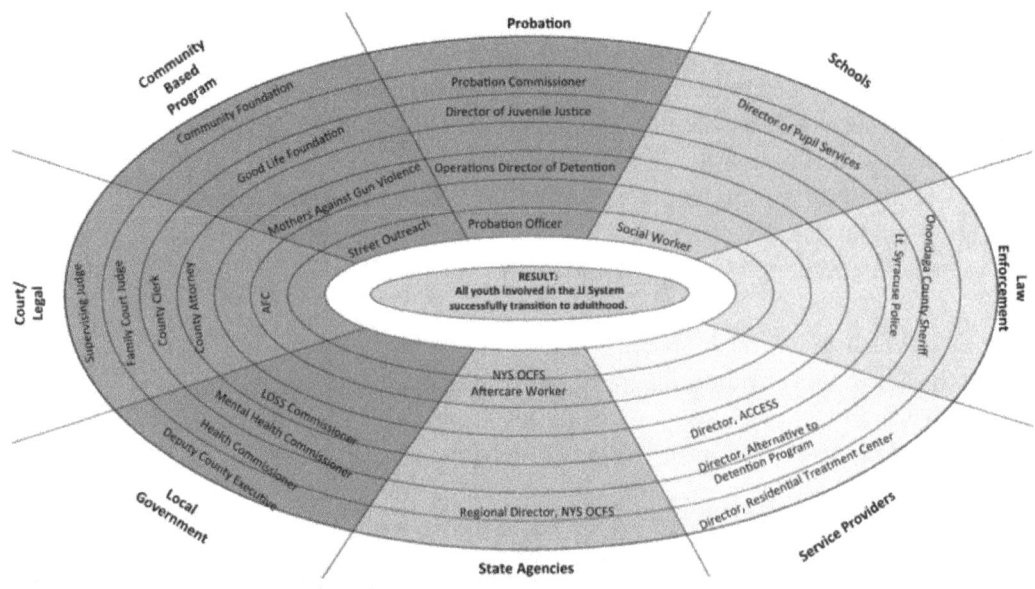

Onondaga County Partnership for Youth Justice

30

As Figure 2.2 shows, those stakeholders who are closest to the result (i.e., direct service providers, like a probation officer or social worker) are mapped in slots closest to the center, while those who are further removed (i.e., those whose work supports those in direct service, like a director of a residential treatment center) are mapped further away. Each stakeholder has a unique contribution to make in supporting the result and a responsibility to make that contribution in alignment with others within their sector and across sectors.

Shift from Defining a Problem to Declaring a Result

However beautiful the strategy, you should occasionally look at the results.

– Sir Winston Churchill

As we learned in Chapter 1, defining a complex public problem can be difficult in that such problems have few obvious solutions and no clear accountability. There are also cultural, social and psychological factors—including individual and collective world-views—at play in identifying exactly what the problem is. Results leaders render these unavoidable difficulties irrelevant by choosing to focus on declaring a desired result instead.

According to Jeffrey Luke, author of *Catalytic Leadership: Strategies for an Interconnected World*, collective efforts to solve public problems often fail because the problem is framed in overly general terms.[4] This may attract important stakeholders, but it makes in-depth exploration and analysis very difficult. The problem becomes just too big. This can lead to disagreements about what the "real problem" even is.

Stakeholders come to the table with a specific definition of the problem that is tied to their interests and the solutions they want to see. People often define the problem to fit their worldview—in a way that protects their turf, advances their interests and stakes, or reflects the way in which they collect and analyze information.[5] But a problem's definition will typically have less to do with data and analysis and more to do with values, traditions, and varying points of view. For example, there may be a stakeholder whose point of view is that parents are solely responsible for their children's success in school and life. Regardless of what the data and evidence may reveal about what contributes to a child's success, the starting point for this stakeholder will be parental responsibility. Therefore, their primary focus will be programs that promote parent engagement and accountability.

Because it is hard to determine what the real problem is in these situations, there is seldom one correct solution for stakeholders to rally behind. Interconnected problems are not only extraordinarily difficult to define, they do not lend themselves to easy solutions. Resources and time always seem limited. Further, most results leaders are dealing with a multiplicity and diversity of stakeholder groups. Each brings a well-defined set of preferences. Naturally, they compete to define the "one right" solution. Conflict emerges in their search for specific, objective criteria for sorting through potentially successful strategies and identifying the "best" solution.

We tend to assume that effective leadership will support stakeholders to embrace a common goal. This may be true, but we have to accept that people may work together only to the extent that in doing so it will help them advance their own interests, goals, and points of view. *Therefore, a fundamental act of results leadership is to define problems and solutions in a way that allows all stakeholders to be in aligned action based on their interests and stakes.* This happens when you shift from a problem statement to a result statement.

For example, notice the shift in tone in the first problem statement to the second, result statement.

- Problem statement: "The problem is that parents are not teaching their kids to read."
- Result statement: "Our result is that all children in our community are reading at grade-level by the third grade."

A result statement shifts the focus from a narrow outcome to a condition that invites stakeholders to make a contribution.

Creating a Population-Level Results Statement

Crucial to declaring a "result in the center" is stating that result in terms of a population and geography.

A population-level result is a result that shows improvement in a "quality-of-life" condition for a whole population of individuals, children, or families in a specified place, or for a place itself.[6] Effective statements of population-level results use plain language to describe an observable condition of wellbeing for human beings—children, adults, families, communities. The quality of life for people will improve to the extent the work succeeds.

Chapter 2: Aligned Contributions—From Fragmentation to Shared Accountability

One simple way of understanding a population-level result is: *People (or Community) + Geographic Boundary + Condition of Wellbeing = Population-Level Result*. Examples of statements of population-level results that are linked to the wellbeing of people and communities include:

- "All children in Atlanta enter school ready to learn."
- "All communities in Maine are safe."
- "All babies in the United States are born healthy."

> Developing a Results Statement Worksheet in the apps/tools section at the end of this chapter is designed to help you write your own population-level results statements.

Example: Informal Care and Grade-Level Reading in Indianola, Mississippi

Competition among service providers, particularly those who do similar work, can be a natural state of affairs. After all, these organizations are chasing the same funding and offering similar services. They strive to stand out through their relationships with their customers and stakeholders as well as their funders. In this context, we can easily understand why it might be very difficult to shift from competition to shared accountability toward a common result—especially in a resource-poor area like the Mississippi Delta.

Let's look at this notion of competition and special relationships in action as evident when the Indianola Promise Community (introduced in Chapter 1) invited a large number of partners, stakeholders, and service providers to join in a day of planning and strategizing toward a results statement of "where all children enter school ready to learn." Prior to the meeting there was concern that these stakeholders and service providers would have a hard time shifting from seeing each other as competitors to viewing each other as partners. The implementation team prepared the room for this meeting carefully by putting data posters on the wall and by having data charts at their tables, so that we could all start the work by reviewing the facts the data revealed about their community.

After the initial data conversation, I invited the approximately 35 participants to share their thoughts. They spoke of the reality of what was happening in Indianola regarding school readiness. We then applied a results frame, or "Results Playbook," to identify gaps, and to name contributing factors and to highlight the possibility of shared accountability to all of Indianola's children.

It was when these participants engaged in a "results in the center" conversation that the switch from competitor to partner began to occur. As they were mapping the service providers, partners, and stakeholders, I could hear them talking about "gaps" and the "children being left behind." When connecting this mapping to the data they had on school readiness, these participants noticed that the community as a whole was falling short on what was needed. It was a powerful moment when these service providers shifted their stance from protecting their program to broadening their gaze and holding all the children in Indianola at the center of their work. The room felt less guarded and suspicious and more taken with a shared concern for their community.

These realizations allowed the participants in the Indianola Promise Community planning day to shift from seeing others as competitors—who felt as if they were going to be blamed for the children in their care not being ready for kindergarten—to seeing how they needed to work with others in a collaborative manner toward a population-level result.

Moving Toward Urgency and Accountability

Once a population-level result has been identified, the work begins to create an actionable plan that allows cross-sector stakeholders and partners to work with both urgency and accountability. All too often, stakeholders come together to work on a common result and instead move directly to focusing on programs already in place: those they are already doing, perhaps due to the pressures of doing something right away or the already-proven opportunities at hand. By focusing directly on existing programs and defaulting into programmatic v. results thinking, leaders find themselves limited in what they can do together. At best, when partners join together in programmatic thinking, they will know what the others are doing and can cooperate with each other and attempt to coordinate their efforts. At worst, the **programmatic thinking** creates misunderstandings and working at cross-purposes, which then may lead to fragmentation and competition.

Results thinking, on the other hand, creates the ability in leaders to put the result in the center and do the necessary work to create an actionable plan where they can make aligned contributions. Doing the necessary work means, among other things, using a shared language and shared concepts that support working collaboratively. This use of shared language and concepts allows leaders to create a shared results frame from which to work, analyzing the best available data to develop appropriate strategies and action, and leveraging past experiences of working collaboratively to work more effectively with others. This shared work is ultimately manifested in a shared results action plan (see Chapter 3) that connects both the passion for the work as well as the discipline needed for execution. While this work happens

---

Programmatic thinking: Leaders' critical-thinking processes in which the selection of people, events, resources, and activities are made to overcome the problems and achieve the goals of a specific program.

Results thinking: The ability of leaders to put the result in the center and work to create an actionable plan where multiple leaders can make their aligned contributions.

concurrently and is dynamic, for the sake of explanation I'll start by first describing the Results Playbook and then the data and analysis needed to create a results action plan.

Meet the "Results Playbook"

I use the metaphor of a "Results Playbook" to help leaders know they are on the same team playing the same game. Good football coaches use a playbook to convey fundamental knowledge of the game to their players, clearly and concisely. Much like a sports team, leaders may know the rules of the game and the position they play, but need coaching (and plenty of practice!) to understand the different roles their "teammates" are playing so they can work together effectively. A Results Playbook helps individual leaders better understand the unique plays they may profit from to advance their game toward that winning goal.

The Results Playbook can also be seen as a physical representation of the work that results leaders engage in, in order to understand their shared work and how best to make progress. It is, in other words, a document for all to refer to, adapt as needed based on new insights or quality improvement, and change if political and/or economic environments require.

One key purpose of a Results Playbook is to create a common set of terms and concepts that allow stakeholders to work in alignment with each other and their work. Leaders can use and adapt a variety of results frames. This book focuses on the frame offered by Mark Friedman in his book, *Trying Hard is Not Good Enough.* According to Friedman, building accountability to results means starting with the "ends" (the designated results) and working backwards, step by step, toward the "means" (the strategies and tasks selected for achieving the results).[7] This approach gives leaders a working understanding—both in their own thinking and in collaboration with others—of how to link their day-to-day work to overarching strategies, and then to the result they are seeking. Because they share a common results frame, everyone grasps that they are accountable to that result in every action they take.

Friedman describes this idea of working backwards to enable leaders to be accountable to two sets of results as:

1. Results for a whole population because of the collective work of multiple partners and organizations; and
2. Results at the program level, where each leader and/or organization makes its contribution to the larger result.

One powerful contribution that Friedman makes in his work is to highlight that no one organization, agency, system, or person is

Part 1: From Fragmentation to Shared Results

accountable to or "owns" a population-level result. Rather, stakeholders and partners who choose to work together on behalf of a population-level result jointly "own" the result, and share accountability for that result through their contribution. The contribution comes through a leader's work at a program level or the work that leaders do in their organization or system. The way to align their contributions—and move from programmatic thinking to results work—is by connecting their programmatic contributions through a set of overarching strategies.

These three "levels"—the population-level result, the strategy level, and the program level—are the foundation for the Results Playbook. By asking a similar set of questions at each level, results leaders begin the initial analysis that helps to shape their shared results work. These questions are:

- What is the result at this level?
- Who is this result for?
- How is progress measured at this level?
- How will you make progress at this level?

Figure 2.3 illustrates what the answers to these questions will look like at each level.

Figure 2.3 **Questions Asked at Three "Levels" are the Foundation for the Results Playbook**

Population Level:
- What is the result at this level? *The population level result.*
- Who is this result for? *All people in a geographic area.*
- How is progress measured at this level? *By indicator or set of indicators.*
- How will you make progress? *Through a set of strategies.*

Strategy Level:
- What is the result at this level? *A strategy level result.*
- Who is this result for? *All people targeted by the strategy.*
- How is progress measured at this level? *By performance measures.*
- How will you make progress? *Through a set of programs.*

Program Level
- What is the result at this level? *A program level result.*
- Who is this result for? *All people targeted by a program.*
- How is progress measured at this level? *By performance measures.*
- How will you make progress? *Through a set of activities.*

Chapter 2: Aligned Contributions—From Fragmentation to Shared Accountability

Creating the Results Playbook

Once the overall population-level result is identified, results leaders must begin the difficult work of establishing both indicators and performance measures—data capturing what is being done, how well those tactics are working, and how the effort is affecting the population in question. These are the key elements of a Results Playbook. This level of analysis helps results leaders see how their contribution fits into the whole and how best they can work together toward that shared result.

We will explore the Results Playbook, shown in Figure 2.4, as well as the analysis required (questions to be addressed), by working from the Results through Overarching Strategies, Programs, and Activities, to arrive finally at Individual Actions that support results leaders.

Figure 2.4 **The Results Playbook**

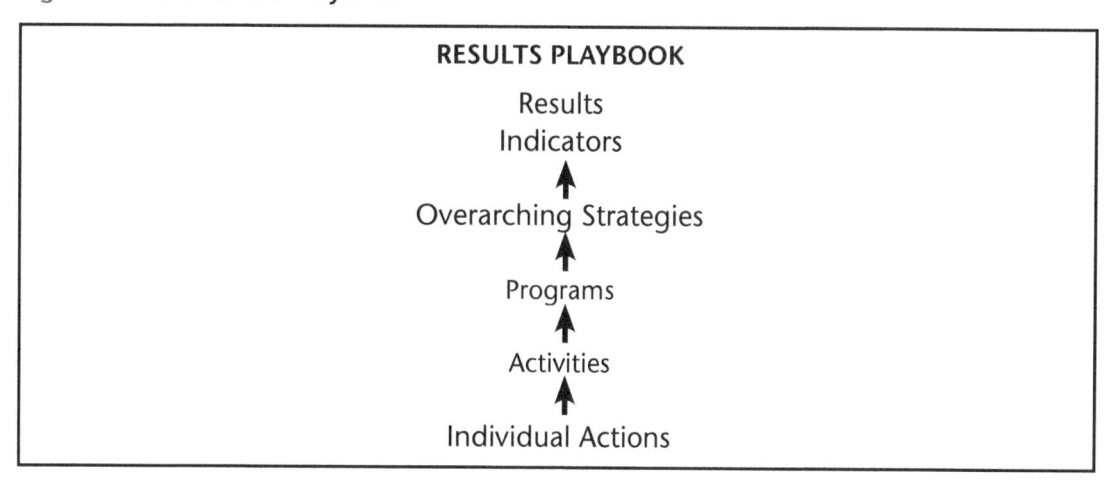

RESULTS PLAYBOOK

Results
Indicators
↑
Overarching Strategies
↑
Programs
↑
Activities
↑
Individual Actions

Preparing for the Results Work

As we saw above, leaders engaging in results work first must make that important pivot from identifying a problem to stating a result. A primary task in this part of the Playbook is to define problems and potential solutions in a way that allows multiple partners and stakeholders, from all their different perspectives, to come together and play the same game.

The leadership task is to identify and convene a diverse set of stakeholders and potential partners and link their concerns about a problem to aligned actions. Often, by using disaggregated population-level data (by race, class, culture, language, gender, etc.) leaders start to see where their collective work needs to focus and how they may contribute.

Part 1: From Fragmentation to Shared Results

Questions to Address
- For what population is the results work being done?
- What does the data reveal about what the problem actually is?

Determining the Result of the Results Work

Population-Level Results: The purpose of the results work is to make progress toward a population-level result. As you will remember, a population-level result is a result that shows improvement in a "quality-of-life" condition for a whole population of individuals, children, or families in a specified place, or for a place itself.

Indicators: To know you are making progress toward a goal requires having an agreed-upon data point or set of data points in order to know—and keep—"the score" in the "results game." These data points or indicators help leaders know they are doing the right work. These indicators are measures that quantify achievement of the result.[8] For example, for each of the sample population-level results in Figure 2.3, the following indicators could be used:

- All children enter school ready to learn. Indicator: the percentage of children who pass the kindergarten readiness assessment.
- All communities are safe. Indicator: the percentage of residents who feel safe, or the rate of crime in a community.
- All babies are born healthy. Indicator: the percentage of babies who are born full-term or normal weight.

Sometimes an indicator is not available or accessible. In that case, results leaders can use a proxy indicator that represents an approximate measure or a process measure to represent the results work. For example, in some communities there may not be a standard kindergarten readiness assessment that directly shows if children are entering school ready to learn. A proxy indicator might be the children enrolled in formal, high-quality, early learning programs.

Questions to Address
- What measures can be used to track progress on the result?
- Is the data available in a timely fashion?
- What does the disaggregated data reveal (e.g., by race, class, gender, language, age etc.)?

Result: A population condition of wellbeing for children, adults, families and communities, stated in plain language.

Indicator: A measure that helps quantify the achievement of a result. Indicators answer the question (to use Mark Friedman's phrase), "How would we recognize this result if we fell over it?"[9]

Strategies: The "Game Plan"

A "results game plan" is a systematic assessment of what needs to happen in order to make progress toward a specified result. The developed strategies are part of the leaders' *theory of change.* In a nutshell, a theory of change states: "If these strategies are executed with fidelity and produce results, then you will see a change in the indicator trend line in a positive direction."

Achieving a population-level result requires multiple strategies, usually a broad mix of direct service, policy, and systems **strategies** to move the indicators in the desired direction. Strategies describe the overarching approach and the coherent actions through which leaders will achieve declared targets. They are the means—the method or "the how"—for progress. Strategies also enable multiple leaders (and members of the programs they lead) to identify their individual contributions toward achieving that population-level result.

> The Developing Indicators Worksheet in the apps/tools section at the end of this chapter is designed to help you develop your own indicators.

Questions to Address

Strategies:
- What works to address the factors driving the current status of each indicator?
- What works to address the disparities that are revealed by disaggregating the data?
- What do research, evidence-based practices, and experience suggest will make a difference?
- What assortment of actions is likely to move the needle on each indicator and contribute to improving the results you are working on?

> **Strategy:** A coherent collection of actions that has a reasoned chance of improving results.

Once the collaborative work related to defining the population-level result, indicators, and overarching strategies is complete, leaders can shift their focus to their programmatic work, confident that that work will contribute to the result in the center.

Programs: The "Building Blocks"

Like Lego™ bricks that interlock to build a sturdy structure, programs organize individual actions and activities into coherent units that support overarching strategies.

Leaders focus on their unique contributions to the result through the programs they lead. This work starts by connecting the leader's programmatic work to the overarching strategy and then identifying the program-level result that a leader and/or an organization will work toward as part of the broader effort. Programmatic work can be

Part 1: From Fragmentation to Shared Results

> Developing Powerful Strategies Worksheet in the apps/tools section at the end of this chapter is designed to help develop overarching strategies.

connected to policy, technical assistance, and systems work as well as providing a direct service. Accountability to program-level results is essential: it is the "Lego™ brick" that supports accountability to a population-level result.

Questions to Address

Program Population:
- Who are the "customers" of the program—in other words, the program population—the people who are served by our efforts, our organization, or our program?
- How do these customers relate to the whole population (e.g., are they a sub-group? What shared trait sets them apart?)
- What is our program result—the impact or difference that we expect to make for these people as a result of our work?
- What are our performance measures—the actual measurable quantification of how much will we do, how well will we do it, and how our efforts will make a difference?

Activities and Actions: The "Nuts and Bolts"

Results leaders think about the formal role they fill in the context of their Results Playbook. In doing so, they create a set of performance measures (their "how much," "how well," and "difference made" measures) that evaluate their effectiveness in that role in achieving a declared goal or target. They use these performance measures to move into execution quickly, and subsequently to assess the quality and impact of their actions. With a set of performance measures to assess work, action commitments become a first-line measure for quality improvement. Greater detail on role and action commitments can be found in Chapter 5.

Questions to Address
- What actions or tasks do I take—in my role—to contribute to the desired result?
- What are the performance measures I use to assess the effectiveness of my contribution (how much, how well, is anyone better off measures)?
- What are reasonable, but challenging targets for my performance measures?

Chapter 2: Aligned Contributions—From Fragmentation to Shared Accountability

If you work your way through the **Questions to Address** for each component of the Results Playbook I've just described, you will be prepared to move on to the work ahead: connecting the playbook to a plan for action. Our "descent down the ladder" of the Results Playbook from Results through Overarching Strategies, Programs, Activities, and Individual Actions is now complete.

Working in High Action and High Alignment

Jolie Bain Pillsbury's Theory of Aligned Contributions makes two fundamental observations:

- Population-level changes cannot be made by a single agency or organization but must be part of a multi-sector, public, and private movement to achieve a given result.
- Outcomes for children, families, and communities are unsatisfactory in part because key stakeholders are engaged in unaligned action on multiple results or when there is no specific identified result.

There are many reasons for stakeholders to engage in unaligned actions or make limited progress together toward a result. As stated in Chapter 1, competition for resources, power, control, and turf are some reasons that make it difficult for partners and stakeholders to work with others within their sector and across other sectors. It is often the case that individual collaborators are not clear on what they can contribute or aware of what others can offer. A leader may be so focused on their program or their role that they may not see who else is connected to the result. Jolie makes some cogent observations on this issue in the following passage.

> There is a lack of context about who else is around the child—a church, a mental health provider, an uncle or aunt, a Boys or Girls Club, even a local merchant who puts washing machines in the school to help kids have clean clothes....
> So many are feeling isolated in their role ... isolated and defensive. The principal thinks he alone is on the hook for grades, on the hook for student wellbeing. So there are barriers around the role design, when the roles are not in a system of shared accountability. *Alone and isolated equals defending yourself from potential action and not revealing the difficulties....* A probation officer often does not have access to

the range of services she needs to help ex-offenders, but she is still on the hook if parolees make a mistake.... They feel alone in that they are only one who is accountable. They will not take risks. In their defensiveness, they are isolated and that prevents them from good conversations with a behavioral counselor who can help them change how they relate with a black boy .... Role barriers also include not getting how you contribute in your role, where your role places you in the system, and being defensive and seeing measurement and numbers as things that are just used to punish.[10]

It is clear that making progress on a population-level result is a dynamic process involving multiple stakeholders—stakeholders who may have competing interests and competing points of view as to the cause and effect of a certain problem. Results leadership takes advantage of the opportunities available when leaders join together in pursuit of for a common result and address inherent inter-group challenges—competition, status, relationships—in order to work in both High action and High alignment. As we learned earlier in this chapter, using a results-in-the-center frame is the beginning of the process of working in High Action and High Alignment.

Better Together

Working in High Action/High Alignment to address a complex social problem means that the combined and coordinated efforts of all stakeholders are effective in ways that would not be possible if each of the partners were pursuing his or her work alone. Again, *The Theory of Aligned Contributions* states:

> When a critical mass of leaders from different sectors come together and make an unequivocal commitment to take aligned actions, they accelerate improvement in the wellbeing of their communities. Aligned actions become aligned contributions when individuals within organizations and communities take actions that complement, support, leverage or correlate with actions that are occurring in other organizations, communities or systems at a scope and scale necessary to contribute to a measurable improvement in a population-level result.[11]

Operating in this manner—in a space of shared accountability to an agreed-upon result—is fundamentally challenging:

- Being in High Alignment with peers is difficult when there is no formal authority dictating direction and strategy and thus individuals cannot rely on their power to control the situation; and
- Being in High Action is difficult because it requires stakeholders to assess what they are doing, how well they are doing it, and what contribution they are making to the result.

Being in both High Alignment and High Action requires using data to assess performance; accountability to acknowledge any mistakes or missteps; and a commitment to focus on execution. None of these behaviors come easily.

Acknowledging Reality

Assessing the current situation is the first step toward working in High Action and High Alignment. This requires the leader to put the concerns of people at the forefront and then to understand the existing practices (including his or her own) intended to address those concerns. In this way, leaders acknowledge the current reality, and the journey to making a difference begins.

The next step is to assess the environment. Elements that leaders might notice include:

- The gap between current realties of people and aspirational rhetoric of organizations and systems;
- The level of attachment leaders place in their current and existing practices;
- The organizational and systems challenges leaders are experiencing as they try to address the concerns of their people;
- New and different practices that, if implemented, would resolve the breakdowns and make progress to address concerns; and
- Resistance from leaders who perceive a net loss of value in the change.

After assessing the environment, the reality of addressing complex social problems becomes clearer. Leaders may encounter these challenges:

- The way stakeholders work together is unsystematic and fragmented. They might, sometimes, work well together but only if it benefits some narrow interest. More often, however, each has a different interest and a very different point of view based on that interest.
- Leaders are pressured (by themselves, their boards, their organizations) to follow a structured and systematic approach to solving complex social problems.
- Too many stakeholders focus on traditional tools, methods, practices and beliefs regarding solving these public problems.

Results leaders might observe other issues specific to the situation as well. With all this as a backdrop, leaders prepare to begin making the shift toward effective collaboration by guiding their groups to work in High Action and High Alignment.

High Action/High Alignment As An Organizing Frame

High alignment is when leaders are working in the same direction and towards the same goal. To be in high action is to engage in executing strategies and implementing programs. The concept of high action/high alignment provides an organizing framework that allows leaders to collectively move forward together with other results leaders. It is an intentional way of being for results leaders; it is a goal when results leaders work together; and it is a set of choices that leaders make in order to address complex problems. Table 2.1 presents this frame by describing what the behavior of a leader in each quadrant might look like.

Leaders use the High Action/High Alignment quadrants to help frame how they will work together. They create explicit and specific criteria that they will use to assess individuals' performances against the standard of High Action and High Alignment behaviors. Once the criteria have been established, leaders then engage in intentional conversations to assess current levels of alignment and action toward the population-level result. Without this intentionality, leaders could work in low action, low alignment, or both. They would thereby sabotage their collaborative ability to make progress toward that result.

Chapter 2: Aligned Contributions—From Fragmentation to Shared Accountability

Table 2.1 **Observable Behaviors in the High Action/High Alignment Frame**

A Leader in High Action, Low Alignment is…	A Leader in High Action, High Alignment is…
• Working actively and independently on his/her work, but not reaching out to build relationships, share resources, and execute in coordination with others • Acting on his/her own agenda, own work plan, own program and/or grant • Displaying lack of interest in adapting to maximize impact	• Having resilient relationships • Acting on collaborative decision • Being accountable for measurably improving results • Implementing shared strategies • Working to strengthen relationships • Focusing on both scope and scale of the results work
A Leader in Low Action, Low Alignment is…	**A Leader in Low Action, High Alignment is…**
• Observing what is going on • Not building relationships • Not taking needed action • Sitting on the fence, perhaps with another agenda or seeing how the political winds will blow	• Joining with others and fostering relationships • Getting to know and connecting with others • Not using the relationships to leverage contributions to the result. • Not acting to implement strategies

High Action/High Alignment in Action

To see this in action, let us return the example of Informal Care and Grade-Level Reading in Indianola introduced earlier. The group of leaders working on the result of grade-level reading had, as stakeholders, representatives from the state and community level. Before attempting to work together, they first had to acknowledge that things were not getting better, and they would have to change precisely the way they were working together in order to be in High Action and High Alignment.

During an intentional conversation about working together, they shared experiences of being in both low action and low alignment with each other and with other partners.

They described their experience of "low action" as:

- Stakeholders doing a lot of talking and meeting;
- Agreement at high level, but never cascading down to the operation level;

See High Alignment/High Action in the apps/tools section at the end of this chapter.

- Working together with a lack of honesty and transparency; and
- Stakeholder representatives constantly changing.

Then they described their experience of "low alignment" as:

- Stakeholders stubbornly holding different points of view and the points of view changing when stakeholder representatives change;
- Stakeholders saying they are all doing same thing but in reality are all in different places;
- Stakeholders engagement is independent from one another;
- A lack of real commitment to the results work; and
- Stakeholders work is duplicative—they are not aligning their contributions and leveraging resources.

From this honest and difficult conversation about working in low action and/or low alignment they acknowledged that working in High Action and High Alignment would demand intentionality and purpose. Now the conversation turned to answering the question: *What are our criteria for working in High Action and High Alignment for the sake of the result? How will we know if we are working in High Action and High Alignment?* They agreed that they would:

- Work to address the real issue—with or without funding;
- Publicly declare their focus to be the result of grade-level reading by working on a shared results action plan—plans, strategies, policies, visual mapping as evidence;
- Publicly identify and acknowledge the gap in grade-level reading;
- Focus on coordination and collaboration without duplication, which meant
  - Publicly supporting each other's work
  - Providing a venue or forum for sharing evidence of work that is going on;
- Use data and performance measures as evidence that change is actually happening; and
- Have their primary focus on the result of grade-level reading—not just their specific program. This meant evaluating the effectiveness of programs and a willingness to change, modify or improve the programmatic work if needed.

This set of criteria was not a magic bullet for working harmoniously. It was, rather, a basis to address their conflicts, differing points

Chapter 2: Aligned Contributions—From Fragmentation to Shared Accountability

of view, issues of accountability, and other dynamics that were bound to rise as they discovered how best to operationalize their shared results action plan.

Being in High Action and High Alignment is an intentional set of choices that results leaders make regarding how they act and how they lead others to behave. Simply put, they engage in conversations to assess the current situation, create specific criteria that describe the desired behaviors of collaborating partners, and then align action toward a population-level result. Bringing stakeholders together to address complex social problems requires a commitment to work together in High Action and High Alignment toward a common result. This commitment enables stakeholders to trust each other to make progress that will have the desired effect on the defined population: the essence of shared accountability.

Questions to Support High Action and High Alignment

When a group of stakeholders comes together, exploring and answering the following questions can support their efforts to work in High Action and High Alignment. First, think of a positive experience when you where is High Action and High Alignment with another.

- What made this experience so positive?

- What do you need so you have work in High Action and High Alignment with others?

- What can you contribute so others can be in High Action and High Alignment?

- What are the practices and behaviors needed so this collaborative work group can be in High Action together? Be specific and concrete.

- What are the practices and behaviors needed so this collaborative work group can be in High Alignment together? Be specific and concrete.

- How will the collaborative work group support each other in these practices and behaviors?

What Does It Take to Be in High Action and High Alignment?

A tremendous amount of learning has occurred over the last three decades about what it takes for organizations and leaders to work together to solve complex problems. This learning can be distilled into three broad areas of focus:

1. The work itself,
2. The individual leader, and
3. The collaborative work group.

Each deserves brief consideration.

The work: The result that brings partners and stakeholders together has to be the primary focus of the work. Using a Results Playbook is fundamental to creating High Action and High Alignment. It allows the usage of a common language, terms, and distinctions to do the data analysis needed to create a results action plan (discussed in detail in Chapter 3).

Individual leader: The leader's commitment to the results work becomes an essential requirement to working in High Action and High Alignment. Leaders use their power, resources, and networks to bring their contribution to a population-level result. This requires self-awareness and understanding (topics explored in Chapter 4). It also requires leaders to pay attention to how they engage effectively with others (the subject of Chapter 5).

The collaborative work group: It is through the efforts of a collaborative work group engaging in High Action and High Alignment that progress toward a population-level result is realized. The collaborative work group demonstrates High Action and High Alignment by creating a "results culture" (see Chapter 6), which supports working toward both scope and scale (Chapter 7).

What the work of the last 30 years has taught us is that in order to make progress on the results, several things must be in place. The work itself requires an organizing frame. Individual leaders must have the capacity to know themselves and how they work effectively with others. Finally, the collaborative work group must be able to create a results culture and execute toward a common results plan at a systems level.

Chapter 2: Aligned Contributions—From Fragmentation to Shared Accountability

Working Toward Results: Impact of Low Action/ Low Alignment

Recently, I had a very honest conversation with Carter Friend, the Deputy Director of the York County Community Action Corporation in Sanford, Maine. As someone who has worked in and around social service agencies, public and private funders, and boots-on-the-ground community organizations that implement various programs attempting to solve population-level problems, he is very well-placed to observe and report on what low action/low alignment looks like in real life and real time. He and his organization had been attempting to use the concepts of results leadership to support family and community results. He started by saying, "the world spends its very full days living and breathing in programs such as early learning, adult literacy, health and wellness—and the people working in these programs are almost always underpaid and asked to do a lot with very little." He acknowledged that many of these programs work well. He could say with confidence that many children in Head Start programs do enter school ready to learn, that many teens with substance abuse challenges benefit from the many programs available for them, and many adults leave employment programs with a job.

He continued by saying that programs "can be very good at doing what they are incentivized to do." The challenge, from his experience, was the lack of strong incentives for these programs to align and the many barriers to doing so. He found this to be true across organizations where capacity, culture, trust, and competition for funding were some barriers he had experienced. For example, organizations can be in competition for resources from state government funding or philanthropic grants. These funding streams can make organizations feel territorial about what they do and how they do their work—even when the work is somewhat similar. He observed that some of these barriers also exist within large organizations and agencies.

He then spoke of systems (i.e., education, healthcare, housing) as organizing frames that touch the same populations, operate in silos, and have few incentives to align. The end result is "multiple *layers* of silos—siloed programs operating in siloed organizations operating within siloed systems." He ended this observation with a smile on his face and said, "This makes alignment not just arithmetically but geometrically more challenging."

I then asked him to speak specifically about the impact of systems, organizations, and programs not working in High Action and High Alignment toward a population-level result.

At the program level he stated that:

- Clients' needs are often very complex. Programs that do not achieve the desired outcome for a client sometimes fail to explore causes outside of their expertise (such as a workforce program not identifying chronic dental pain as a barrier to successful employment). In the context of this complexity, programs will often measure the number of people they serve or they connect with but may fail to address the other barriers preventing their participants from succeeding.
- Sometimes, however, programs do recognize other barriers to participant success. Instead of collaborating with others who already do that work to address those barriers, some organizations add a new program element to what they do. Often, it is the desire to create larger funding streams, to increase power and influence in their community, or just to grow into larger organizations! This may drive organizations and programs away from their core competency, which creates an inefficient use of resources and increased competition for resources—and still may miss the needs of their program participants.
- System drivers—such as funding through reimbursement rates—often create scenarios where multiple programs serve a particular client group and offer no or limited services to another client group. This misalignment causes some groups to be underserved.
- Finally, lack of being in High Action and High Alignment creates a duplication of services in the same neighborhood. Carter gave the example of two school-based afterschool programs targeting the same population, offering similar services that missed opportunities to leverage strategies and resources to increase the number of participants served.

At a whole-population level Carter stated that:

- Lack of being in High Action and High Alignment causes providers working in multiple systems to fail to coordinate efforts of their services. This also results in important systems issues not being identified. For example, young people could get lost in transition from one program to another or one system to another.
- His experience in employment and workforce serves as

a powerful example. He noticed that the lack of working in High Action and High Alignment created barriers and confusion for people who needed a range of services to secure employment (i.e., job training, language, interviewing skills, internships). Not being in High Action/High Alignment also creates a lack of coordinated outreach to businesses, resulting in missed opportunities to produce the desired results (such as hiring more, say, at-risk teens). In at least one instance, a results-focused approach helped address these issues and increased alignment.

This honest conversation reveals the impact of working in low action and low alignment. Some programs will work to the extent they are incentivized to do so. The problem is that there are few incentives, and many barriers, to collaborating in High Action and High Alignment. This creates negative effects at the program and population level. I challenged this leader to use data about the current state of education outcomes and co-create a shared Results Playbook with his partners and stakeholders. He could then support these partners and stakeholders as they confronted their challenges in working in High Action and High Alignment. Those who chose to stay and work were worth working with. The others could choose to come back and join when they could make their aligned contributions.

To counter this tendency to move away from High Action and High Alignment, Carter now starts his results work with a data conversation that illuminates the current state of things in a particular community. (Chapter 3 offers a way to use similar data to help move your Results Playbook into a shared results action plan.) He then uses the framework of a results action plan as the basis for work in aligned action toward a result. The leadership challenge is to address the individual, collective, and systems barriers that reveal themselves when working with others toward a shared result. Part 2 of this book offers an exploration of what is required of the individual leader and the collaborative work group to work at a systems level.

Chapter 2 Summary

We have now explored the three conceptual building blocks on which shared accountability rests: Result in the center, population-level results, and the High Action/High Alignment frame. In subsequent chapters, I will bring these building blocks together to examine what shared accountability looks like, and how to get there.

Chapter 2 Applications: Tools and Worksheets

1. Results in the Center Worksheet 54
2. Developing a Result Statement 56
3. Developing Indicators Worksheet 58
4. Developing Powerful Strategies Worksheet 60
5. Results Playbook 62
6. High Alignment/High Action 64

To download these apps, visit the book's online resources:
http://ChooseResultsBook.com/resources.html

Part 1: From Fragmentation to Shared Results

Putting Results in the Center Worksheet
Developed by Jolie Bain Pillsbury

Working towards a population level result requires leaders making aligned contributions. The Results in the Center chart is a process that supports a group of results-based leaders to move towards the result. It allows leaders to visual display contributions partners and stakeholders make towards that result and from what section. It also allows leaders to see what sectors are missing or over-represented.

A simple four-step process can be used to define and clarify stakeholders' contribution to a result.

1. Identify the population and the result you will put at the center of your work.
    a. This step is complete when the desired results and population are clearly defined and placed at the center of the chart and
    b. The various sectors that have a contribution to the result are identified

2. Map where you are in relation to the result and your potential partners.
    a. Once the result, population, and sectors are identified, a leader places him or herself (in their role and organizations) in the appropriate place on the chart
    b. Guidance: Those who are closest to the population and result (i.e., if grade-level reading is the result, teachers and teachers aides would be placed in the education sector in the space closest to the result. School principals, school superintendents, school board of education would be placed in subsequent spaces further away from the result)

3. Identify the others with whom you will align to make progress toward the result.
    a. All partners and stakeholders who are engaged in the results work place themselves in the appropriate spaces on the chart

4. Identify other potential contributions.
    a. Leaders then identify other potential partners and contributors to the result and place them on the chart
    b. Leaders then make commitments to reach out to others to join in the results work

Chapter 2: Apps/Tools

Non-profit
Public Human Services
Faith
Public Education
RESULT
Community
Public Health
Philanthropic
Business

Theory of Aligned Contributions in Action (DRAFT β5) © Jolie Bain Pillsbury

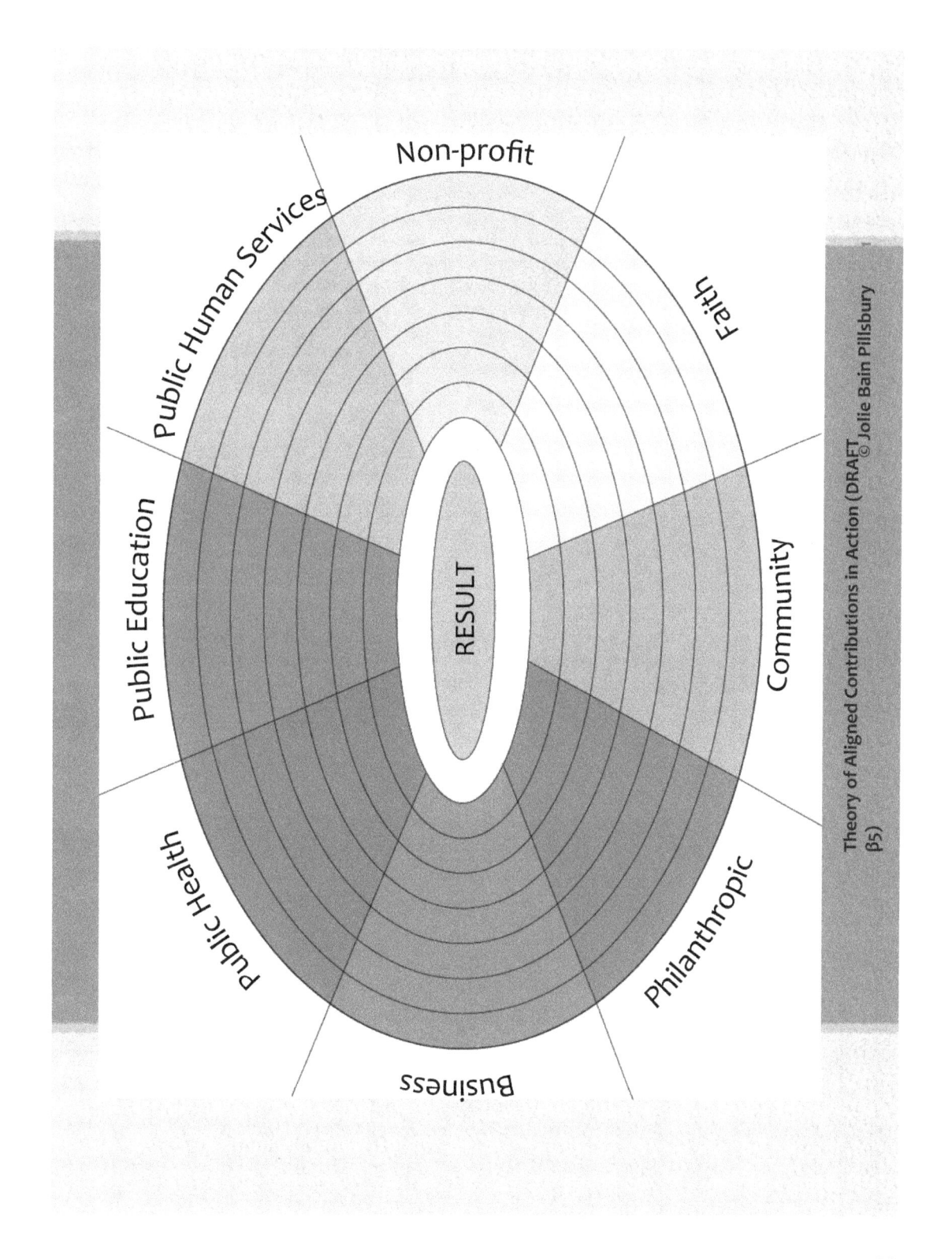

Part 1: From Fragmentation to Shared Results

Developing A Result Statement
Worksheet developed by Phyllis Rozanski

Results-Based leaders identify a condition of wellbeing for people as a way to define and focus their collaborative work. This condition of wellbeing – as declared through a results statement - involves identifying the result to be achieved for a population within a specific place such as a neighborhood, city, county or state. This is in contrast to a stakeholder's contribution to a population level result - which focuses on a client population served through a program, agency or system. It is the clarity of the end condition – the condition of wellbeing - sought that serves to unite individuals, organizations, and collaborative bodies to make their contributions, align their actions and resources. The clarity of the result statement provides the basis for selecting the indicators that will measure the progress to the result. This tool helps groups create population level Results statements.

Result Definition for a Whole Population
A Result statement consists of three parts:

- **Population:** Individuals such as children, youth, families, households, residents and so forth. The description can also include specific groups such as all children under the age of five, all immigrants, or all families living below 200% of poverty, etc.

- **Place:** Connected to the population is the place or geographic area of the population. For example, this can be a neighborhood, city, county, state or the nation.

- **Results/Outcomes:** These are the end conditions or the quality of life conditions desired for the population. For example, families are economically successful, children are healthy and prepared to succeed in school, and neighborhoods are safe for families and children.

Chapter 2: Apps/Tools

This worksheet offers a simple way to create shared agreement on a population level result that a group of leaders can align their work towards.

How to Use
1. List the proposed Result statement in the table provided
2. Rank the result by the three criteria
3. Score the result
4. Decide to use the result or to revise the result to reach a higher score

Proposed Result	Criteria: Insert a *(3) High, (2) Medium or (1) Low*			Score
	Population Defined	Place Defined	End Condition Defined	*1 = Low* *2 = Medium* *3 = High*
1.				
2.				
3.				
4.				

Part 1: From Fragmentation to Shared Results

Developing Indicators WORKSHEET
Worksheet developed by Phyllis Rozanski

Purpose
The purpose of this tool is to: 1. Identify potential indicators 2. Decide on a set of quality indicators and 3. Prioritize the indicators especially naming the specific indicators that the group will hold itself accountable to improve. It helps to name the criteria at the beginning of the conversation to provide a lens for the conversation.

Indicator Definition
An indicator quantifies the achievement of the result related to the population named in the result. Indicators take the form of percentages, rates, ratios or averages, etc. As a practice, indicators are not stated in number values because numbers do not provide a method to measure the impact for the whole population.

Criteria for Indicator Selection
- ✓ **Easy to Understand**: Is the indicator clear and simple so that it can be easily understood by people from different walks of life?
- ✓ **Importance**: Does the indicator have primary relevance to the result? Would people make a direct connection of the indicator to the result? Could it stand for the result?
- ✓ **Field Use**: What evidence exists regarding the use of this indicator to the population result? Which policy groups, foundations, collective impact entities are using this indicator? How widely accepted is this indicator?
- ✓ **Data Capacity:** Can the indicator be collected on a scheduled basis? Is there access to the data for the population and place included in the result? Who are the data sources? Is there capacity to collect the data? Can the data be collected for specific population groups?

Sort Indicators by Importance
Indicators include three types:
- ✓ **Impact Indicators:** The collaborative or organization commits to improve the trendline on these indicators and regularly tracks progress.
- ✓ **Contextual Indicators:** Groups use these indicators to provide other measures on the population named in the result such as the percentage of adults with high school degrees in order to better understand the conditions of the population.
- ✓ **Future Indicators:** These indicators could potentially be either of the two types above. However, there is a lack of access to, availability of or capacity to collect the data.

Chapter 2: Apps/Tools

Strategy/Program: _____ Target Population: _____

If a program, what is the "Program Result" for the target population:
_____

Tip: Start with your difference made measures. 2. Fewer measures are better -not everything that can be measured should be measured. 3. Sync the "how well measures" with the "how much measures."

How much (HM), how well (HW) or better off/difference made (DM)		Insert: *High (H), Medium (M) or Low (L)* for each					Action to Take *Use it, delete it, repair it or Add to Develop Data List*
Measure	Type	Clarity	Importance	Measurability	Availability	Access	
1.							
2.							
3.							
4.							
5.							
6.							
7.							
8.							
9.							
10.							

Actions to Take:

Part 1: From Fragmentation to Shared Results

Developing Powerful Strategies WORKSHEET
Worksheet developed by Phyllis Rozanski

Purpose
Strategies are the means to change the indicator trend line to improve the well-being of children, families, residents or communities. Therefore, strategies have to be "powerful" enough to impact the indicator trend line or in RBA language "turn the curve." The purpose of this tool is to help groups scrutinize their strategy selection using five criteria.

Strategy Definition
A strategy is the overarching approach (based on a set of coherent actions) that has the power to improve the indicator trendline or reach set targets of improvement. Strategies have to be specific and actionable. Strategies are the means, the method or "the how." A strategy can take the form of public policy change, an initiative, a campaign or implementation of a program on a larger scale. Strategies are developed based on identifying the factors that are increasing and decreasing the Impact indicator trend line and the ensuing theory of change.

Criteria for Strategy Selection
- ✓ **Reach:** Will the strategy reach the children, families, or residents that we have identified? Will the strategy reach specifically, those experiencing disparities based on race, ethnicity, place or special circumstances such as English language learners or formerly incarcerated individuals? Will it reach our targeted population(s)?
- ✓ **Scale:** When implemented what is the expected "level" of scale in terms of the number of the targeted population to impact the trend line? For example, the strategy to form an employer's alliance to hire ex-offenders will affect 800 or 20% of ex-offenders returning to the community annually.
- ✓ **Success Probability:** Does the strategy have "good enough" evidence that it works for the targeted population? What is the research, evidence or best practice to predict success?
- ✓ **Community Fit**: Does this strategy fit the values of residents, stakeholders and partners? Does it fit the culture and interests of the community?
- ✓ **Capacity**: Do we have the necessary infrastructure and resources to implement the strategy successfully? Do we have the resources or can we access them? Do we have the critical partners needed or can we recruit them?

How to Use
1. Use the primary factors identified through the factor analysis coupled with the theory of change to list potential or existing strategies
2. Rank each strategy by applying the criteria
3. Score the strategies by totaling up the number for each criteria and decide on which strateg(ies) to implement

Chapter 2: Apps/Tools

Proposed Strategy	Criteria: Insert a *(3)* High, *(2)* Medium or *(1)* Low					Total Score
	Reach	Scale	Success Probability	Community Fit	Capacity	
1.						
2.						
3.						
4.						
5.						
6.						
7.						
8.						
9.						
10.						

Tip: *The scoring is a guide to inform decision making. This conversation can lead to gathering more evidence about a specific strategy, clarifying the theory of change, gathering more data etc. Additionally, groups will often move to a formal decision making step to reach consensus and commitment from its leadership, members and/or partners to move forward to implement the proposed strategies based on action commitments to take to achieve implementation.*

Part 1: From Fragmentation to Shared Results

Results Playbook:
A Bridge from Programmatic to Results Work
© Raj Chawla

Programmatic thinking, at its best, is very effective in creating programs that create positive outcomes for those who engage with the program. With this type of thinking, leaders focus on their programs and how to improve what they do. To make progress towards a population level result[1], however, requires leaders to move beyond the singular activity of programmatic thinking to that of population level results thinking. By engaging in results thinking, leaders acknowledge that their work is to make progress at a population level and that no one agency, system, sector, or person is accountable for or "owns" a population-level result. Rather, all stakeholders and partners all have a contribution towards a result and their contribution is through their programs.

Contents
I. Three Levels of Work
II. Result and Indicator
III. Overarching Strategies
IV. Programs and Activities

Joining with other organizations and sectors to work towards a population level result with aligned contributions is a complicated and difficult process. It often requires leaders to move past competition and fragmentation in order to create an actionable plan where all can make their aligned contribution.

A first step towards an actionable plan is development of a "results playbook". A results playbook is, on the most surface level, a metaphor used to help results leaders know they are on the same team playing the same game. It is also a physical representation of the steps and hard work needed to get to an actionable results plan. It helps results leaders engage in results work by connecting their programmatic contributions to a shared population level result through a set of overarching strategies.

I. Three Levels of Work
These three "levels"—the population level, the strategy level, and the program level—are the foundation for the results playbook. By asking and answering a similar set of questions at each level, results leaders begin the initial analysis that helps to shape the shared results work. These questions and answers are:

Population Level:
- Question: What is the result at this level? Answer: The population level result
- Who is this result for? All people in a geographic area
- How is progress measured at this level? By indicator or set of indicators
- How will you make progress? Through a set of strategies

Strategy Level:
- What is the result at this level? A strategy level result
- Who is this result for? All people targeted by the strategy
- How is progress measured at this level? By performance measures
- How will you make progress? Through a set of programs

Program Level
- What is the result at this level? A program level result
- Who is this result for? All people targeted by a program
- How is progress measured at this level? By performance measures
- How will you make progress? Through a set of activities

---
[1] Mark Friedman, Trying Hard is Not Good Enough

II. Working Towards a Result and Indicator

The goal of the results work is to make progress towards a population-level **result**. A population-level result is a result that shows improvement in a "quality-of-life" condition for a whole population of individuals, children, or families in a specified place, or for a place itself.

Question to Address to identify a population level result:
- What is the "quality-of-life" condition for a whole population of people that is desired? What is the geographic boundary for this work?
- *Example: All children in "our community" enter school ready to learn*

To know you are making progress towards a result requires having an agreed-upon data point or set of data points in order to know "the score" in the results work. These data points or **indicators** help leaders know they are doing the right work

Questions to Address to identify population level indicators:
- What measures can be used to track progress?
- What data available in a timely fashion?
- What does disaggregating the data (e.g., by race, class, gender, age etc.) reveal?
- *Example: Kindergarten readiness assessment*

```
RESULTS PLAYBOOK
Results
(Indicators)
↑
Overarching Strategies
↑
Programs
(Performance Measures)
↑
Activities
(Performance Measures)
↑
Individual Actions
(Performance Measures and
Action Commitments)
```

III. Developing Overarching Strategies

Achieving a population-level result requires multiple strategies—usually a broad mix of direct service, policy, and systems strategies to move the indicators in the desired direction. They are the means—the method or "the how"—for progress. Strategies also enable multiple leaders (and the programs they lead) to identify their aligned contributions toward achieving that population-level result.

Questions to Address to identify overarching strategies:
- What key factors are contributing to the status of each indicator? What works to address those factors?
- What works to address the disparities that are revealed by disaggregating the data?
- What do research, evidence-based practices, and experience suggest will make a difference?
- *Example: High quality formal early learning experiences*

IV. Programs, Activities, and Individual Actions

Leaders focus on their unique contributions to the result through their programs and activities as well as their individual actions. In doing so, they create a set of performance measures (their "how much", "how well", and "difference made" measures) that will support achieving a declared goal or target.

Questions to Address to identify programs and activities:
- Who are the "customers" of the program—the people who are served by the work?
- What is the program-level result—in other words, the impact or difference that is expected to make for these people as a result of programmatic work?
- What activities does the program carry out in service of the result?
- What are the performance measures?
- *Example: The number of children in a local head start early learning program*
- *Example: The implementation of evidence-based curriculum*

Questions to Address the individual actions:
- What actions or tasks do I take—in my role—to contribute to the desired result?
- What are the performance measures I use to assess the effectiveness of my contribution?
- What are reasonable, but challenging targets for my performance measures?
- *Example: The classroom teacher holding fidelity to an evidence-based curriculum*

Part 1: From Fragmentation to Shared Results

High Alignment/High Action
© Jolie Bain Pillsbury and Raj Chawla

Aligned contributions occur when leaders work together to take effective action that is complementary, mutually supportive, and leveraged to produce measurable improvement in a result.

The Four Quadrants of Aligned Contribution

		Low	High
Takes actions that contribute to results	**High**	**High action, low alignment** A leader working actively and independently to contribute to the result, but not reaching out to build relationships with others to achieve complementary efforts. • A leader acting on their own agenda • A leader uninterested adapting to maximize impact	**High action, high alignment** A leader with resilient relationships acting on collaborative decisions and being accountable for measurably improving results. • A leader implementing shared strategies • A leader working to strengthen relationships
	Low	**Low action, low alignment** A leader observing what is going and not engaging in either relationship building or taking action that can contribute to result. • A leader sitting on the fence • A leader not connecting with others	**Low action, high alignment** A leader joining with others and fostering relationships, but not using the relationships to leverage contributions to the result. • A leader not in action to implement strategies • A leader getting to know and connect with others

Works to be in alignment with others

To What End?

High Action/High Alignment is only possible if you and those you want to work with seek to achieve a common result that cannot be achieved alone. Authentic agreement on the result defines the purpose and meaning of the work and allows people to answer the question to what end? The pull of the common result is strengthened when people can vividly describe what the result looks like and how you will know when you have it.

> **Contents**
> Four Quadrants
> To what end?
> High Action
> High Alignment
> Where are you?
> What are you willing to do?

> Is there a result you are committed to achieving that you cannot achieve alone?

High Action

Even with authentic agreement to a clearly understood common result, what people do doesn't add up. The Four Quadrants of Aligned Contributions is used to get groups moving together in the same direction and actively matching up their actions to achieve results.

High action captures actions that both contribute effectively to the result and are frequent enough and large enough to make a measurable difference. High action requires leaders to examine what they do, how much they do, and whether what they do contributes to the result.

> Are your actions timely and sufficient to make a difference?

High Alignment

Achieving alignment with peers is hard when you are in the habit of being the "boss" or the expert and can tell people what to do. The work of alignment requires listening to other points of view and modifying your own; understanding the limits of your authority and accepting other people's authority; living with shared decision making: and, accepting other ways of learning and doing. Taking the time, the energy and the risk necessary to change how you work in relationship with others is the work of high alignment.

> What are you willing to do differently in how you work with others to align your action?

4. Where are you now?

Look at the four quadrants of aligned action. Consider the result you share with others that is worth changing for. What quadrant are you in now? Where do you perceive others to be? Share your assessment with others and understand their assessment. What do these assessments tell what you need to do and what others might need to do to get to or stay in aligned action?

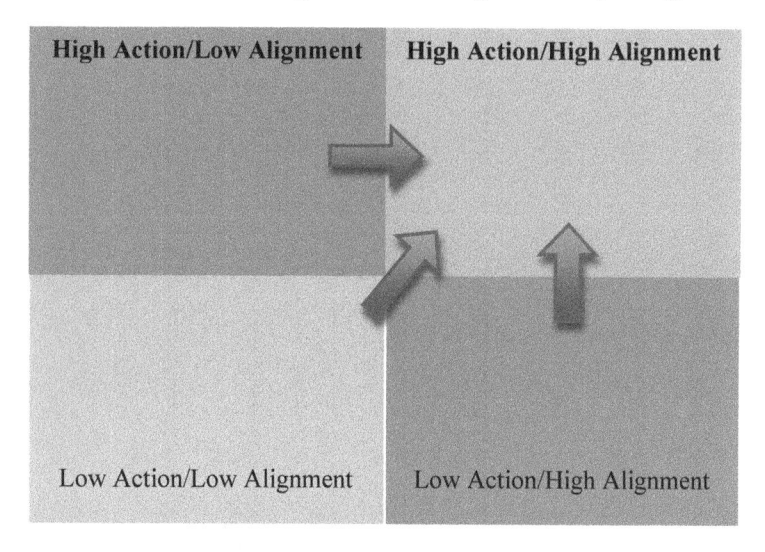

High Action/Low Alignment	High Action/High Alignment
Low Action/Low Alignment	Low Action/High Alignment

> What quadrant are you in? Where are others? What do you and others need to do?

5. What will you each do to move into or stay in aligned action?

Through your conversation discover what will you need to do to either get to aligned action or stay in aligned action? Make a commitment to aligned action that specifies what you will do, how you will do it, when you will do it, and how what you do will match up with or contribute to what others do.

> What is your aligned actionable commitment?

CHAPTER 3

Moving Toward Execution— The Results Action Plan

*Vision without action is a daydream.
Action with without vision is a nightmare.*

– *Japanese proverb*

Results leaders use a Results Playbook to begin engaging in shared work. As mentioned in Chapter 2, leaders have the opportunity to make progress towards a shared result by:

- Placing the population-level results in the center of all their work;
- Creating a Results Playbook to generate both urgency and accountability towards a shared result; and
- Making their aligned contributions, working in High Action and High Alignment as they proceed.

The Results Playbook allows multiple stakeholders and partners to use common language and frames to explore how their work might contribute to the overall results. The development of a Results Playbook is essential to help frame the work to be done. *However, the playbook is, in and of itself, insufficient to provide an actionable plan for partners and stakeholders.* It may provide the broad strategies that are needed to make progress on the result, but more work needs to be done to develop strategies that are connected to the underlying causes contributing to the problem itself.

For results leaders to make sure they are on the right path and doing the needed work, they will gather the appropriate or best-available data and do the appropriate analysis to make sure the strategies are the "right" ones; the targets set create the needed urgency; and realistic timelines are developed to track progress.

It is only in using data and engaging in thoughtful analysis that leaders using the Results Playbook can successfully create a results action plan. For example, the ability to disaggregate the data on race and gender may illuminate the need for leaders to focus their work to address specific disparities. Key elements of the playbook are found in the results action plan, including the "north star" statement of population-level result, indicator(s), overarching strategies, and stakeholder contributions. It is this Results Action plan that reveals the urgency of the work; allows the shared work to be measured across time; and creates the opportunity for quality improvement efforts. If we were to look at the whole endeavor as a multi-person relay race, the Results Playbook would be the team's runners' individual and collective plans involving strategies and choice of individuals for each leg, evaluation and overview of the competition, and goal-setting for each baton carrier. The results action plan is the actual execution or running of the race with the population-level result being the team's final arrival at the finish line.

I'm about to go into a fairly detailed discussion of using data in results leadership. Don't worry if you don't understand exactly how each component of the data-driven approach works on first read-through. You will find an in-depth example from my work in Indianola, Mississippi toward the end of the chapter that demonstrates how the parts come together in results work.

Results playbook + (Data + Analysis) = Results Action Plan
What is holding you back from placing a population-level result at the center of your work, creating a results playbook using data and analysis, and seeing your work group making their aligned contributions? Return to this question after reading this chapter.

Commit to Using Data

> *By putting results and data at the heart of the work, results leaders are willing to risk relationships, reframe loyalties, and confront their own losses. They are also asking their stakeholders and partners to do the same.*
>
> – Raj Chawla

Commitment to using data is fundamental to results work. This includes data that:

- Provides insights about the people and how they are doing (population level and indicator data);
- Offers deeper understanding about why things are the way they are (called factor analysis);
- Creates urgency by naming targets connected to time (baseline and target data); and
- Creates accountability of stakeholders' specific contributions (performance measures).

But even data can be subject to conflict. Our worldviews and interests are tenacious and can often remain below the surface yet still influencing how we respond to data. The need to convince others of the "right" data or the "correct way" to interpret data creates tension and drains time and energy from results work. Sometimes it can seem like different people are seeing different realities and are competing to prove the rightness and wrongness of these realities instead of working toward solving the problem the data describes.

Results leaders can work through these battles by thoughtfully defining the result and indicators and thinking strategically about how to use data to advance the group's collective understanding of how best to move forward. Several factors—and we'll see specific examples of each as we discuss them—deserve consideration including:

- The types of data—specifically quantitative and qualitative data;
- Disaggregation and visualization of the data in order to analyze it from multiple perspectives; and
- Using the data to inform the three levels—population, strategy, and program—that results leaders operate.

Types of Data—Qualitative and Quantitative Data

Results leaders focus on the two types of data—qualitative and quantitative data—needed to make informed decisions about their results work. It is important for leaders to know the benefits and the limits of both as they work together toward results.

Qualitative data is information about *qualities*—information that can't actually be measured. Qualitative data tend to be narrative (a results story), holistic (speaks to the whole picture), and longitudinal (brings in history and long-term trends). For example, qualitative data may highlight what it is like to live in a community where there are limited transportation options or to describe the experiences of a teacher in an overcrowded and under-resourced classroom. The purpose of qualitative data is to provide a perspective on the complex public problem from the reality of the individual, the community, and/or the culture, capturing as fully as possible how its participants feel or live it.[1]

Quantitative data is information about *quantities*—things that can be measured. Quantitative data is expressed numerically and statistically. Examples of quantitative data used in results work include indicators and performance measures (both discussed in Chapter 2). This type of data can be used to construct tables of raw data and graphs to help interpret that data.

Table 3.1 offers a quick snapshot of qualitative and quantitative data.[2]

Results leaders value both qualitative and quantitative data to create urgency or to demonstrate work accomplished. In results work, it is expected that leaders will use both kinds of data to inform strategy development and to measure the effectiveness of program contribution and impact of on-the-ground activity. For example, it is a normal practice in results work to disaggregate quantitative and qualitative data and to engage in a factor analysis to tell the "story behind the data" to support decisions about how to move forward.

Disaggregation and Visualization of Data

In order to effectively analyze the data, results leaders pay particular attention to both disaggregating the data and then presenting the data in a way that deepens the understanding of what the data reveals.

Disaggregation: Disaggregation provides leaders clearer and more precise information from which to work. Disaggregating (breaking apart) a large set of data (for example, high school graduation rates, teen pregnancy rates, arrest rates) makes visible smaller subsets (for

Table 3.1 **Characteristics of Qualitative and Quantitative Data**

	Qualitative Data	**Quantitative Data**
Concerned with…	• Understanding human behavior from the informant's perspective • Assumes a dynamic and negotiated reality	• Discovering facts about social phenomena • Assumes a fixed and measurable reality
Methods of collection and analysis	• Data is collected through participant observation and interviews, self assessments, and self reports • Data is analyzed by themes from descriptions by informants • Data is reported in the language of the informant	• Data is collected through measuring things • Data is analyzed through numerical comparisons and statistical inferences • Data is reported through statistical analysis
Benefits	• Suggest possible relationships, causes, effects, and dynamic processes • Allows for ambiguities and contradictions in the data, which are a reflection of social reality	• Can be interpreted with statistical analysis for scientific objectivity • Is based on measured values and can be checked by others, or replicated • Hypotheses can also be tested because of the use of statistical analysis
Limits	• The problem of adequate validity or reliability is a major criticism. Because of the subjective nature of qualitative data and its origin in single contexts, it is difficult to apply conventional standards of reliability and validity	• Context: Quantitative analysis does not take place in natural settings. It lacks context and nuance in the choices that participants make. • Confirmation bias: The researcher might miss phenomena because of focus on theory or hypothesis testing rather than on the theory of hypothesis generation

example, by race, gender, class, geography). This disaggregation provides leaders with information about underlying issues, concerns, or focal points within the larger population.

It allows leaders to explore questions about what is working and for whom and what is not working and for whom. It can reveal disparities based on race or ethnicity, gender, income, geography, culture, sexual orientation, etc. It allows leaders to explore causal factors relevant to specific populations and to design specific strategies to address those factors. It can also be a door that leads to larger systems dynamics that may be alive in an organization, a community, or a sector.

Table 3.2 gives an example of how leaders might disaggregate their data to create deeper understanding of the community in determining areas of focus in their work. This table examines their population by race/ethnicity and poverty levels.

Table 3.2 Whole Population: All Children in State. Indicator: Children Reading on Grade-Level at 3rd Grade

Race/Ethnicity	% of children reading on grade level by race and ethnicity	Poverty Level measured by Federal Poverty Guidelines	% of children reading on grade level by poverty level
White __%			
African American __%			
Latino/Hispanic __%			
Asian __%			
Native American __%			
Other __%			

Chapter 3: Moving Toward Execution—The Results Action Plan

An example of disaggregation comes from the initial work that Jim Czarniak did in the juvenile justice system in an Upstate New York county (introduced in Chapter 2). When Jim looked at the population of the children in the juvenile justice system in his county, he could see that African American and Hispanic children were over-represented—a trend which continued for those children in probation and supervision. With this data, the work was to identify specific strategies to address this disparity. His team would have to do the hard work to look at policies, the rules and regulations that organizations use to implement their work, the ways the cross-sector systems engaged with each other all to address the disparity revealed by disaggregating the data. Figure 3.1 offers an example of population disaggregation.

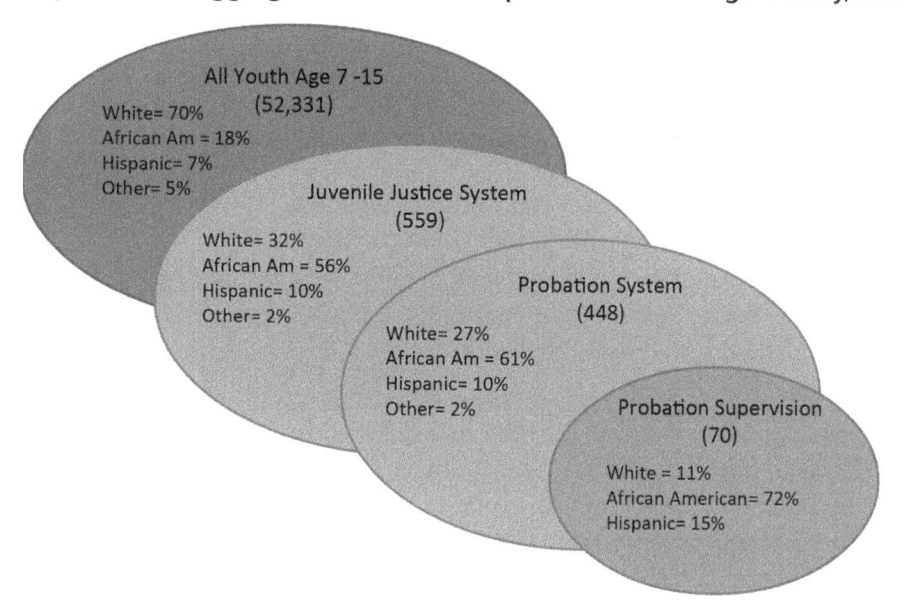

Figure 3.1 Population Disaggregation Revealed Disparities in Onondaga County, New York

All Youth Age 7-15 (52,331)
White= 70%
African Am = 18%
Hispanic= 7%
Other= 5%

Juvenile Justice System (559)
White= 32%
African Am = 56%
Hispanic= 10%
Other= 2%

Probation System (448)
White= 27%
African Am = 61%
Hispanic= 10%
Other= 2%

Probation Supervision (70)
White = 11%
African American= 72%
Hispanic= 15%

Data Visualization: Effective collaboration requires taking data and offering it in a way that is useful to understand and interpret. Data visualization and presentation is the visual representation and presentation of data to enhance understanding of the data. When partners and stakeholders can see their data presented visually, they are better able to grasp difficult concepts, identify new patterns, and deduce key messages. Effective data presentation allows for leaders to comprehend the information quickly, see emerging trends, and communicate the work to others.

Some of the most useful of the many possible formats for data presentation are described in Table 3.3.

Part 1: From Fragmentation to Shared Results

Table 3.3 **Data Presentation Formats**

Description	Example
Bar Graphs: Can be used to display comparisons, rankings, and change over time. As the name states, it uses bars to compare data among categories. They are popular because they allow people to recognize patterns or trends far more easily than looking at a table of numerical data.	
Line Graphs: Can be used to display a sloping line representing change over time. This is useful displaying trends and making projections. Line graphs are effective in comparison of several lines. For example, trends for a whole population and a disaggregated population.	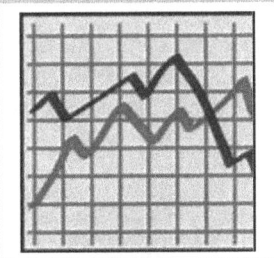
Pie Charts: A circular chart divided into wedge-like sectors, illustrating proportion. This type of presentation displays parts of the whole. The size of each part of the whole displayed as a percentage makes the relationships among the parts and between the parts and the whole easily observable.	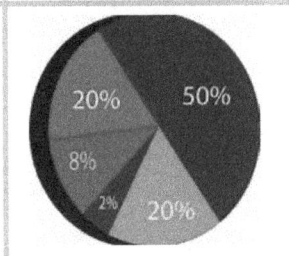
Maps: Displaying your data with mapping is a quick and powerful way to display trends and services by region. This type of data presentation can be simple or complex and will allow stakeholders to compare services, measures, demographics and other data elements quickly.	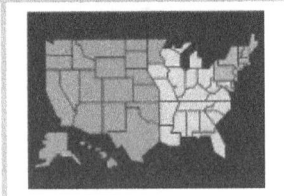
Dashboard: A dashboard is a collection of important data assembled to create a single visual display. Dashboards can include information about one part of a system, an entire system or a combination. Dashboard data changes as the data changes—this can be done in real time to allow the leaders to track progress over time.	

Chapter 3: Moving Toward Execution—The Results Action Plan

How Results Leaders Do Data Analysis

Moving from a Results Playbook to a shared results action plan requires leaders to engage in data analysis in order to sharpen the focus of their work at three "population" levels:

1. **Whole population:** the entire "headcount" of individuals, children, or families in a specified place;
2. **Strategy population:** the individuals, children or families affected by a specific strategy; and
3. **Program population:** the individuals, children, or families impacted by a program (which may include multiple strategies).

This data analysis allows leaders to accomplish several essentials:

- Focus their work through a better understanding of the population;
- Identify the goal of their work by identifying a baseline and target—at all three levels;
- Use factor analysis to determine the best strategies to develop by focusing on the factors that contribute to the problem; and
- Create timelines—at all three levels—to create both urgency and accountability to the work, and make transparent the need for coordination between individual actions across strategies and programs.

Engaging in this level of data analysis allows leaders to track progress of their collaborative work, engage in any quality improvement needed (discussed in greater detail in Chapter 6), and support the development of a results culture (discussed in Chapter 5). Now, let's take a closer look at what's involved as results leaders perform their data analysis.

Data Analysis to Understand the Population

When we disaggregate population-level data—by race, class, culture, gender, ethnicity, geography, etc., most often disparities are revealed. Results leaders are interested in whole population, strategy population, and their program population and will engage in analysis at all three levels. This allows them to see where there may be disproportionality in their work. This analysis encourages leaders to explore what might be the factors that contribute to the disproportionality and consider possible solutions to implement.

Disaggregating data at the population level is the first step in this analysis.

Data Analysis to Identify Baseline and Trend Data for Indicator

Leaders collaborate to adopt a baseline of the indicator in order to answer the question "where are we?" Baseline data and trend data report on both a whole population and a "sub" population, disaggregated to reveal disparities.

Baseline: A baseline assessment is an evaluation used to obtain general information about the present state of a result. It is the first data point that will be compared to future data points. For example, if the work is focused on health and one indicator is diabetes rates for people within a defined community, the baseline would be the percentage of the population diagnosed with diabetes at the start of the results work. A baseline allows leaders to set future targets for their results work. To make a positive change, one of the first things leaders need to agree on is the starting point for their work and then to determine any trends.

Trend Line: A trend line is used to represent the behavior of a set of data to determine if there is a certain pattern. It is an analytical tool used to see if there is a relationship between two variables. The main purpose of a trend line is to determine if a set of points exhibits a positive trend, a negative trend, or no trend at all. It can be useful to predict unknown or future data points. Figure 3.2 shows an example of a trend line with two variables—temperature and day. The data points show a positive trend. The dotted lines after day 11 predict future data points based on the positive trend.

Using data to answer the question, "Where are we now?" provides leaders with a history of past performance in relation to the indicator they are using to measure progress. For example, an adopted result might be, "All children read on grade-level by 3rd grade," and an indicator, the percentage of children who pass a reading level assessment. The "Where are we now?" measure would simply show what percentage of children currently are passing this assessment, while also providing data on recent trends by looking at previous scores—i.e., is this measure going up or down?

Having this data serves two purposes. First, it allows leaders to determine the current status of a group of people or a community. Second, it creates the needed urgency for action by asking: "Are things okay the way they are?"

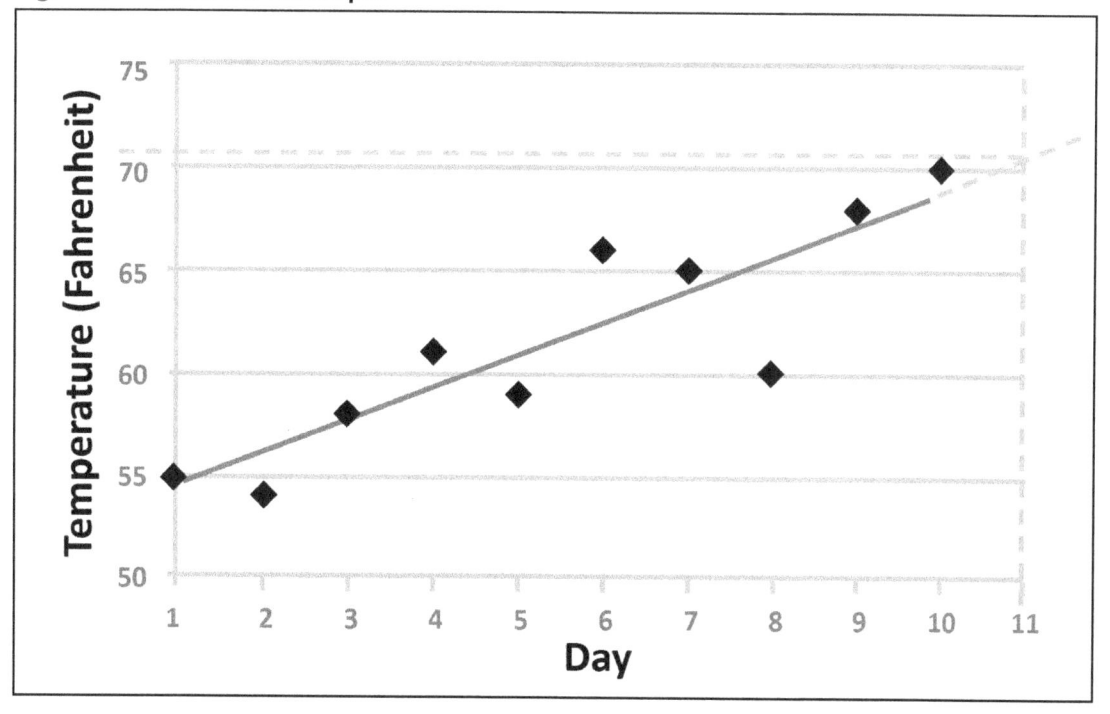

Figure 3.2 **Trend Line Example**

With baseline data in hand, leaders are able come together to assess the data and answer the following questions:

- What does the available data say about what is happening relative to the result we want to achieve?
- How extensive are the problems we aim to solve? What populations are affected most?
- How do we know if things are getting better or worse?
- What additional data do we need?

In addition, baseline and trend data can and should be disaggregated by race, class, culture, or any subset of the whole population. This allows leaders to understand what is working and not working, and for whom.

An example of base and trend line, disaggregated by race might look like the graph in Figure 3.3. This graph shows a baseline data point for juveniles in residential placement by race and Hispanic origin as well as a downward trend line. It also shows a disparity by race (top line) where non-Hispanic African American juveniles are overrepresented in this population.

Part 1: From Fragmentation to Shared Results

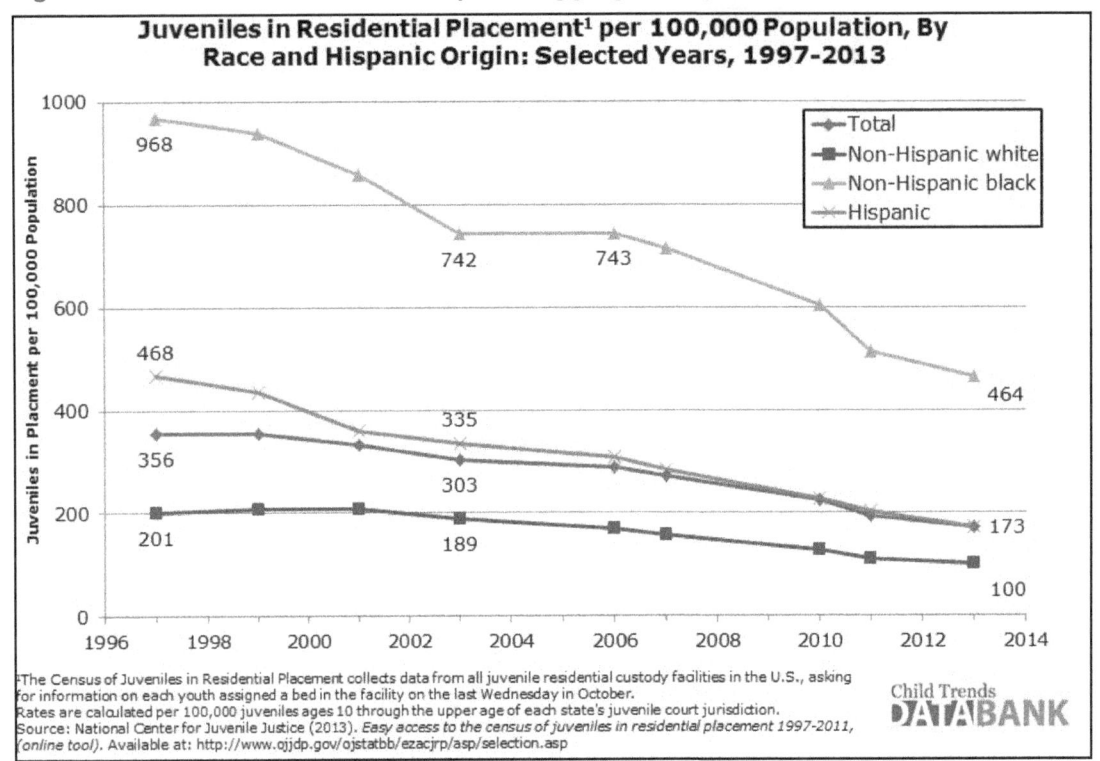

Figure 3.3 **Base and Trend Line Example Disaggregated by Race**

Juveniles in Residential Placement[1] per 100,000 Population, By Race and Hispanic Origin: Selected Years, 1997-2013

- Total
- Non-Hispanic white
- Non-Hispanic black
- Hispanic

Non-Hispanic black: 968 (1997), 742, 743, 464 (2013)
Hispanic: 468, 335, 173
Total: 356, 303, 100
Non-Hispanic white: 201, 189

[1]The Census of Juveniles in Residential Placement collects data from all juvenile residential custody facilities in the U.S., asking for information on each youth assigned a bed in the facility on the last Wednesday in October.
Rates are calculated per 100,000 juveniles ages 10 through the upper age of each state's juvenile court jurisdiction.
Source: National Center for Juvenile Justice (2013). *Easy access to the census of juveniles in residential placement 1997-2011*, (online tool). Available at: http://www.ojjdp.gov/ojstatbb/ezacjrp/asp/selection.asp

Child Trends DATABANK

Agreed-upon indicator target: Using baseline data allows leaders to assess what progress might look like over time. In other words, leaders can use such data to anticipate future trends—*if nothing is done*—and to envision a new and different future—should the trend line start moving in the positive direction—*if SOMETHING is done.*

The simplest way to recognize a target is to ask, "Where do we want to be?" This allows leaders to set the stage for the hard work ahead. For example, if the trend line shows a steep decline in an indicator over the last five years and factor analysis (explained below) reveals deeply entrenched factors, then leaders might define success as slowing down the decline and then gradually "turning the curve" in the positive direction.

It can take time to move an indicator in the right direction, particularly if the trend line has been going the wrong way for a long time. If leaders do not use baselines and factor analysis to illuminate current conditions, they can set themselves up for failure or open their work to criticism by creating unrealistic expectations.

Targets allow leaders to create urgency in their work and to assess their progress. Targets can be both inspiring and daunting at the same

Chapter 3: Moving Toward Execution—The Results Action Plan

time. They define what is to be done and by when. If baselines force the question, *"Are we satisfied with the way things are?"* then targets provide clarity of purpose and answer the question, *"Where do we want to be?"*

In setting targets, leaders need to consider the following factors:

- The degree of desired change—expressed both as a percentage and a whole number. For example, leaders might agree that they want to move the grade-level reading indicator from 40% (for a whole or target population) to 50%, or from 400 to 500 children in a population of 1000;
- The criteria for choosing the target—consider past performance, comparison to other similar work, estimations and expectations; and
- The time period—i.e., the end date of a measurement cycle.

The example in Figure 3.4 shows a starting point of 51.5% rearrests in 2006. From this baseline, trends can be determined and then targets can be set.

In short, results leaders analyze how populations, strategies, and programs are performing by using a baseline and trend line, and agreed-upon target, examining data for a designated measurement cycle.

Figure 3.4 **Trend Line Example with Baseline, Target, and Actual Performance in Time Period**

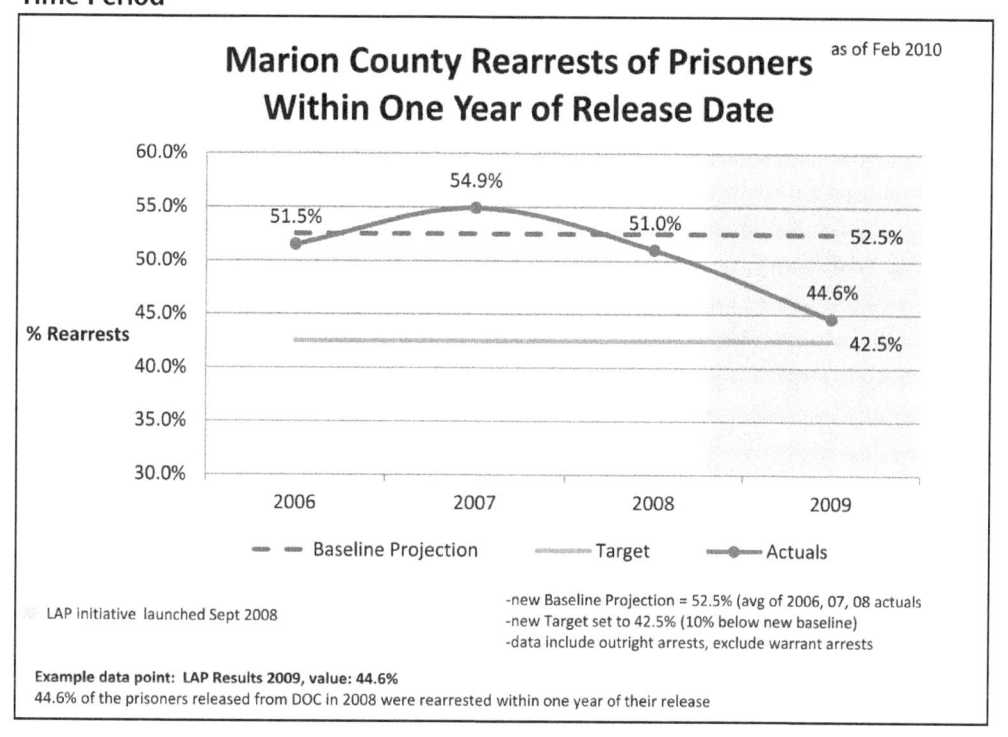

Marion County Rearrests of Prisoners Within One Year of Release Date (as of Feb 2010)

% Rearrests:
- 2006: 51.5%
- 2007: 54.9%
- 2008: 51.0%
- 2009: 44.6%

Baseline Projection: 52.5%
Target: 42.5%

LAP initiative launched Sept 2008

- new Baseline Projection = 52.5% (avg of 2006, 07, 08 actuals
- new Target set to 42.5% (10% below new baseline)
- data include outright arrests, exclude warrant arrests

Example data point: LAP Results 2009, value: 44.6%
44.6% of the prisoners released from DOC in 2008 were rearrested within one year of their release

Jim Czarniak is so committed to targets he uses the notion of target setting even as he introduces himself to a new audience. He'll say, "Hi, my name is Jim and I'm a results leader." After the crowd's response of "Hi, Jim," he'll add "It is 113 days until my next target!"

He will then go into greater detail about his targets. Again, in his words: "Sometime I'll let partners and stakeholders know that our county has 120,000 children and 850 of those children are not living at home. I let them know I want to reduce that number. I will ask my partners in the mental health, juvenile justice, and homeless sectors to join in getting 85% of the children not living at home back with their families by the end of 2018. I know that by having a target it allows all of us to do our part to be successful."

Data Analysis Identifies Priority Strategies: Factor Analysis and Criteria Setting

The heart of any actionable results plan is the strategies that are identified, developed, and then implemented. As we saw in Chapter 2, strategies become a theory of change in shared results work. In creating a results action plan, results leaders take the time to examine the slope of the trend line of their work and determine if things are getting better, worse, or if they are about the same. Then, they take the time to look below the surface to determine what exactly is going on. The work needed to answer the second question, known as factor analysis,[3] is perhaps the most important analysis results leaders can do as they work towards results. This problem-solving methodology seeks to address the contributing factors to a situation.

Factors are the underlying or structural reasons behind the problem or issue results leaders are seeking to address. Trying to identify why the problem has developed is an essential part of developing a results action plan. We do this in order to develop the appropriate strategies and to engage all necessary stakeholders.

By engaging in the work of factor analysis, results leaders are able to:

- Determine the current state of a program or population result;
- Look at what is contributing to the current state;
- Examine the underlying conditions and contributors; and
- Identify the strategies that specifically address the underlying conditions.

For example, by engaging in a factor analysis process, results leaders can identify individual, community, and/or systems strategies such as[4]

- Strategies to support individual knowledge, awareness, attitudes, and behavior:
  - Parents may need more knowledge about nutrition.
  - Children may need to learn refusal skills to avoid smoking.
  - Service providers may need greater cultural awareness.
- Strategies to explore community and system causes such as:
  - Cultural factors—customs, beliefs, and values;
  - Economic factors—income, land, and resources;
  - Political factors—decision-making power, engagement.

Factor analysis: This work allows results leaders to identify the multiple strategies needed to make progress on the results work. Because the factor analysis reveals the complexities of the public problem, it increases the chances of choosing the right set of strategies.

Leaders take three initial steps in their factor analysis work:

1. Define the current state of the population for the result:
   - Is the trend line better, worse, or the same? Is the disparity increasing or decreasing?
   - How do you know if the state is getting better or worse?
2. Define what is contributing to the current state:
   - What factors are contributing to the trend line going in the right direction, those making a positive contribution to the current situation?
   - What factors are contributing to the trend line going in the wrong direction, those making a negative contribution to the current situation?
3. Which factors are contributing to existing disparities?
   - Explore underlying factors:
   - What is the underlying reason the problem or solution is occurring?
   - What's helping to shape that underlying reason behind the problem or solution?

> The Factor Analysis Worksheet in the apps/tools section at the end of this chapter is designed to help you and your partners determine the actionable factors that are contributing to your trend line.

In the Apps/Tools section the end of this chapter, you will find a Factor Analysis Worksheet that you can use to support your work to identify the priority strategies needed for your results work. The Five Whys worksheet included there should be helpful as well. Chapter 4 uses a version of factor analysis to go deeper into an individual leader's intent and purpose for engaging in this kind of work.

Criteria setting: Once results leaders have established the possible set of strategies to implement, they use a set of criteria that allow them to make sure these strategies could support the hard work required to make a difference at a population level. An example of Criteria for Strategy Selection is shown in Figure 3.5.

By selecting overarching strategies based on factor analysis and then using a set of criteria to refine strategy selection, results leaders create the foundation for executing their results work. The final task is then to determine how performance of strategies will be measured.

Paola Maranan, Executive Director for the Children's Alliance in Seattle, Washington, was introduced to results work as a participant in Annie E. Casey's results program titled Leadership Institute for State-based Advocates. This leadership program was designed specifically to provide state advocates with the technical skills for advocacy coupled with key results leadership tools and methods. One key focus for Paola was to move her organization—its trustees, staff, and partners—toward a greater emphasis on equity. "I have always felt we needed to be doing everything we could to improve conditions for kids of color, and I wanted to explore how we could do that," she said.

Paola was initially skeptical about the population-level results approach, but over time she said she had a "light-bulb moment." She told me, "I realized this was how our organization and its people were going to hold ourselves accountable for real change for children of color. It's one thing to say you care about equity, and it's another thing to hold yourself accountable for making equity a reality." By engaging with their partners and stakeholders in first analyzing the disaggregated data to highlight where there were disparities, and then to use that data to do a factor analysis, they were able to work in a way that created greater alignment toward a shared result.

Data Analysis to Assess Performance

The way to create High Action and High Alignment (leveraging each other's work) in results work is through performance. Performance and performance measures were discussed in Chapter 2 and deserve consideration as part of a results action plan—specifically performance measures related to strategies.

As I said earlier, data highlights the current state of the problem. In doing so, it forces leaders to consider, "Are things okay the way they are?" Which begs the answer, "Certainly not!" Coming to this shared realization creates urgency and accountability in all stakeholder leaders, work groups, partners, and systems.

Figure 3.5 **Criteria for Strategy Selection**

Criteria for Strategy Selection

Impact: Refers to the impact the strategy will have towards the results work.
- Will the strategy reach the children, families, or residents that leaders have identified? *For example, to reduce recidivism through more and better jobs and associated training, does the strategy reach both the incarcerated and employers who could contribute to their successful reentry into the community after release?*
- Will the strategy reach, specifically, those experiencing disparities based on race, class, culture, gender, etc.? *For example, developing a training strategy for ex-offenders designed to develop the necessary skills for employment in a specific sector where more jobs exist in their neighborhoods v. those where, say, another ethnic identity is predominant.*

Reach: The portion of the target population that will benefit from the successful execution of the strategy.
- When implemented, what is the expected "level" of impact in terms of the percentage of people? *For example, the strategy to form an employer's alliance to hire ex-offenders will affect 800 or 20% of ex-offenders returning to the community annually.*

Success Probability: Does the strategy have "good enough" evidence that it works for the targeted population?
- What is the research, evidence, or best practice to predict success? *For example, developing an employment strategy designed to provide jobs that pay a livable wage based on research that shows this correlates to reducing recidivisim.*

Community Fit: Does this strategy fit the values of residents, stakeholders, and partners?
- Does it fit the culture and interests of the community?
- Were the voices or interests of the stakeholders incorporated in developing the strategy? *For example, incorporating the interests of ex-offenders when exploring the factor analysis and strategy development.*

Capacity: Is there the necessary infrastructure and resources to implement the strategy successfully?
- Are the needed resources available or accessible?
- Are the critical partners ready to do the work?
- Who else needs to be recruited? *For example, preparing employers as well as ex-offenders for successful on-boarding and training of new hires.*

Used with permission by Phyllis Rozanski

Part 1: From Fragmentation to Shared Results

Connecting the key elements of the Results Playbook (result, indicator, overarching strategies) to the analysis of data (population-level analysis, adoption of a baseline and target for the indicator, and factor analysis) allows results leaders to create a shared results action plan. The final pieces of any such plan are those that create both the urgency and the accountability of the work. Thus, it is absolutely essential to use data to assess performance as strategies move forward. Through performance assessment, leaders create the conditions for individuals to work in High Action and High Alignment.

Results action plans highlight at least two levels of accountability: **Performance measures** and timelines that track progress and create urgency of work-performance at the population and program level. Just as we examined the components of data analysis earlier, we now complete our consideration of the results action plan with a look at these two final pieces of the plan.

Performance Measures

Once leaders identify a strategy or set of strategies, connect the programmatic work to those strategies, and identify their role in those programs, execution begins—and measurement of how those strategies performed. Results leaders are always paying attention to the performance of the strategies, the programs, and the individuals in their role through performance measures—metrics used to identify the quantity, quality, and impact of the work being done. The three simple questions used to assess performance are:

- How much did we do/are we doing (this is a "quantity" question)?
- How well did we do it/are we doing it (this is a "quality" question)?
- What difference did we make/are we making (this is an "impact" question)?

Performance measure: A measure of the impact of a strategy, a program, agency, or service. It is also a measure of the impact of a leader in his or her role. The most important performance measures tell us whether anyone is better off.

Strategy Performance: As stated earlier, strategies are the means to the end—the result. Thus, performance measures provide:

- A way to know if a strategy, the programs that support the strategy, and its implementing leaders are making a difference;
- Clarity about how to define "success" for the strategy, program, and/or individual actions in role;
- A continuous, pervasive, and insightful way of assessing

the work and the contribution a program is making to the larger, population-level result;
- Information about whether anybody is better off because of the strategy and its supporting programs—and how;
- A sense of whether the strategy or program can or will meet its targets; and
- A way to evaluate if any one individual's activities are producing the desired results.

Program Performance: Once leaders identify a program population and a program result (linked, of course, to the overall population-level result), the more difficult work of establishing performance measures for the program can begin.[5]

Without knowing their performance measures, results leaders would not know what their contribution has been to the result; what is working and what isn't; and appropriate areas for quality improvement processes. I once worked with a leader whose contribution to a result of all children entering school ready to learn was focusing on children who were deaf or hearing impaired. While there were a variety of strategies designed to support this particular population, her specific contribution was to support teacher development, so they could work most effectively with deaf or hearing-impaired children.

Developing performance measures for a program can be laborious and rather complex. A more detailed guide to setting performance measures for quantity, quality, and impact can be found at the end of Chapter 2.

Results leaders use a template to help hold their program. This template will be foundational to help leaders make their contribution in the population level results action plan.

Measuring individual performance in role: Leaders also use performance measure data to track their own performance. To be effective in their work, results leaders must be clear on role and task expectations as well as the role and task expectations of others they work with for people to function at their peak effectiveness. While there is a deeper exploration of role in Chapter 5, the following set of questions can help results leaders become clearer on their own performance measures.

Role and Key Tasks performed in role:
- What is your role? Who authorized you to perform it?

See Strategy Template in the apps/tools section at the end of this chapter. Results leaders use a template to help identify the key elements of strategy development. Chapter 7 will explore the various ways strategies are used to execute the work. This template will be foundational to help leaders move the Results Playbook to a population-level results action plan.

Developing Quality Performance Measures Worksheet in the apps/tools section at the end of this chapter is designed to support the development of performance measures.

Part 1: From Fragmentation to Shared Results

> See Program Template in the apps/tools section at the end of this chapter.

- What is the purpose/function of your role in advancing the results plan?
- Who do you need to align with so you will be successful in role? Who needs to align with you so they can be successful?
- What data are you using to measure if you are being successful in your role?
- What are your role performance measures?

Timelines

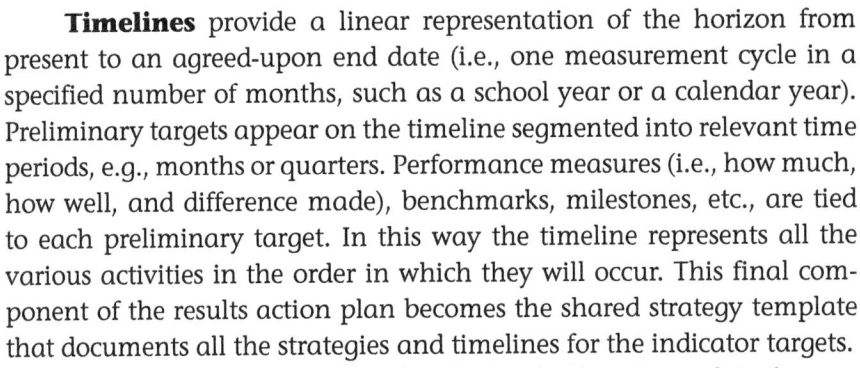

Timelines provide a linear representation of the horizon from present to an agreed-upon end date (i.e., one measurement cycle in a specified number of months, such as a school year or a calendar year). Preliminary targets appear on the timeline segmented into relevant time periods, e.g., months or quarters. Performance measures (i.e., how much, how well, and difference made), benchmarks, milestones, etc., are tied to each preliminary target. In this way the timeline represents all the various activities in the order in which they will occur. This final component of the results action plan becomes the shared strategy template that documents all the strategies and timelines for the indicator targets.

> **Timelines:** Graphic representations of the passage of time as a line beginning at the present date, extending to an agreed-upon end date for one measurement cycle. Timelines document the milestones to be reached along the way.

As highlighted in the Results Playbook, data is used to focus a group's work on a goal specific to a population, by identifying a baseline and target, agreeing on indicator targets, and using factor analysis to determine the best strategies to pursue based on the factors contributing to the problem. Data points over time reveal whether progress is being made on the population-level result (the condition of wellbeing) that brings these results leaders together. All the work undertaken across multiple programs is thus strategically designed to move the indicator in the target direction.

It should now be clear how—and why—results leaders do data analysis. Why? To understand the population, develop potential strategies, choose which to prioritize, and monitor that performance stays in High Action and High Alignment after execution begins on those strategies. How? Through gathering the right data, disaggregating it, and conducting factor analysis, criteria selection, and tying the results action plan to a timeline with milestones and benchmarks.

When combining the Results Playbook with data and analysis you will be able to create a results action plan that supports partners and stakeholders working toward shared results. Below is a template for a population-level results plan.

Population-Level Results Action Plan Template

Leaders use the results action plan to hold or contain the work they are doing together. The results action plan not only reveals the intent of the work (the result), it holds the analysis done to help focus the work. Because the results action plan is public, it also serves as a vehicle for accountability and transparency by declaring targets and placing targets on a timeline.

> A Population-Level Results Action Plan Template appears in the apps/tools section at the end of this chapter. It is designed to help you and your partners hold the results work at a high level. This template is a distillation of the work done by Jolie Bain Pillsbury.

Executing the Results Action Plan in Indianola

When I started working with the Indianola Promise Neighborhood team, as lead faculty and part of a robust implementation team[6] that included representatives from the Promise Neighborhood Institute and the Annie E Casey Foundation, they were already a well-formed team working with the Mississippi Delta Health Alliance. The Delta Health Alliance operated programs throughout the Mississippi Delta with a particular focus on health and education. The Indianola Promise Neighborhood team's work was focused on children's education, specifically children entering kindergarten ready to learn and continuing to work towards college and career readiness through their K-12 education. I recall when the Promise Neighborhood team members were first introduced to the Results Playbook and their initial discomfort with the whole population-level result.

Their journey to creating and executing a results action plan began with their ability to hold the central idea in doing results work—being accountable to both the population-level result and their program-level result. They developed their "Result in the Center" chart to see who else should be invited to join them to make an impact at the population level. They could see that many sectors and systems were needed to make sure that children succeeded in school.

Once they agreed on the results and their set of indicators, they started to create their Results Playbook. Instead of jumping from the result and indicator right to the programs they were already running (defaulting to programmatic thinking), they paused to conduct a factor analysis and examine what overarching strategies might be needed and to identify the stakeholders and partners needed to execute those strategies. (In other words, they engaged in results thinking). They quickly saw that they needed to engage the health sector, the housing sector, and the community sector, among others, to ensure that the children of Indianola would be successful in school. They could also see, through disaggregating data, that their programmatic work only impacted a portion of children in their community. They would have to engage with others within the education sector to ensure that all children in their community succeeded. As the team shares their story, you will notice the hard work they did to engage with their partners in order to do their work in High Action and High Alignment. You will notice how they used the discipline of data to create targets measured against time.

In December 2017, a broad coalition of community partners came together at the Indianola, Mississippi Public Library. Delta Health Alliance, the sponsor of the Indianola Promise Community (IPC), announced at the gathering that, in the fall of 2017, 64 percent of the city's kindergartners started the school year ready to learn, up from just 25 percent in 2013.

That's big news anywhere, but especially in Indianola, located in one of the poorest counties in the Mississippi Delta. Increased school readiness augers well for increased rates of third-grade reading proficiency, which research indicates will translate into higher rates of students graduating from high school ready for college and career success.

Focusing on population-level results

IPC's Results Action Plan was and is a call to action. It states that all children in Indianola will enter kindergarten ready to learn.

This is a bold and urgent goal. Just four years earlier, only one in four children in Indianola entering kindergarten was assessed as ready and on track for reading success by third grade.

As their baseline indicator for that result, IPC uses the percentage of children who passed the Sunflower County Consolidated School District's early literacy assessment, which determines which kindergarten students need academic intervention as well as those on track to read proficiently by the end of third grade.

Whole population analysis

IPC's work to disaggregate data revealed 73 percent of the incoming kindergarten class came from single-parent families and nearly half from households earning less than $10,000 annually.

The analysis also showed that a majority of single moms sending their kids to kindergarten had college experience and that 26 percent had earned an associate, bachelor's, or graduate degree, compared to 11 percent who hadn't finished high school.

In addition, the data revealed that boys, who made up 58 percent of the incoming class, were less likely to be ready for kindergarten than girls.

Adoption of baseline and target for improvement

Although the December gathering celebrated Indianola's progress in kindergarten readiness, 64 percent is still far short of the action plan's goal of all children starting school ready to learn. Partners thus set a target for a 70 percent school readiness rate by the end of 2018.

Whole population factor analysis and strategy selection

Factor analysis conducted by the IPC team allowed them to design intervention strategies in partnership with the community's pre-K program providers, the school district, social service agencies, and child and family advocates.

For example, IPC partners identified a need for a pre-K curriculum that was aligned to the school district's early literacy assessment. In May 2015, Head Start and private childcare providers began to implement an evidence-based curriculum they identified with support from IPC and other stakeholders. Today the curriculum is taught to more than 450 preschoolers in Indianola and Sunflower County. In addition, Head Start and other providers share pre-K student data with each other and Delta Health Alliance to assure quality implementation of the curriculum.

The partners also determined that pre-K students and families needed multiple "touches" from a variety of programs outside of childcare centers to assure school readiness. They crafted a strategy to enroll families receiving home visits from IPC staff in the Dolly Parton Imagination Library program, which provides free books every month to families with children from birth to age five.

Summer learning was identified as another key factor for school readiness, especially the summer before children enter kindergarten. (Research shows that ongoing skill-building in summer programs helps children retain and practice what they've learned during the previous months.) A six-week summer program, called Promise School, was developed by the school district, pre-K providers, Delta Health Alliance, and Head Start. Data collected from students attending Promise School has shown they outperform children who don't participate in the program not only on the kindergarten early literacy assessment, but on grade-level reading proficiency assessments in first through third grade.

Strategy work plan

Each strategy has its own set of targets and performance measures that are tied to the overarching result of all children being ready for school. For example, partners have set a target of 90 percent of pre-K programs in Indianola using a curriculum aligned to the early literacy assessment. The number and percentage of students meeting age-appropriate developmental markers at age three and age four are the performance measures partners will use to determine if they're on track to meet the target.

Figure 3.6 represents the fifth year of a results action plan that the Indianola team developed for their school-readiness work. Note that years 1 through 4 of this plan would look much different in terms of their baselines, targets, and strategies.

Chapter 3: Moving Toward Execution—The Results Action Plan

Figure 3.6 **Population-level Results/Indianola K-readiness Results Action Plan**

Component	Content
Part 1: Population, Result and Indicator with focus on a Call to Action	**Call to Action** • **Whole Population:** Children in Indianola • **Result:** Children enter kindergarten ready to learn • **Indicator(s) with Trend Line:** **Percent of Students Kindergarten Ready** 2013: 25%, 2014: 44%, 2015: 52%, 2016: 49%, 2017: 64%

Part 2: Whole Population Analysis	**Whole Population**
	• Disaggregated Data:
	  - 95% African American
	  - 55% male
	  - Majority of kindergarten students come from single parent families (73%)
	  - Half (48%) of kindergarten students come from families who make less than $10,000 annually
	  - Girls are more likely than boys to be ready for kindergarten

Part 3: Adoption of Baseline and Target for Improvement	**Adoption of Baseline:** *Where are we now?* 64% *What does the data tell us?* The trend is in the right direction and we need to accelerate the pace of change Set **Target for Improvement:** Where do we want to be? What's the goal—where do you want to be by when? 2018 target—70%

Part 1: From Fragmentation to Shared Results

Part 4: Whole Population Factor Analysis	**Factors** • High quality pre-K programs • Layered enrollment in IPC programs • Summer transition programs **What works to address factors?** • Evidence based curriculum and assessment • Targeted dual enrollment in programming • Alignment of summer programming **Who can contribute to what works?** • Delta Health Alliance • Pre-K providers • Save the Children Head Start • Sunflower County Consolidated School District Additional disaggregated data about the whole population (i.e. demographics, disaggregated data initial set, and additional from data development agenda)
Part 5: Strategy Selection	**What are the Strategies?** • What strategies address the factors and reflect what the leaders can contribute? Dual Enrollment Strategy Coordinated Summer Transition Strategy Alignment of Curriculum/Assessment Strategy *How do we get there?* Dual Enrollment Strategy Leader: Dr. Moore, Delta Health Alliance Coordinated Summer Transition Strategy Leader: [Name], DHA, and [Name], Sunflower County Consolidated School District Alignment of Curriculum/Assessment Strategy Leader: [Name], DHA

Chapter 3: Moving Toward Execution—The Results Action Plan

| Part 6: Strategy Group Work Plans | **Strategy: Aligned Pre-K Curriculum and Assessment**
 Strategy Population:
 Childcare programs and children attending Pre-K in Indianola

 Strategy Result:
 All childcare programs in Indianola have an aligned curriculum and assessment and are implementing with fidelity with a final result in center that children are ready for Kindergarten

 Strategy Target:
 90% of Pre-K programs in Indianola are using an aligned curriculum and assessment

 Strategy Performance Measures:
 Number and percentage of centers using aligned curriculum/assessment <ul><li>Current status: 4 of 5 centers (80%), including private child care centers, the state Pre-K collaborative, and Save the Children Head Start program.</li></ul> Number and percentage of students meeting age-appropriate development markers at three and four years old. <ul><li>Current status: 38% of three-year-old children in Indianola are meeting age-appropriate development markers across multiple domains</li><li>Data Development Agenda: Need to obtain the finalized data for four-year-old children meeting development markers</li></ul> Number and percentage of students dually enrolled in a home visitation program and Imagination Library <ul><li>Current status: 90% of home-visitation participants are dually enrolled in Imagination Library.</li></ul> Number and percentage of students who participate in evidence-based summer transition program before entering kindergarten <ul><li>Current status: 70% of 2017 kindergarteners participated in the summer transition program before entering kindergarten</li></ul>
 continued |

Part 1: From Fragmentation to Shared Results

Part 6 continued	**Strategy Partners:** Save the Children Head Start Private Childcare Centers Sunflower County Consolidated School District Delta Health Alliance Sunflower County United for Children
Part 7: Strategy Implementation Timeline	**Path to Achieving Target (Impact)** **Timeline and Milestones of Performance Measure to Achieve Scope and Scale to Advance Strategy Execution (Impact)** **In the next 3 months these key milestones need to be completed:** Conduct environment scan of Head Start, private childcare centers, and Pre-K Collaborative programs in Indianola to determine current curriculum and assessment, and barriers to possible alignment Use Delta Health Alliance to provide resources for curriculum/assessment to private childcare centers in Indianola Identify possible resources for centers in greater county (outside of Indianola) Engage Save the Children Head Start to provide access to professional development regarding curriculum to private childcare centers in Sunflower County Encourage Save the Children Head Start and childcare centers to share quarterly data with Delta Health Alliance Have Delta Health Alliance use quarterly assessment data to provide targeted referrals to additional IPC programming Ensure continuous improvement cycle by having Delta Health Alliance provide quarterly reports to partners

Chapter 3: Moving Toward Execution—The Results Action Plan

Results Leaders: Josh Davis, Karin Scott, Carolyn Willis and Deborah Moore

One of the biggest lessons Indianola Promise Community leaders say they've learned from using a results action plan is how to work in true collaboration with the 16 community partners who are helping drive the increase in Indianola's school-readiness rate.

For some, it meant learning a totally new leadership style.

Josh Davis, DHA's former Vice President for External Affairs, said his individual challenge was to abandon the traditional, hierarchal leadership style he had learned in school and used throughout his career in the nonprofit sector. The tactics and tools of results leadership made sense but were not effective for him, Davis said, until "I was personally able to allow myself to be open to judgment, critique, and advice, and to be vulnerable." This personal journey was "profound and deep and reflective" because he had to deal with temporary real and perceived losses of trust and confidence from those who expected him to function as a more traditional leader where "the buck stops with you and you are looked at as the problem solver .... if you don't have the answer then you find out how to get there."

Results leadership allowed him to move toward a more collective and collaborative leadership model with childcare and early education providers, schools, local government, and social service organizations involved in the Indianola Promise Community.

> *We have seen our work be successful by us moving away from the hierarchal form of dictating and allowing others to contribute.*
>
> *– Josh Davis, former Vice President for External Affairs, Delta Health Alliance*

Karin Scott started her job as Research and Evaluation Director for DHA (she is now the Associate Vice President for Strategic Data) thinking her job was to make sure that data collected was in compliance with the requirements of the federal Promise Neighborhood Initiative, "as opposed to asking questions about the data we needed to make better decisions to move the work forward,"—being responsible to the government v. being responsible to the work.

Asking those kinds of questions required her to learn to be a different kind of leader, and she wasn't sure at first if she had the skill or confidence to make the transition from focusing on compliance to focusing on results. Eventually, diligent practice of results leadership allowed her to make full

Part 1: From Fragmentation to Shared Results

Results Leader

use of population factor analysis with IPC partners. "I saw how it could be used to inform strategy development, how what I thought was a one-off tool or skill could start to reinforce conversations focused on results."

Carolyn Willis, the current vice president for Delta Health Alliance and project manager for the Indianola Promise Community, says she, too, has changed the way she works. Learning and applying the tools and methods of results leadership has helped her to adopt a less task-driven, "just get it done" approach and instead to allow the realities of child-care providers and school principals to inform strategies to achieve population-level results.

"The personal challenge is to not interject myself and my wants into this but to… recognize the challenges and barriers of others that have not been considered and to bring their realities into the room as well as their data," Willis said. "My previous work was all about taking personal ownership, and giving the work back was the most difficult hurdle for me. When you learn to do that, it then becomes more of a team effort to get things done. You do not have to own the whole process. I still struggle with that. I still think I could do it faster and just get it done."

Dr. Deborah Moore, the former Associate Vice President for Community Relations, Indianola Promise Community, says, "The results approach gives the work back to the group. You are not coming up with ideas, you are not saying what the ideas are … stakeholders and partners develop their own strategies and their own ideas, and the programs to move the needle on whatever those issues are. That is empowerment in itself."

For her, becoming a results leader has meant more than learning a skill. "This work is kind of contagious…when people start to feel empowered and they feel like they can make decisions about their own lives," she said. "They are moving from talk to action themselves. The more people who can do that in a community, the more accelerated this work becomes."

Putting results at the center has allowed the Indianola team to practice a new way of doing business, to move beyond relation building and toward data-driven decision making. The fact that kindergarten readiness and third-grade reading indicators are moving in the right direction has helped embed the new approach across child-care centers and the school district. There are still plenty of challenges ahead, the team acknowledges, especially given the changing mandates from state policy-makers, the new and ongoing economic and social challenges the community faces, and the changing and competing interests of the leaders within the community.

However, the results of their work is undeniable as shown in Figure 3.7.

As you can see, there is still work to be done so that all children in Indianola enter school ready to learn. As happens with all teams, there have been some role changes. Josh Davis and Deborah Moore are no longer

Chapter 3: Moving Toward Execution—The Results Action Plan

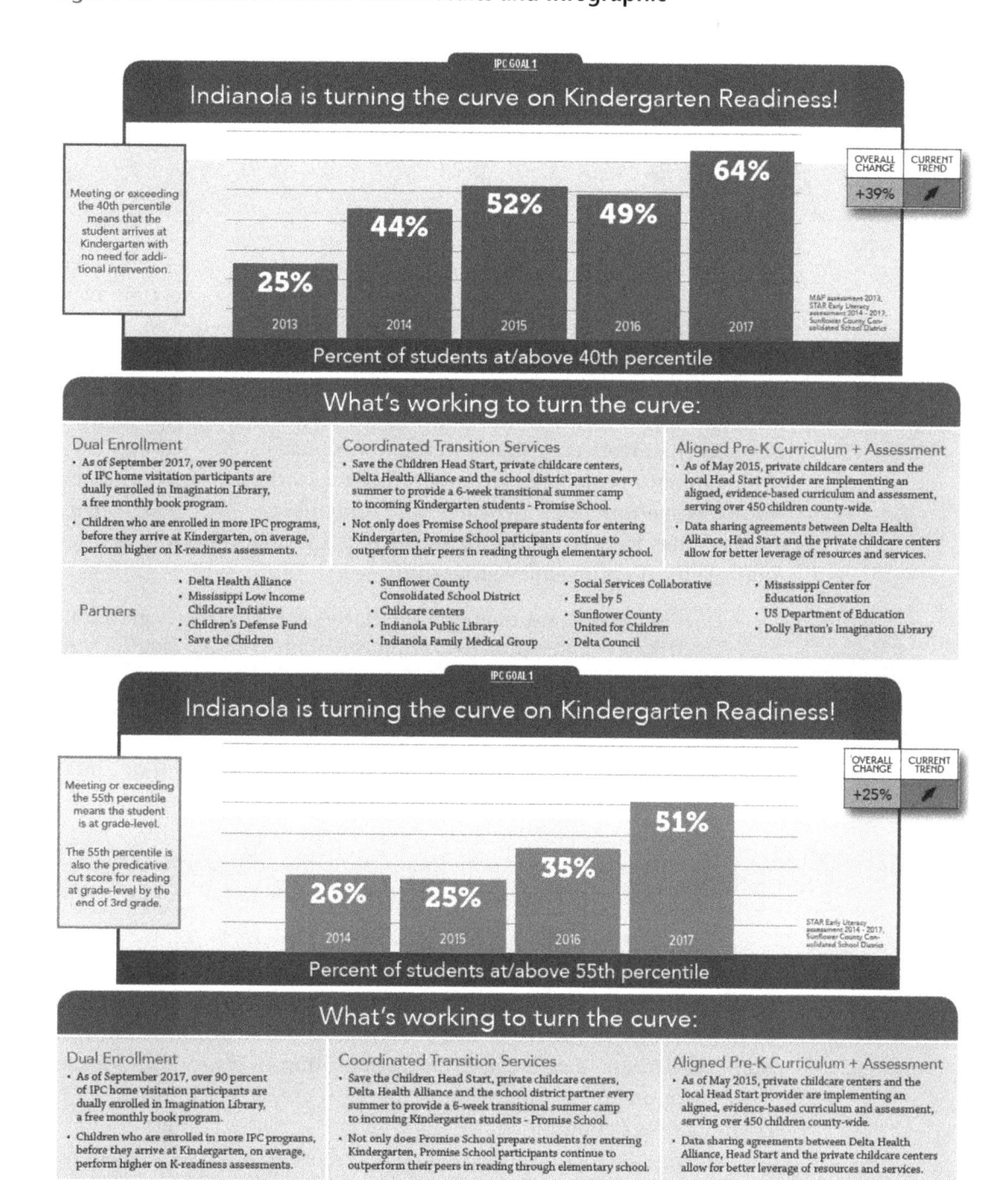

Figure 3.7 **Indianola Promise Team Results and Infographic**

IPC GOAL 1
Indianola is turning the curve on Kindergarten Readiness!

Meeting or exceeding the 40th percentile means that the student arrives at Kindergarten with no need for additional intervention.

2013	2014	2015	2016	2017
25%	44%	52%	49%	64%

Percent of students at/above 40th percentile

OVERALL CHANGE: +39%

MAP assessment 2013, STAR Early Literacy assessment 2014 - 2017, Sunflower County Consolidated School District

What's working to turn the curve:

Dual Enrollment
- As of September 2017, over 90 percent of IPC home visitation participants are dually enrolled in Imagination Library, a free monthly book program.
- Children who are enrolled in more IPC programs, before they arrive at Kindergarten, on average, perform higher on K-readiness assessments.

Coordinated Transition Services
- Save the Children Head Start, private childcare centers, Delta Health Alliance and the school district partner every summer to provide a 6-week transitional summer camp to incoming Kindergarten students - Promise School.
- Not only does Promise School prepare students for entering Kindergarten, Promise School participants continue to outperform their peers in reading through elementary school.

Aligned Pre-K Curriculum + Assessment
- As of May 2015, private childcare centers and the local Head Start provider are implementing an aligned, evidence-based curriculum and assessment, serving over 450 children county-wide.
- Data sharing agreements between Delta Health Alliance, Head Start and the private childcare centers allow for better leverage of resources and services.

Partners
- Delta Health Alliance
- Mississippi Low Income Childcare Initiative
- Children's Defense Fund
- Save the Children
- Sunflower County Consolidated School District
- Childcare centers
- Indianola Public Library
- Indianola Family Medical Group
- Social Services Collaborative
- Excel by 5
- Sunflower County United for Children
- Delta Council
- Mississippi Center for Education Innovation
- US Department of Education
- Dolly Parton's Imagination Library

IPC GOAL 1
Indianola is turning the curve on Kindergarten Readiness!

Meeting or exceeding the 55th percentile means the student is at grade-level.

The 55th percentile is also the predicative cut score for reading at grade-level by the end of 3rd grade.

2014	2015	2016	2017
26%	25%	35%	51%

Percent of students at/above 55th percentile

OVERALL CHANGE: +25%

STAR Early Literacy assessment 2014 - 2017, Sunflower County Consolidated School District

What's working to turn the curve:

Dual Enrollment
- As of September 2017, over 90 percent of IPC home visitation participants are dually enrolled in Imagination Library, a free monthly book program.
- Children who are enrolled in more IPC programs, before they arrive at Kindergarten, on average, perform higher on K-readiness assessments.

Coordinated Transition Services
- Save the Children Head Start, private childcare centers, Delta Health Alliance and the school district partner every summer to provide a 6-week transitional summer camp to incoming Kindergarten students - Promise School.
- Not only does Promise School prepare students for entering Kindergarten, Promise School participants continue to outperform their peers in reading through elementary school.

Aligned Pre-K Curriculum + Assessment
- As of May 2015, private childcare centers and the local Head Start provider are implementing an aligned, evidence-based curriculum and assessment, serving over 450 children county-wide.
- Data sharing agreements between Delta Health Alliance, Head Start and the private childcare centers allow for better leverage of resources and services.

Partners
- Delta Health Alliance
- Mississippi Low Income Childcare Initiative
- Children's Defense Fund
- Save the Children
- Sunflower County Consolidated School District
- Childcare centers
- Indianola Public Library
- Indianola Family Medical Group
- Social Services Collaborative
- Excel by 5
- Sunflower County United for Children
- Delta Council
- Mississippi Center for Education Innovation
- US Department of Education
- Dolly Parton's Imagination Library

Reprinted with permission from Karin Scott and the Indianola Promise Team

with the Indianola team. Carolyn Davis is now the vice president for Delta Health Alliance and project manager for the Indianola Promise work. The current team is working on the results and indicators in the school pipeline again, with some successes and some failures. In addition to their work in Indianola, the team has expanded their work to the county level as a way to forge greater scope and scale in their efforts.

Chapter 3 Summary

Chapter 3 concludes Part 1 of this book. You have now completed your study of the vocabulary and concepts needed to perform as a results leader in the social sector. The Results Playbook approach introduced in Chapter 2 is complemented by the results action plan introduced here, which allows multiple stakeholders and partners to see how their work contributes to the overall results.

Gathering and analyzing data allows leaders to verify that the strategies, performance measures, and timelines they've chosen are the "right" ones to achieve the intended population-level result. Leaders analyze the data to achieve four aims:

1. To understand the population, by gathering the right data (both quantitative and qualitative) and disaggregating it to see multiple perspectives;
2. To identify baseline and trend data for the selected indicator;
3. To identify priority strategies, through factor analysis and selection of criteria to measure; and
4. To assess performance as execution moves forward. Timelines at the population, strategy, and program levels create both urgency and accountability to the work.

Data informs all three of the levels on which results leaders operate—population, strategy, and program. How that data is presented is important, because the right presentation allows everyone to more easily grasp what the data is trying to say. Data analysis prepares leaders to understand the population in a way that focuses their work on the strategies most likely succeed, enabling them to create results action plans.

A template for a results action plan followed by a case study of the Indianola Promise Community's concluded this chapter.

Chapter 3 Applications: Tools and Worksheets

1. Factor Analysis Worksheet 100
2. Strategy Template 104
3. Developing Quality Performance Measures Worksheet. .105
4. Program Template. 107
5. Results Action Plan Template 109

🛠 To download these apps, visit the book's online resources:
http://ChooseResultsBook.com/resources.html

Factor Analysis Work Sheet
Raj Chawla

When leaders from different sectors and/or from different roles within systems come together to work on a population level result, they bring with them different experiences, mental models, and knowledge about the work that is in front of them. They also bring with them an awareness of the different factors that contribute to the way things are and what works to address those factors. Given the complexity of the work and the fact that there may be many contributing factors that are contributing to the current situation, results leaders will take the time to engage in a factor analysis.[1]

Factors are the underlying reasons behind the problem or issue that results leaders are seeking to address. Engaging in a factor analysis allows leaders to create strategies that seek to address the identified factors. This process is an essential step in developing a results action plan.

This technique may disclose factors at various levels, including individual, family, community or broader social system levels. Thus, leaders may need to develop strategies that address causes at each of these levels. , For example:

- Existing knowledge, awareness, attitudes and/or behaviors factors of individuals, families, and communities.
- Cultural factors such as customs, beliefs, and values
- Economic factors such as income, housing, and other resources
- Political factors such as representation, decision-making power, policies

Get the right people in the room
Prior to engaging in a factor analysis process it is important to gather key stakeholders and partners who can contribute to the work. Key stakeholders include people who are affected by the current problem and are in a position to contribute to the solution. Together they explore a broader range of possible factors that may be at play – and not be limited by unconscious assumptions and/or untested or disproven mental models. These multiple perspectives allow results leaders to see the "whole" problem, appraise it through shared intelligence, negotiate a broad mix of needed strategies, and engage in the work.

Four Steps to identify factors:
Step 1: Collect and Analyze Data
The first step in the analysis is to gather data, specifically population level trend line data that has been disaggregated by race, gender, class or other groups. This allows leaders to see the population level trend and the disaggregated trend.

Questions to explore:
- Are things getting better, worse, or about the same for the whole population?

---

[1] Based on the "Turn-the Curve" activity in Mark Friedman's Trying Hard is not Good Enough

Chapter 3: Apps/Tools

- Are things getting better, worse, or about the same for the disaggregated populations?
- How do you know if the state of things is getting better or worse?
- Where would the trend line go if nothing were to be done?
- How long has the problem existed?
- What is the impact of the problem and on whom?

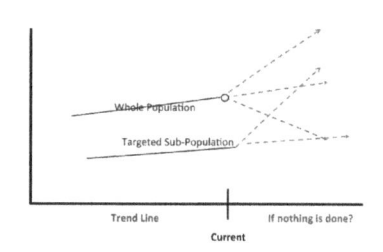

Step 2: Identify the contributing factors
Identifying contributing factors allows results leaders to create a shared meaning as to why things are they way they are. Stakeholders and partners may have differing perspectives and points of view and, thereby, offer an important perspective of what is happening. This step can also reveal gaps in understanding and knowledge of why things are the way they are.

Questions to explore:
- What current factors are contributing positively to the trend line?
- What current factors are contributing negatively to the trend line?
- How do we know these are positive or negative factors? What is the evidence?
- Use multiple examples of positive and negative results to identify additional contributors
- Are there unique factors that specifically contribute positively or negatively for the population as a whole or for sub-populations?
- Which factors are contributing to existing disparities and how do you know? List both the contributing factors that are positive (or making the situation better) and negative (or making the situation worse).

Step 3: Ask the "multiple-whys" questions:

This technique examines key factors by asking the question "why?" several times to find out what caused it. The purpose of asking "why" is to have a good enough understanding of the factors to make informed choices about which ones are actionable by a stakeholder and/or partner, are relevant for the population being impacted, meets the strategy criteria Each time an answer is given, it is followed-up by another "why?" question. After, each answer leaders might see an opportunity to take action right away that can help move the trend line in the right direction..

For example, if the current situation is that too few children in a particular community are attending college ready, leaders would ask "why?" Once factors have been identified, there is an opportunity to go deeper into one that is deemed important and relevant. Asking why to a factor will illicit an answer, it is followed up by another "why?" question until you are satisfied

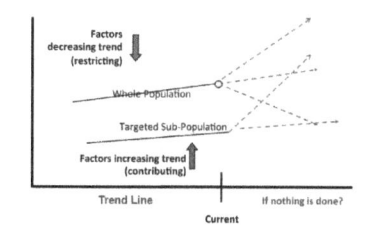

Part 1: From Fragmentation to Shared Results

you have identified multiple factors of the problem. Include both positive and negative contributing factors for a whole and subpopulation and drill down by asking:

- Why does the contributing factor exist?
- Are there conditions or contributors that are unique to sub-populations?
- How is this driving the trend line? (Use the Multiple Why Work Sheet below)
- If this factor shifted, what impact would that have and how big a contribution would that make to turn the curve?
- For which factors is there evidence (research, experience, knowledge) that can inform how best to proceed?
- What are the 2 or 3 factors that, if shifted, would address systems-level changes?

See the "multiple-whys" work sheet at end of this document

Step 4: Develop strategies to address the factors

The next step is the generation of potential strategies. These strategies are connected directly to the factors that have been identified.

- For what factors, if addressed, is there evidence of strategies that are effective?
- For what factors, if addressed, would there be greatest gain towards the result?
- What can partners contribute to the strategies that work for specific factors?
- What will it take to develop and execute effective strategies?
- What set of strategies can be developed/implemented that directly address the most salient factors?
- What level of activity is needed to achieve change? To get to scope and scale?
- Complete a Strategy Chart for these strategies using this format:

Strategy Name:
Strategy Population:
Strategy Result:
Strategy Target: -
Strategy Performance Measures:
Strategy Partners:

- Review the strategies identified on your preliminary strategies inventory
- Use a set of strategy criteria to help identify strategies to develop and implement

Chapter 3: Apps/Tools

Multiple "Whys" Worksheet
Students Not Attending College

One Key Contributing Factor
Financial: Students not applying to college

Each time you ask "why," look for an answer that is grounded in fact: it must be an account of things that have actually happened – not events that might have happened. Make sure that your answer is grounded in fact, and then ask "why" again. **After each answer determine is there is an action that can be taken by a partner and/or stakeholder.**

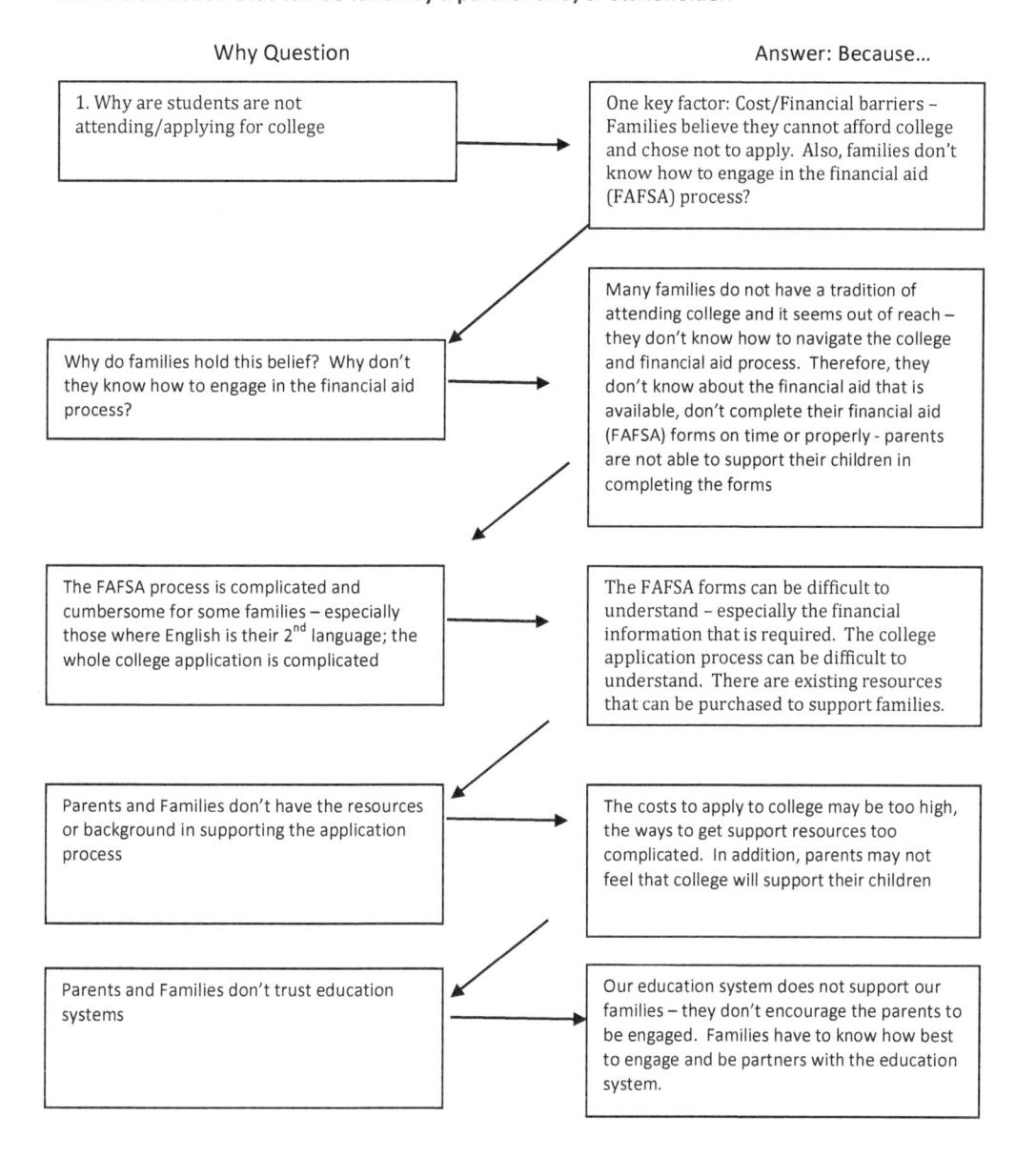

Why Question → Answer: Because…

1. Why are students are not attending/applying for college
   → One key factor: Cost/Financial barriers – Families believe they cannot afford college and chose not to apply. Also, families don't know how to engage in the financial aid (FAFSA) process?

Why do families hold this belief? Why don't they know how to engage in the financial aid process?
   → Many families do not have a tradition of attending college and it seems out of reach – they don't know how to navigate the college and financial aid process. Therefore, they don't know about the financial aid that is available, don't complete their financial aid (FAFSA) forms on time or properly - parents are not able to support their children in completing the forms

The FAFSA process is complicated and cumbersome for some families – especially those where English is their 2nd language; the whole college application is complicated
   → The FAFSA forms can be difficult to understand – especially the financial information that is required. The college application process can be difficult to understand. There are existing resources that can be purchased to support families.

Parents and Families don't have the resources or background in supporting the application process
   → The costs to apply to college may be too high, the ways to get support resources too complicated. In addition, parents may not feel that college will support their children

Parents and Families don't trust education systems
   → Our education system does not support our families – they don't encourage the parents to be engaged. Families have to know how best to engage and be partners with the education system.

Part 1: From Fragmentation to Shared Results

Strategy Template

Strategy Name: _____

- Priority Factor(s) Strategy Addresses: _____

- Strategy Population: _____

- Strategy Result: _____

- Strategy Performance Measures:

    o How Much _____
    o How Well _____
    o Difference Made _____

- Strategy Partners:

    o _____
    o _____
    o _____
    o _____

Path to Achieving Target (Impact)

Timeline and Milestones of Performance Measure Targets to Achieve Scope and Scale to Integrate Strategy Execution (Impact)

Strategy	Jan	Feb	Mar	Apr	May

Chapter 3: Apps/Tools

Developing Quality Performance Measures
Worksheet developed by Phyllis Rozanski

Purpose

All too often, organizations have either too many or not the right mix of measures, i.e. they have too many "how much" measures and not enough of "make a difference" measures. The purpose of this worksheet is to help programs decide on the measures that best describe the effectiveness of their strategies and/or programs. This worksheet can be used to identify new measures and/or to inventory existing measures.

Criteria for Measure Selection
- **Clarity**: Simple, clear, and understandable
- **Importance:** To the population result(s) we seek to impact and to our leadership, stakeholders, funders, staff, partners
- **Measurability**: Stated as a number, percent, rate, ratio, average, or dollar amount
- **Availability**: Data can be collected regularly at the end of a program or on a schedule such as daily, weekly, monthly, or quarterly
- **Access:** Data can be retrieved easily by the people who need it to inform their decision making, to make reports, etc.

How to Use
1. List the potential measure or existing measure
2. Designate the Type using the initials: *HM, HW, or DM*
3. Rank the Measure under each criteria: *High (H), Medium (M) or Low (L)*
4. Assess the ranking and identity the action to take: *Use it, delete it, repair it, or gather more information, or other (specify)*

Example

How much (HM), how well (HW) or better off/difference made (DM)		Insert: *High (H), Medium (M) or Low (L)* for each					Action to Take Use it, delete it, repair it
Measure	Type	Clarity	Importance	Measurability	Availability	Access	
% of residents retaining employment after 6 months	DM	H	H	H	L	L	*Conduct follow-up to get the data*

105

Part 1: From Fragmentation to Shared Results

Strategy/Program: _____ Target Population: _____

If a program, what is the "Program Result" for the target population:
_____

Tip: Start with your difference made measures. 2. Fewer measures are better -not everything that can be measured should be measured. 3. Sync the "how well measures" with the "how much measures."

How much (HM), how well (HW) or better off/difference made (DM)		Insert: *High (H), Medium (M) or Low (L)* for each					*Action to Take* Use it, delete it, repair it or Add to Develop Data List
Measure	**Type**	**Clarity**	**Importance**	**Measurability**	**Availability**	**Access**	
1.							
2.							
3.							
4.							
5.							
6.							
7.							
8.							
9.							
10.							

Actions to Take:

Program Template

Program Name: _____

- Contributing to Strategy:
    - _____
    - _____

- Program Population: _____

- Program Result: _____

- Program Performance Measures:
    - How Much _____
    - How Well _____
    - Difference Made _____

- Program Partners (if any):
    - _____
    - _____
    - _____
    - _____

Part 1: From Fragmentation to Shared Results

Results Action Plan Template
As synthesized by Jolie Bain Pillsbury

Component	Content
Part 1: Population, Result and Indicator with focus on a Call to Action	**Call to Action** • Whole Population: • Result: • Indicator(s) Trend Line
Part 2: Whole Population Analysis	**Whole Population** • Disaggregated Data • Highlighting relationship among and between whole/system/program populations • Identification of Disparities
Part 3: Adoption of Baseline and target for improvement	**Adoption of Baseline:** *Where are we now?* *What does the data tell us?* **Set Target for Improvement:** *Where do we want to be?* *What's the goal—where you want to be by when?*
Part 4: Whole Population Factor Analysis	<table><tr><th>Factors</th><th>What works to address factors</th><th>Who can contribute to what works</th></tr></table>Additional disaggregated data about the whole population (i.e. demographics, disaggregated data initial set and then additional from data development agenda) Factor Analysis Worksheet: • Identify factors impacting the trend line and • What works to address the factors
Part 5: Strategy Selection	**What are the Strategies?** *What strategies that address the factors and reflect what the can contribute?* *How do we get there?* List of strategies and the leaders in the strategy groups. Summary matrix of scale—e.g., contribution of each strategy to the overall target—sums up the "collective impact".

Part 6: Strategy Group Work Plans	**Strategy Name:**_
	    Strategy Population:
	    Strategy Result:
	    Strategy Target:
	    Strategy Performance Measures:
	    Strategy Partners:
	    Strategy Scale:

Chapter 3: Apps/Tools

	Strategy Population Factor Analysis: *Target population (disaggregated) linked to a deeper factor analysis and identification of what works.*
Part 7: Strategy Implementation Timeline	**Path to Achieving Target (Impact)** **Timeline and Milestones of Performance Measure Targets to Achieve Scope and Scale to Integrate Strategy Execution (Impact)** | Strategy	Jan	Feb	Mar	Apr	May
---	---	---	---	---	---

PART TWO

Executing to Scope and Scale

Leaders come together out of a shared concern they hold for the future. They hope for an opportunity to make an aligned contribution in the knowledge that what can be created collaboratively is greater than what can be achieved separately.

This coming-together evokes a set of dynamic relationships that must be tended in order for High Action and High Alignment to make a measurable difference toward a result. In Part 2, readers use the four-perspective frame, each mapped to adjoining quadrants, to examine this set of dynamic relationships. Leaders need to understand these four quadrants and their inter-relationships or the ability to make progress toward a population-level result is greatly jeopardized.

The four perspectives are:

1. Me
2. Me with You
3. Us
4. Us in the World

I like to visualize the four perspectives as quadrants of a whole, as shown in the figure on the next page. Each perspective is the subject of a chapter in Part 2.

Part 2: Executing to Scope and Scale

Four Perspectives Visualized as Quadrants

Me	Me with You
• Values, purpose, intent • Worldviews and mental model • Being a learner	• Honoring our word • Honoring our role • Honoring our relationships
Us	**Us in the World**
• Creating a shared results culture • Shared work rituals • Shared language	• Working towards scope and scale • Leveraging systems • Engaging in quality improvement efforts

Chapter 4, "Me—Leader Readiness, Working on the Self," explores where leaders' work must begin—with the relationship of the individual leader to the result itself.

Chapter 5, "Me with You—Work Group Readiness," introduces the learning required of the individuals who make up the collaborative work group. Each must master skills and behaviors, such as integrity, commitment, and resilience.

Chapter 6, "Us—Creating a Results Culture," reconnoiters the terrain of work group culture—how the relationships between individuals function to create impact on the result in the center and what leaders and stakeholders need to know to avoid the problems that often beset collaborative work.

Chapter 7, "Us in the World—Working Towards Scope and Scale," considers collaborative work in context of the larger systems it is trying to influence in order to make a measurable difference.

The accompanying table (see facing page) identifies these relationships and the effect of awareness of the principles of results leadership on the work. You may use this as an assessment tool to judge the benefit your work group may gain from coming to awareness of this results leadership approach.

Part 2 concludes with a brief final chapter calling on you to put into action what you've learned.

Relationships and Effect of Awareness of the Principles of Results Leadership

	Relationship	Without Awareness	With Awareness
Individual Leader "Me"	To the result	Unaware of blind spots Competition with other mental models	Intent, purpose Acknowledgment of partial "truth", willingness to join others mental models, Learning and reflecting
Individual Leader "Me with You"	To the result With collaborative partners	Not aware of impact of individual actions and behaviors with others	Honoring your word with others—making requests, promises, and commitments Honoring your role with others—knowing and working with your boundaries of authority, role, and task Honoring your relationship with others—intentionally building resilient relationships
Collaborative Work Group "Us"	To the result To the results work group	A culture that avoids conflict, values relationships over results	A results culture that creates a shared language, shared rituals, and artifacts that re-enforce the commitment results and leaders making their aligned contributions
Collaborative Work Group "Us in the World"	To the result To larger external systems and structures	Avoids the larger systems change; focuses only on the margins	Working together to create both the scope and scale of the work, leveraging the work to create systems change, and engaging in quality improvement practices throughout the work

CHAPTER 4

"Me"—Leader Readiness and Working on the Self

Knowing other is intelligence
Knowing yourself is true wisdom
Mastering others is strength
Mastering yourself is true power

– *Tao Te Ching #33*

Several years ago in the late summer, I was in Elkhart, Indiana, in a room full of community leaders and stakeholders who were interested in ex-offender re-entry into their communities. Specifically, they wanted people incarcerated in the criminal justice system to get the treatment and support they needed while in prison and to have the support and services they needed to connect back to their community after their release.

In addition to defining their organizational and community roles, these leaders introduced themselves as both politically and socially conservative. I didn't know their interests or even their various purposes for being in the room. What to expect of them? Were they here to make sure that people in the prison system paid their dues? To make sure the ex-offenders were not a risk to society when they got out? To make political gains in their community by declaring they were tough on crime? They spent the remainder of this first session working to both understand the elements of a Results Playbook and to create a results action plan.

The second session with these leaders happened in mid-November. It was a powerful and robust session during which they developed overarching strategies connected to education, health, employment, community, and policy. At the end, as an acknowledgment of the upcoming Thanksgiving holiday, I asked for each leader to share what he or she was thankful for. Many in the room told a story of a family member—a son, a nephew, a daughter—or a close family friend or business partner who was in the prison system. They felt it was their duty, their responsibility, their caring as a family member or friend to support not only the person they knew but all who were in prison.

This potent conversation reminded me of the power of purpose to connect leaders to the results as well as to each other. It also revealed to me the flaws in my mental model: the assumptions I carried about working with those I had assessed as more politically conservative than I—about who does this type of work and why—and the unconscious biases I carried.

The conversation also gave me an opportunity to learn as well as to coach as I worked with these leaders. I learned about the uniqueness of their community, came to better understand the values and beliefs that shaped how these residents worked and lived with each other. I learned how partners and stakeholders worked together, and how they held accountability and resilience.

For results leaders to be effective in addressing a social problem, we need to be aware of all the factors that conversation brought to my mind that day. The inner workings of any human can be complex—even contradictory—and require a lifetime of inquiry and discovery. As my reflection on that conversation reveals, results leaders need tremendous self-awareness to endure the challenges inherent in working collaboratively with others.

In this chapter, we explore three pillars of self-awareness that will support you in your role as a results leader. Given the challenges leaders are sure to experience in doing results work, it is important that they:

1. Connect to why they choose do this work—the intent and purpose of their own leadership journey.
2. Reflect on and understand how their worldviews—their mental models—help to shape what they see and what they don't see.
3. Engage as lifelong learners to gain better understanding of the complex public problems that are being confronted.

Let's get started.

The Leader's Foundation: Intent, Values, and Purpose

As results leaders making a contribution to population-level results, the first step toward self-awareness is deeply understanding why we do the work we do. This understanding allows us to connect to both our intent and purpose: Why we choose to do what we do; and thus, how we show up in the world. Intent and purpose arise from who we think we are or who we want to be. These somewhat abstract concepts connect to and shape our identity. They help us bring our own unique flavor to how we play our various roles, such as mother, father, community member, or leader. Intent and purpose allow us as leaders to connect to the result we seek to make real and help to shape the contribution we will make.

Perhaps most importantly, the intent and purpose from which we act reveal the values we hold important. But what are values, exactly? Values can be thought of as priorities: internal compasses or springboards for action that shape our moral imperatives.[1] Values are not the actions themselves nor are they specific checklists of acceptable or unacceptable behavior. Rather, values are implicit or explicit guides for action. When shared by a group, values become mores that function as a system of criteria by which behavior is judged and sanctions applied.[2]

According to Forman and Ross, in their book, *Integral Leadership: The Next Half-Step*,[3]

> ...[C]ore values are our answers to the question, "What is most enduringly important to me?" They are the deep values that influence what we see, whom we choose to interact with, and how we behave. When we consciously understand and intentionally cultivate these crucial filtering and meaning-making frameworks, we can engage them to enhance our personal and professional performance. We can simultaneously provide deep and lasting feelings of satisfaction and reward across groups and organizations.

Two leaders could hold similar values but differ in their ideas regarding how best to achieve the desired result and thus would have to allow for more than one "way" to make progress towards the result. Therefore, it is important to articulate intent, values, and purpose, creating defined "guardrails" to help keep us from being sidetracked by feelings of insufficiency, tension, conflict, and vulnerability. Purpose won't act as a barrier

Part 2: Executing to Scope and Scale

The Five Whys worksheet in the apps/tools section at the end of this chapter is designed to support your connection to purpose and intent.

to these feelings, but it will support us in navigating them so we can work more effectively toward results. Clarity of purpose combined with the ability to articulate that purpose to others helps create the possibility of producing something greater together. This clarity provides stability and serves as a foundation for the hard work ahead.

The ability to probe below the surface of why you choose to do what you do, asking *why* multiple times, may reveal to the leader or to others the depth of the purpose of their work. The "Five Whys" technique, borrowed from the world of quality improvement, is a simple reflection for leaders that may help reveal or name the purpose or intent of engaging in this work.

Results Leader: Dr. Deborah Moore

I first met Dr. Moore during an initial engagement designed to support the Indianola Promise Neighborhood team efforts to move their work from large-scale programming to a results focus, which required that many stakeholders and partners make their aligned contributions. The first piece of hard work the Indianola team had to engage in was truth-telling about and among themselves. I labeled the work the Indianola team currently was doing "smallball," and I knew that Dr. Moore agreed. She knew that the team would have to take on the hard work to name their current reality—namely that of working in a grants culture—and challenge the team to a new reality: working in a results culture.

During our sessions together, I invited the team to focus on putting results in the center and working in High Action and High Alignment toward that result. During team time, the Indianola leadership team would have long conversations during which they would speak to what they wanted, and what they would need to do to create a new future. They looked at the population-level data, the trends over time, and their programmatic performance measures, and knew that they had to work differently. For example, some of their "on-the-ground" efforts were duplicative and too narrow in scope and their population-level targets too small to make a real difference. I knew these were difficult and, often, painful conversations for the team.

Over the three to four years of working with Indianola, I always admired Dr. Moore's ability to show up and do the hard work. She was willing to try new ways of working, new ways of thinking, and new ways to challenge herself and her team. During one of my trips there, I noticed she was a bit subdued, but still working hard. I asked one of her co-workers if everything was okay. I was told that Dr. Moore had experienced two sudden deaths in her family just a week or so earlier. Yet here she was, putting all of that aside in order to do the hard results work for her community.

I found some time over a lunch break to tell her how sorry I was for her loss and how amazed I was that she was here working as hard as ever for the children in Indianola. I asked her why.

She went on to tell me her story and her connection to the Mississippi Delta.

> I was born in Cleveland, Mississippi. I am a native. I have never left the area. I have visited a lot of different places, but I have always desired to live in the Delta. I grew up in poverty. I was the product of a two-parent household, both of whom were individuals who did not have an academic education but who were educated in their own right. I had ten brothers and three sisters.
>
> What I remember most: I was taught to be responsible and to value education. The Christian values of treating people the way you want to be treated. Those teachings molded and shaped me.
>
> Mom and Dad valued education, to go as far as you could. My brothers grew up during sharecropping days and had to be out of school or drop out of school.
>
> What I am most proud of about my family is that they developed a path for me and my sisters to obtain an education. They sacrificed a lot for us. That is why, when I look at black men and boys, I remember what they have sacrificed. They may have had to drop out but they are still productive citizens because of their morals and values.
>
> To do this work, there has to be a passion that goes along with having skills. You look at the data and you see only half of kids arriving at kindergarten ready and you cannot understand the urgency unless you have a passion for the work. You have to have drive and interest that aligns with the results approach. With this result work, we are empowering others to do the work. You are giving them the power to do it. You are allowing them to use their own power to do the work.

I understood the strong foundation on which Dr. Moore stood—her values and her purpose. They were so strong that the deaths of her family members, however painful, could not hold her back from doing her work. I always felt proud to work with Dr. Moore, and that day I knew that she would give back to the children and families of the Delta the same way her parents and brothers had given to her.

Part 2: Executing to Scope and Scale

As Dr. Moore's story shows, a leader's personal clarity about his or her intent, values, and purpose—and their ability to articulate that clearly to others—provides the foundation for meaningful collaborative work.

Finding Your Inner Compass

Being a results leader can be a difficult journey—one that requires reflection as well as action. It requires working well with others, even those you may not enjoy working work with. It requires patience as well as urgency. Connecting this journey to your values, your purpose, and how you make meaning of your life is important. It is in that spirit that taking a regular pause to reflect on the following questions may be helpful in finding your inner compass.

- Why is it that you choose to do this work?
- Why does this result matter to you?
- Who else does your work matter to?
- What do you hope to gain by doing this work?

Mental Models: A Gateway for Understanding Yourself and Working With Others

We don't see things as they are;
we see them as we are.

– Anaïs Nin

Each one of us has a perception of reality, of how the world works—an interpretive lens that provides understanding, guides thinking, and directs decision-making. My interpretive lens supports me in the successes I achieve and contributes to the failures I endure. For example, one of the messages my father gave me when I was growing up as an immigrant in Atlanta, Georgia, was that I had to be twice as good as someone else in order to be considered equal. As I incorporated this message into my own mental model of the world, I found that I often worked really hard. At school this meant focusing on grades, In community it meant trying to fit in and make good decisions. This message also had its down side; sometimes I felt that I would never be as good as others, that I would be found to be a fraud, and that I was really an outsider.

It is these interpretive lenses that can cause a group of stakeholders to have diverse (and sometimes conflicting) opinions on both the causes of a set of complex public problems they are confronting and on possible solutions to those problems.

Peter Senge, in *The Fifth Discipline: The Art and Practice of the Learning Organization*,[4] calls these lenses **mental models** and suggests they "are deeply ingrained assumptions, generalizations, or even images that influence how we understand the world and how we take action." Mental models are internal structures and therefore not easily known. They are constructed from a lifetime of experiences and are part of who we are. We are often unaware of how they guide our actions—and thus require us to pay attention to things not easily known or named. Mental models are developed from a broad mix of influences including innate traits and abilities, emotional reactions, beliefs, and values. Our mental models come from our education and training, our personal experiences, and the influence of others on us including family, friends, mentors, and experts. Mental models emerge from both our conscious and unconscious worlds. With so many contributing factors, it is not surprising that every individual has his or her own unique set of mental models!

Mental models: Deeply ingrained assumptions, generalizations, and other internal structures derived from a lifetime of experience that act as lenses or filters affecting our interpretation of the world around us.

Mental models help us to make sense of our experiences. They allow us to quickly deduce how to respond to the circumstances directly in front of us, to make the necessary decisions, and to determine what, if any, risks or dangers are present. Our mental models are so deeply ingrained that in the course of day-to-day activities, they influence many things we do and decisions we make—all without our conscious thought. Sometimes, we are able to identify and put into words the thinking behind our actions. More often, we find it very challenging to recognize or name what arises from deep in our subconscious.

Whether or not we are consciously aware of them, our mental models are the filters through which we see the world. They influence what we see and what we don't, what we value and what we don't. They create our blind spots and help to shape our strengths. They create the boundaries—and, therefore the limits—of our understanding. They affect how we understand the circumstances we face, the others who are connected to those circumstances, and even ourselves.

Given that results leaders are working on complex public problems, we must stay mindful of both the benefits and the limits of our mental models, listed below in Table 4.1.

Table 4.1 **Benefits and Limits of Mental Models**

Benefits	Limits
Allow you to quickly organize information and make decisions	Are not always based on facts or quantifiable information (and may therefore be inaccurate)
Make it possible to use best available data to engage in complex problem solving	Can blind you to facts and ideas that challenge or defy your deeply held beliefs
Enable you to interpret the language and actions of others in order to engage in dialogue and discussion	Are not always accurate whzen generalizing from one type of action or behavior to another

Opportunities abound for leaders to "bump into" each other's mental models without realizing it, for example, the different mental models that a social worker and a lawyer may have when they engage with a family in crisis. A lack of awareness of mental models makes collaborative work more challenging. For these reasons and more, it is important to explore mental models—both our own and others'—to bring to the surface how they shape our thinking.

As we dive deeper into working with this concept, it is important to remember that mental models[5] are usually:

- Incomplete, simplified explanations for complex situations;
- Constantly evolving;
- Permeated with errors and contradictions; and
- Based on a degree of vagueness that allows them to be used even if incorrect.

Working With Mental Models

According to cognitive scientists, humans engage in two types of thinking—intuitive and reflective.[6] *Intuitive thinking* is associated with instincts and quick responses. *Reflective thinking* is deliberate and conscious. One simple way to understand this is to consider how we unconsciously lean on our mental models when our intuitive thinking is activated.

For example, most Americans would use their intuitive thinking if they were listening to the morning weather forecast on the radio and heard that the midday temperature would be 85° Fahrenheit. They would dress comfortably for a warm day without conscious thought. On the other hand, if the meteorologist announced 30° Celsius, Americans would have to use their reflective thinking to convert Celsius to Fahrenheit to determine whether to dress for a cold, warm, or hot day.

We always have access to both our intuitive and reflective thinking. Because our intuitive thinking is unconscious and based on mental models that are quite possibly flawed, we are susceptible to making mistakes that impact and influence our thinking.

Cognitive Bias

Technically speaking, a cognitive bias is a pattern of deviation in judgment, whereby inferences about other people and situations maybe drawn in an illogical fashion.[7] Therefore, a **cognitive bias** can be understood as a mistake in reasoning, evaluating, or understanding that affects the decisions and judgments people make due to the mental models we carry. It usually occurs as a result of holding onto one's preferences and beliefs regardless of contrary information. Good data is the best antidote to cognitive bias, as the following story shows.

I was with a group of state legislators who were working on targeted policy that would support their constituents. They were interested in learning and applying key results leadership tenets in their work. One of the most important practices I offer to results leaders is the use of data. Facts and figures help everyone assess the current situation and track progress toward the result.

This idea of cognitive bias also influences leaders' ability to use and interpret data. As always, I asked these leaders to bring five to seven PowerPoint slides showing the data they used in assessing how successful they were in their work. I was not surprised by the pushback I received from their staff about this request. The complaints could be grouped as follows:

- Too much information—therefore they didn't know what to bring or what to believe;
- Too little information—therefore they didn't know how to interpret or make meaning of what was available;
- Unreliable information—what was available didn't reflect the realities of their constituents, so they didn't trust it; and
- Irrelevant information—decisions frequently had to be made quickly and they did not have time to identify the relevant data, assess its meaning, and then make a decision.

Because of these beliefs, these legislators were susceptible to several cognitive biases that might impact their decisions. Those who felt there was too much information might fall to a confirmation bias—seeing only the evidence that supports their point of view. Those who

> **Cognitive bias:** A mistake in reasoning, evaluating, remembering, or other cognitive process, often occurring as a result of holding onto one's preferences and beliefs regardless of contrary information.

felt there was too little data or didn't trust the data could fall to a framing bias—mistaking their view of the problem for the real need. Finally, those who felt that the information was irrelevant could fall to an overconfidence bias—a self-delusion that everything is working well or everything is collapsing.

To continue the story, the day of our gathering arrived. Each legislator did bring some data on education, health, and community indicators, which I asked them to post on the wall. Then I invited them to explore their colleagues' data—to notice what was happening in communities other than their own. This 30-minute activity of exploration, of asking questions about the various legislators' constituents, of answering questions about their own data and their own constituents, led to a very heated conversation about the use of data in their work. They noticed that some of it was not disaggregated. This lead to a conversation from the legislators about race: For some it was about the difficulty of getting data that revealed racial disparities. For others, it was about actually naming the disparities and identifying the legislative work that needed to be done. For others, it was not connecting the disparities of race to gender. It was as if no one could see the full picture of the complex public problems their communities were facing and therefore any single person could only offer partial solutions.

About half the group expressed frustration at not having enough data or the appropriate data to make informed decisions. While they expressed frustration at the lack of response they often got from the various agencies that supplied the data, they shared that they were able to make do by knowing their constituents and trusting their staff to help them make the right decisions.

The other half of the group expressed frustration about what the data was saying. They felt the data was blaming the constituents who were most impacted by failed policies and dysfunctional systems. This feeling of "blame the constituents" led them to doubt the data. Instead they trusted their own experiences and the stories they heard during hearings and testimonies.

The leaders' reaction illustrates the limits of mental models in making decisions. All these legislators were relying on their own experiences and points of view to understand what the data was saying and what subsequent actions to take. This ability to be data-informed is important for a leader to adapt quickly to a complex environment; to learn what is working and what isn't; and to make decisions based on the facts in front of them.

As you move forward with your results work, I invite you to use the Cognitive Bias Table provided to help ensure you are hearing different

See the Cognitive Bias Table in the apps/tools section at the end of this chapter. It is offered to help avoid several types of bias that leaders confront.

perspectives and voices in your work, and to increase the likelihood that the decisions being made take into account cognitive biases.

Implicit Biases

Implicit bias refers to the attitudes or stereotypes that unconsciously affect a leader's understanding, actions, and decisions.[8] These implicit biases, and consequent assessments both favorable and unfavorable, reside deep in the subconscious. They are different from known biases that individuals may choose to conceal for the purposes of social and/or political correctness.

The implicit associations individuals harbor can create feelings and attitudes about other people based on characteristics such as race, ethnicity, age, and appearance. These associations develop over the course of a lifetime, beginning at a very early age through exposure to direct and indirect messages.

A few key characteristics of implicit bias include:

- They are pervasive. Everyone possesses them, even people with avowed commitments to impartiality, such as judges.
- Implicit and explicit biases are related but distinct mental constructs. They are not mutually exclusive and may even reinforce each other.
- The implicit associations we hold do not necessarily align with our declared beliefs or even reflect stances we would explicitly endorse.

We generally tend to hold implicit biases that favor our own in-group, though research has shown that we can still hold implicit biases against our in-group.

Addressing disparities due to race, class, and/or culture factors is a fundamental task for results leaders. Therefore, acknowledgment of implicit biases that impact the work is essential.

Consider the impact of implicit bias in the following examples:

A 2016 *USA Today* article[9] described a study by the Yale Child Study Center that suggested that teachers who care for very young children may judge those kids' behavior differently based on race. Previous research had found that preschool boys were expelled almost five times more often than girls, and that black students were about twice as likely to be expelled as their white or Latino classmates. This more recent research showed that when teachers do not know the background of a child and family, white teachers rated white students' behavior as "more severe" than black students, while black teachers rated black students' behavior as "more severe." Knowledge of the background of

Implicit bias: Attitudes or stereotypes that affect our understanding, actions, and decisions in an unconscious manner.

See the Mental Models and Implicit Bias worksheet in the apps/tools section at the end of this chapter to help avoid the implicit bias that leaders may confront.

> **Working with Mental Models and Implicit Bias Worksheet**
> One way leaders can learn to work with mental models and implicit bias is to reflect on their experience and interactions. A tool in the appendix to this chapter offers several prompts for this reflection. Using those questions, journal about the mental models and implicit biases you are holding, and invite other stakeholders and partners to think together. Concerning the populations you work with, what are some of the disparities you believe your community is facing? What is the evidence that this disparity exists?

the child and family created empathy in the teacher—but only if the teacher and child were of the same race. When teachers learn about implicit bias, they can consciously work toward minimizing it in their own classrooms.

In my own work, I recall encountering implicit bias regarding Hispanic family values. In discussing the impact of bias in her results work, one leader admitted that there was an unstated belief that Hispanic families did not value education as much as they valued work. This unconscious mental model negatively impacted the focus and implementation of education strategies designed to engage parents and schools. Once this leader became aware of that implicit bias, she was able to challenge some unstated assumptions and create strategies specific to Hispanic families and children.

Mental Models as Political Lenses

In his book, *The Three Languages of Politics*, Arnold Kling[10] suggests that mental models allow us to quickly reach closure—a state of high confidence that we and those who agree with us have the right answer—on an issue. That same quick closure, albeit giving us an immediate "what's next" step, may also allow us to assess those who disagree with us as unreasonable. Kling claims that, generally speaking, people who identify politically as progressive, conservative, or libertarian have three distinct mental models which allow them to see the world in a particular way.[11] According to Kling:

Progressives...
- View most favorably those groups who can be regarded as oppressed or standing with the oppressed; and
- View most unfavorably those groups who can be regarded as oppressors.

Conservatives...
- View most favorably the institutions that they believe constrain and guide people toward civilized behavior; and
- View most unfavorably those people who they see as trying to tear down such institutions.

Libertarians...
- View most favorably those who defer to decisions that are made on the basis of personal choice and voluntary agreement; and
- View most unfavorably those people who favor government interventions that restrict personal choice.

There are, of course, many nuances and subtleties associated with these and other political points of view. However, a general understanding of these mental models could help explain the different values, habits, and beliefs that are associated with those who hold each of these views, and the different languages they speak. Without awareness of these different mental models, there could be unintended consequences: missed opportunities for leaders to make aligned contributions, and possibly unnecessary "battles" among those with different values.

Mental Models in Action: Progressive Advocates Learn to Be "Bilingual Advocates" with Conservatives

The following example demonstrates the difference an overt awareness of mental models can make.

A conservative state senator from a very conservative state spoke to a group of state-based advocates who were engaged in a results leadership program with me. These leaders spoke the language of passionate progressive advocates (quite different from the senator) using data and narratives to make a case for children and families on issues of education, health, housing, and poverty. Generally speaking, these advocates held a mental model that current and historical policies, as well as the way systems are designed to function, had created a negative impact on the children and families they were interested in supporting. Therefore, their work was to create the collective action needed to implement just and fair policies and change the way systems worked.

This state senator told the advocates that passion does matter—that the advocates have a story to tell and data to support that story. However, if these advocates couldn't become "bilingual" in his state their chances of success were limited. His use of "bilingual" was of course metaphorical in that he was challenging them to acknowledge a different political language than they might usually speak. He then challenged these leaders to get out of their comfort zone and deal with people they may assess as different, or those they may view as the enemy—that from his experience everybody has a set of fears they want to address and a set of principles they want to honor.

This meant, according to the senator, seeking out and speaking to conservatives in a language they could understand. His direct advice was to avoid using words like "collective," to focus on accountability, contribution, and responsibility. This state senator was inviting the state-based advocates not to change their result but rather advocate for their result in a language or frame that conservatives could understand. In other words, the senator was naming a prevailing mental model of individual accountability and family responsibility in his state that these advocates would need to work with in order to make their desired changes.

Without our knowing it, our words can evoke conscious and unconscious mental models, ignite reactions, and put stakeholders into boxes. That lack of awareness limits both the thinking and contribution from potential stakeholders. With awareness, results leaders can limit reactive thinking, cut through the political tribalism that can derail results work, and invite key stakeholders to make their aligned contribution to the results that are in the center of the work. For example, it is quite evident that the two mental models highlighted in the story above can, and often do, collide with each other. Without awareness and understanding, leaders who hold these mental models can seemingly operate in two different worlds. The work of results leaders is to have the self-awareness of their own mental models, recognize the mental models that others may carry, and engage in the hard work of collaborating for a shared result.

Becoming a Learner: The Way To Manage Cognitive Biases

Leaders today, many of us, are in the roles and positions we are in because of our education, experience, know-how—in sum, our accumulated expertise. As we join with others to form an organization, a collaborative, a community, a country, or a planet, our mental models help shape the actions we can take collectively and, therefore, the results we can create together. To become results leaders, we need a path that takes us beyond the "box" of our mental models, including all our various implicit and explicit cognitive biases. That path forward appears when leaders become learners.

The Learning Cycle[12] shown in Figure 4.1 provides a framework for thinking about how we learn from experience. In this frame, we see learning take place in each and all of three loops:

1. Single-loop: Am I doing the things I do correctly?
2. Double-loop: Am I doing the right things?
3. Triple-loop: How do I decide what is right to do?

All three are important and needed. Results leaders have to get better at what we do (single-loop learning) in order to get results more efficiently. But, at some point we will likely realize that single-loop learning is insufficient because it merely leads to improvements in how technical work is accomplished. The time comes, especially when we work with others on complex problems, when we must move into double- and triple-loop learning.

As leaders begin to ask, "Are the things I'm doing the right things?" (double-loop learning), we expand the way we see the world. This is the only way to gain access to new ways of doing things, new actions that yield new results.

Some leaders, some of the time, begin to examine their thinking process (triple-loop learning). This is the most challenging and difficult type of learning a leader can engage in. Triple-loop learning offers the possibility of new ways of seeing and interpreting what is in front of us. Even deeper learning takes place. Who we are shifts into alignment with a new reality.

Learners first engage in the act of learning, then the practice of applying the new learning, and finally reflection on both the learning and the practice. This reflection engages the questions of single-loop, double-loop and triple-loop learning.[13] There are many variations of learning cycles that all highlight key fundamental steps of planning, acting, and reflecting. To live in this continuous cycle of learning, practice, and reflection is extraordinarily powerful for leaders.

If you are to become a results leader, you must commit to lifelong learning. To this end, it's helpful to understand how these three types of learning impact your leadership ability. Let's take a closer look at each, including the behaviors and actions you might notice when each type of learning is taking place.

Figure 4.1 **The Learning Cycle**

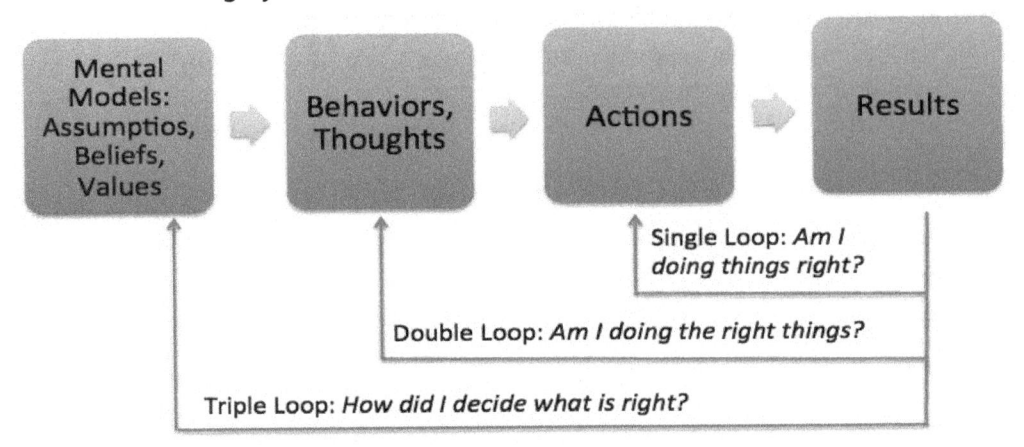

Mental Models: Assumptios, Beliefs, Values → Behaviors, Thoughts → Actions → Results

Single Loop: *Am I doing things right?*
Double Loop: *Am I doing the right things?*
Triple Loop: *How did I decide what is right?*

Am I Doing Things Right? Single-loop Learning

In single-loop learning, a leader's focus is *external*. It is all about *changing* or *improving overt actions to improve the results*. A leader might learn new skills, methods, or rules, and use that new knowledge to take incremental steps toward doing "something" better.

For instance, a tennis coach might work with a novice player on how to hold the racquet, where to place the feet, and how to swing the racquet to meet the tennis ball at the appropriate contact point. Then will come the practice to get the footwork just right, to hold and swing the racquet just right, and so on. The coach will continue to improve the novice player's actions to get the desired result: getting the ball over the net.

Single-loop learning starts by looking at the actions taken to produce results and seeing how those actions could be improved.[14] It can be seen as a three-step process: Separating facts (data) from opinions (interpretations and evaluations), clarifying assumptions, and dealing with assumptions.

Single-loop learning in practice includes:

- Having an action or process map that explains step by step what is supposed to happen;
- Using performance measures to track progress of work;
- Implementing a rapid-cycle quality improvement process to determine efficiency of work; and
- Learning from case studies, best practices, stories and examples for carrying out the same task.

To make an analogy to learning a physical skill—when your tennis coach has you practicing forehand after forehand in order to improve, you are engaging in single-loop learning. If you are the coach, focusing on learning to impart tennis skills more effectively, you might track your students' scores in practice matches as a measure of your performance.

The process map allows a results leader to map all the different elements that might need to go under the efficiency magnifier, while case studies and examples can reveal hidden aspects that are preventing greater efficiency.

The bottom line for single-loop learning is the quest for efficiency and effectiveness in the right work—reducing useless or inefficient effort, speeding up the process, and ultimately doing what you are already doing, but doing it better.

Am I Doing the Right Things? Double-loop Learning

In double-loop learning, the leader's focus shifts from *external* to internal where he or she begins the process of *improving "thinking" to produce different actions and thus get different results.*

A leader might observe that certain goal-driven strategies are not producing the right results when actually deployed, and therefore might decide to reassess those strategies. Dealing with assumptions is the bridge to double-loop learning. This learning is not about the action but rather about the leader. To change inaccurate mental models, a leader must recognize the need to change internally and be willing to modify the old ways of thinking. It has been my experience that leaders tend to go to double-loop learning when they fail to produce the desired results through single-loop learning.

Double-loop learning in practice means:

- Naming the existing mental models, points of view, and/or preferences you have that help inform the current actions you take;
- Identifying other mental models, points of views, and/or preferences others (in similar roles or positions) may have to inform similar actions;
- Examining and practicing other potential ways to do the same task; and
- Bringing a different group people around the table to gain a wider range of perspectives.

To return to our tennis analogy, a coach might notice limited progress in her trainee's forehand. She might go to a "coaching to foundational skills" seminar where she is filmed coaching and playing and having other coaches examine her style of playing and coaching. She might realize that she tends to focus more on the swing and placement and not enough focus on footwork. Upon returning to her trainee she changes her coaching focus to the footwork needed to hit an effective forehand.

As I've said, no one person, organization, or agency "owns" the result or has the answer to the complex social problems at hand. Because of the complexity of the problems and the cognitive limits of mental models, the act of learning is essential for a results leader to be able to be in High Action and High Alignment to the result. Like single-loop learning, the purpose that drives double-loop learning is the quest to be even more effective at addressing the problem. But here, the quest leads to doing things differently, to produce different and "better" results because the original way of working was ineffective.

How Did I Decide What Is Right? Triple-loop Learning

In triple-loop learning, the leader's focus continues *inward to question what is actually behind a leader's thinking process.*

This type of learning is long term in scope and forged through trial and error. For a leader embarking on addressing complex social problems this may mean adapting his or her identity in ways that are often uncomfortable, such as:

- Disrupting a culture of politeness—one that does not name the "elephant" in the room;
- Placing results over relationships—where a leader is willing to align contribution with those who are committed to results and let go of relationships that are focused on other interests; and
- Being vulnerable—to not knowing, to holding the role of learner, to asking for and giving support, in order to make progress on a population-level result.

Triple-loop learning in practice means:

- Having an awareness of the conscious and unconscious assumptions that shape perceptions and interpretations;
- Thinking about the evidence base (data) that informs decisions; and

- Going through experiences such as engaging in reflective practices, coaching, sabbaticals, etc. that invite reexamining one's profound beliefs about intent, values, and purpose.

To close our tennis analogy, a coach engaged in triple-loop learning might observe that with a number of her novice players, she is being too polite, holding the pleasantness of the tennis lesson above the result of improved sports performance. She might call a pause in the lesson to discuss with her students their unspoken rules of engagement and clarify the desired results.

The bottom line in triple-loop learning is to expand who we are—to create a sense of awareness that expands our world, our identity, and our ability to create change in the world.

Your Comfort Zone
In triple-loop learning, everything you want is just outside your comfort zone. What steps could you, as a results leader, take to achieve greater awareness of your own thinking process?

Jenny's Learning Cycle: An In-Depth Example

A colleague of mine, Jenny, shared a story about her journey to triple-loop learning. She is a talented leader who works for a national organization focused on the economic empowerment of low-income people. She holds in high regard the practices needed to produce results and is able to work from a Results Playbook to support her team, colleagues, and stakeholders in working towards shared accountability. She runs meetings that support action and accountability. So what could Jenny have to learn? As it happens, a lot.

Single-Loop Learning: Am I doing things right? Over the years Jenny continued to deploy the skills, model the behavior, and sharpen her practice to hold results meetings and work with others towards shared accountability to a result. There were many practice sessions and hours of pre-work to hone her skills.

Her ability to do things right gave her tremendous credibility in her organization. She was often called upon to lead important meetings. She willingly pushed other members of her leadership team to hold a results frame and to engage their stakeholders in using performance measures to track progress on their work. She was known as the go-to person if you needed to create accountability and make progress. Demand for her skill set grew to the point where she had to do not only her work but the work of others as well.

At this point she realized that even though she was the consummate results leader, she had to address the question: Was she was doing the right things? Specifically, she knew she had to let go of sole ownership of being "the only results leader in the room" so to speak. It was time to encourage others to start learning the practices needed to become results leaders themselves.

Double-Loop Learning: Am I doing the right things? It was here that Jenny entered into double-loop learning. She knew that holding expertise was not moving her results work forward and was—in fact—holding her organization back. She initiated a process where key leaders in her organization learned more directly to embody the practices and model the behavior of results leadership. Now a leadership cohort—not Jenny alone—engaged team members, stakeholders, and partners in results work.

But the organization still deferred to Jenny's expertise. Her team members were carrying out the technical aspects of results leadership but deferred the more challenging adaptive aspects to her. They would ask Jenny to "fix" others within the organization who were perceived as the sources of the conflict: people who were not aligned to the results work, people who were not in High Action and High Alignment towards the result.

Jenny wanted her colleagues to succeed and wanted results practices to be the norm across her staff. Therefore, she agreed to do the "fixing" of those tough issues. Soon she began to notice that she was now invited to lead the "hard" meetings, to hold the difficult conversations, to address the most difficult challenges within her organization. She was, in short, back in her original position of being the "go to" when it came to the most intransigent problems. How did this happen?

Jenny realized that she was unwilling to disappoint her team members, that she was unwilling to have her colleagues fail at the practice of results leadership, and that she was unwilling to be seen as someone who failed at something. Jenny needed to step into the space of triple-loop learning.

Triple-loop Learning: How am I deciding what is right? Jenny had to go deeper to understand why she was not succeeding. She had to examine her mental models. She had to ask the question: What was her contribution to the "over-reliance on Jenny" to do all the hard work?

She started by investigating her fears, her strengths and weaknesses, and how they shaped her behavior and her actions with others. This revealed that she enjoyed being known as the expert and the individual capable of engaging in the difficult conversations, of revealing the conflicts, of dealing with problematic staff and stakeholders. This expertise gave her status, power, and room to maneuver in the organization.

Her willingness to have others learn what she knew revealed some of her strengths—her wanting others to do their best and everyone to contribute to the results work. She was willing to spend her political and social capital to teach other team members the practices that would replace their "reliance on Jenny" with their own leadership. In conversation, examination, and reflection, she realized that part of the identity she held was that of super-competent expert who never disappoints others. It was this identity that she was holding when she—again and again—took on the hardest work within her system.

Jenny finally realized how her "superleader" identity allowed her to operate in a zone of safety. There, she could not be criticized, attacked, or made to feel less than. However, if she was truly going to lead a results organization, sometimes she was going to have to disappoint people by not doing their hard work for them. She was going to have to challenge them to risk their own failure and learn from it. She was going to have to risk getting out of her zone of safety and risk losing her identity.

This deep learning allowed Jenny to launch her colleagues into their own learning cycles, accepting occasional failure as part of their growth. Now Jenny could help others hold their own role and authority in their organization. Ultimately, Jenny allowed the entire organization to examine why their culture was conflict averse, the impact of this behavior on producing results, and what would be required to change that culture.

The Leader as Learner

As Jenny's story illustrates, results leaders acknowledge that they do not know all that they need to know, to be working in High Action and High Alignment. Just as important, they acknowledge the limits of their mental models. They accept the challenge to become lifelong learners, continually moving beyond the comfort zone bounded by their gaps and limitations.

Acknowledging Not Knowing

The acknowledgment of not knowing determines how open the leader will be to new learning. It is here that leaders have to embrace vulnerability.

Deep learning—learning about yourself, your mental models, your values and beliefs—requires being vulnerable. When we place ourselves in the role of learner, we intentionally step out of role of expert, the experience of presumed competence. When we engage in learning we are communicating to others that what we know is insufficient and that we want to grow, to become better.

> **Reflective Questions to Support High Action and High Alignment**
>
> It takes confidence to admit you don't have the answers to everything. It takes confidence to let others know you are willing to examine your mental models and worldviews. Some questions to ponder as you step into your vulnerability:
>
> - Am I being honest with myself about my fears, strengths, weaknesses, about my behavior and the way that I interact with others?
> - What cognitive biases do I hold that are inhibiting progress towards the result?
> - In what ways is my identity connected to my mental models? What am I willing to risk?

Identifying Your Enemies of Learning

In this space of both vulnerability and empathy, a leader must explore his or her "enemies of learning"—those invisible barriers that exist due to our conscious and unconscious mental models. These powerful forces can block a leader from fully incorporating a new learning or insight, thereby impacting what that leader contributes to the collaborative work and to the result.

Some enemies of learning include:[15]

- **The inability to admit ignorance.** This may sound like "I don't need to know that," "That isn't relevant," or "I already know this." It may be connected to a leader's inability to abandon existing assumptions about what he knows and to experience the vulnerability needed to be fully a learner.

- **Believing "This is who I am—I cannot learn this."** This may sound like "I'm too set in my ways to try this learning," "You cannot teach an old dog new tricks," or "I'm not smart enough to do what you are asking." This enemy of learning may be connected to a lack of self-confidence.
- **Being blind to blind spots.** This is a common enemy of learning in that we just don't know what we don't know. This new learning exists in our blind spot and can be a source of re-occurring patterns. "Why am I facing the same problem again?" If a leader finds him- or herself in a familiar failure, it may just require a declaration of not knowing and asking for feedback and/or coaching.
- **Failing to prioritize learning.** This may sound like "I don't have time," "Things are too hectic to stop and learn something new," or "I have too many people depending on me now and I'll just do what I know how to do." Being over-committed or over-burdened can be a defense against thinking. It can block those new practices, skills, or behaviors needed to produce results.
- **Confusing learning with acquiring information.** This may sound like "Tell me what I need to know in bullet form," "Just tell me what to do," or "Let me read an article on this." Learning is deeply rooted in sense of self, of identity, of underlying assumptions of how we make meaning of the world. Learning should be challenging.
- **Not giving others permission to teach.** This may sound like: "I don't trust you," "You don't have any authority to teach me," or "I can only learn from those who are experts." In dealing with complex social problems, leaders are working with others who have different life experiences, different points of view, and different values, habits, and beliefs. To grant others to teach you is to invest trust in that person. A leader must be able to trust others and then step into the vulnerability needed to authorize them to teach.

For the sake of the result, practitioners of results leadership willingly explore these invisible barriers to learning itself.

Activate a Learning Cycle, Find a Teacher

The built-in biases associated with mental models are often associated with cognitive blindness—we don't know what we don't know. It is, therefore, important to reach out to someone from outside who can provide new possibilities for action. To overcome "enemies of learning," leaders can activate their own learning cycle—for example, by using data to measure their own progress; by getting feedback from others; and by reading the books of those they respect. In addition, they can seek out someone to serve as instructor, teacher, or mentor—someone identifiably a results leader, someone who habitually puts results in the center and who works in High Action and High Alignment with others toward that result.

Trust is a key aspect in a relationship with any teacher, coach, or mentor. How to generate and maintain trust is discussed in detail in Chapter 5. Trust is enhanced when there is clear communication about the boundary or domain of the learning, and commitment to a timeframe for the learning.

To generate the trust needed, leaders must assess the competency, the honesty, and the reliability of the person they ask to be their teacher or coach. The following questions can support greater clarity and trust:

- Does this person know what I do not know? What evidence do I have?
- Does this person know how to teach what they know? What evidence do I have?
- Has this person accepted my request to be taught? How do I know?
- Is this person's commitment to teach me sincere? How do I know?
- Is this person reliable? How do I know?

See Reflective Practice: A Catalyst for Aligned Action apps/tools section at the end of this chapter.

Once a teacher or coach has been identified, then the leader goes on to do the hard work of learning new practices, challenging ingrained mental models, and forming new habits, all to support making progress towards the result. Just as important, the leader intentionally engages in continuous practice and reflection to better understand the application and impact of the new learning.

I often invite the leaders I work with to start a journaling, or reflective, practice. This might mean jotting down some thoughts or reflections at the end of a meeting, the end of a day, or after engaging with a difficult person. At the end of this chapter you will find a tool that speaks to reflective practice. Take some time for yourself and for reflection. My promise to you is that this will help you as a lifelong learner.

Chapter 4 Summary

"Leader readiness" has been my theme for this chapter, and I hope you are now feeling ready to move into the work of results leadership—or at least, the learning required to fill your gaps and address the limitations of your mental models.

I have talked about the leader's foundation, why we do what we do, the values, purpose, and intent that give meaning to our work. I have discussed the concept of mental models—their benefits and limitations; their function as political lenses; and the need to recognize and move past them.

Finally, since leaders must be lifelong learners, I have introduced you to the Learning Cycle, with its ever-deepening single-loop, double-loop, and triple-loop levels. I have encouraged you to reflect on your own cognitive biases, to risk being vulnerable, and to find a teacher or coach to help you work to overcome your "enemies of learning."

Feeling overwhelmed? Don't be! You may be "the leader," but you are not alone, or without support on this path. In the next chapter, we turn our attention to the group you'll lead.

Chapter 4 Applications: Tools and Worksheets

1. The Leaders Foundation: Five Whys 142
2. Cognitive Bias 143
3. Mental Models and Implicit Bias Worksheet 146
4. Reflective Practice: A Catalyst for Aligned Action 147

To download these apps, visit the book's online resources:
http://ChooseResultsBook.com/resources.html

Part 2: Executing to Scope and Scale

The Leaders Foundation: Five Whys
Raj Chawla

One simple reflection a leader can do borrows from the world of quality improvement: *The Five Whys,* an iterative interrogation technique. A leader may engage in this exploration for several reasons:
- To be clear on the values and beliefs they hold (their "whys");
- To realize the impact those "whys" have on the work they do; and
- How those "whys" shape their worldviews.

The Five Whys reflection is a springboard for exploring mental models and a way to step into being part of a learning organization.

Response	Digging Deeper for Purpose	What values and beliefs do you notice?
The reason this results work is important is….	This is important…	
Because…(e.g., I can make things better; lives are at stake; this is my calling, etc.)	And why is this important	
…Because	And why is this important	
…Because	And why is this important	

Cognitive Bias

Synthesized by Raj Chawla

In dealing with complex social problems, leaders are often making decisions and judgments with the best available data—this may be too much data, too little data, and/or contradictory data. These decisions and judgments are made with all the pressures that come with making a contribution to a population-level result. By using ones' own experience and the collective experience of colleagues and team, leaders can take mental shortcuts in making decisions—these shortcuts are often unconscious and can be effective in keeping the work on track.

There are times, however, when these mental shortcuts contribute to or cause misjudgments or wrong decisions. Mistakes that lead to misjudgments or wrong decisions—the limits of ones' world view, social pressures, time constraints, individual motivations, and emotions—can be attributed to what scientists call *cognitive biases*. Slowing down, understanding that all people have cognitive biases, and engaging in thoughtful processes can help leaders avoid poor decisions and judgments related to the results work at hand.

The following table highlights a few examples of cognitive biases.

\multicolumn{3}{c}{Challenge: Too much information}
Cognitive Bias	**What it looks like**	**Actions to Take**
Availability Bias	• Relying on immediate examples that come to mind when evaluating a specific topic, concept, method or decision. • Tend to heavily weigh judgments toward more recent information, making new opinions biased toward that latest news.	• Look at evidence, research • Examine the information: Is it valid because you have recently received it? Who from? Why did they give it to you? • Ask "who will benefit from this judgment?"
Anchoring & Adjustment	• Relying too heavily, or "anchoring," on one trait or piece of information when making decisions • Assuming a starting point and thinking about adjustments from there	• Use multiple perspectives • Engage in root cause analysis • Consult diverse sources
Confirmation	• Looking for supporting evidence that confirms your belief or point of view • Picking out pieces of data that make you feel good because they confirm prejudices, beliefs, mental models	• Recognize the pervasiveness of this bias • Examine all evidence with equal rigor and vet your sources • Be wary of overconfidence and use a

Part 2: Executing to Scope and Scale

		Devil's Advocate • Look for contrary evidence and be open to alterations
Framing	• Mistaking your view of the problem for the real need. • Viewing a need in the real world as a "problem" only you can work on or have the answer	• Holding a results frame with a focus on a population level result • Engaging with those who may have a different point of view and seeking aligned contributions • Challenge other people's framings

Challenge: Not Enough Information or Meaning		
Cognitive Bias	**What it looks like**	**Actions to Take**
Guessing At Patterns	• Seeing patterns that don't exist • Quickly spotting the trend or the big picture	• Engage in root cause and factor analysis • Examine the prevalent mental models within a group or community • Use heterogeneous groups • Use the power of diversity
Authority Bias	• Tendency to attribute greater accuracy to the opinion of an authority figure and be more influenced by that opinion	• Look for counter opinion – particularly those whose voices are marginalized or not included • Examine the world views and interests of expert or authority
Selective Perception	• Knowing what you're looking for • See things from our own personal perspective • Only perceives what you feel is right, completely ignoring the opposing viewpoints. • Organize and interpret events/information based on this perception	• Do the math • Intentionally get different points of view
Recallability ("Availability")	• Assessing the frequency or probability of an event by the ease with which instances or occurrences can be brought to mind. • Inadvertently assuming that readily	• Test your hypotheses and do the math • Carefully examine all of your assumptions to ensure they're not unduly influenced

Chapter 4: Apps/Tools

	available instances, examples or images represent unbiased estimates of statistical probabilities.	by your memory. • Get actual statistics whenever possible, and avoid being guided by impressions

Challenge: Contradictory Information		
Cognitive Bias	**What it looks like**	**Actions to Take**
Status Quo	• Bias against anything new • "Business as Usual" • "If it ain't broke, don't fix it"	• Remind yourself of the results • Look for alternatives • Bring in different voices – particularly the voices of those impacted by the decisions • Don't exaggerate switching costs
Sunk Cost	• Treating the resources already spent on one alternative as a real cost of abandoning it for something better • Treating the resources already spent on one alternative as an estimate of the resources you'll have to spend all over again to start a new one.	• Listen to people not involved in original decision • Explore the "losses" stakeholders might resist if change is to happen • Reassign responsibility • Examine performance measures and other metrics
Cognitive Overconfidence	• Self delusion • Decisiveness • Refusal to be haunted by doubt	• Examine the sources of information you tend to rely on? Are these fact-based, or do you rely on hunches? • Identify who else needs to be involved in gathering and assessing information?
Risk Aversion	• Missed opportunities • Preference for reducing a small risk to zero over a greater reduction in a larger risk • "A bird in the hand is worth two in the bush" • Avoid probability of ruin	• Look for objective statistics: Do the numbers! • Examine losses to power, prestige, and/or competence that might influence decisions

Part 2: Executing to Scope and Scale

Mental Models and Implicit Bias Worksheet
Developed by Marian Urquilla

1. Journal your individual thoughts: What are some of the mental models you're holding about why disparities exist in the population you are working with? (How do you privately explain to yourself the persistence of disparities?)

2. Working with other stakeholders and partners, think through the following questions: What are some of the disparities your community is facing? For each one listed, describe the evidence (observation/data) that this disparity exists?

   Disparity   Observations/Data

3. Working with these disparities, as a team discuss the following: What are some of the spoken and unspoken mental models that your group has in explaining these disparities or to describe what it would take to address them? What do people say out loud and what do they say behind closed doors?

   Spoken Explanatory Mental Models   Unspoken Explanatory Mental Models

4. From the list you just generated, choose some of the most prevalent mental models for explaining a particular disparity and discuss the following questions:

   - Where do these mental models come from?
   - How do they impact or influence the work towards producing results?
   - What needs to happen to address the limits of these mental models?
   - How does your work disrupt or contradict (or align with) these mental models?

Chapter 4: Apps/Tools

Reflective Practice: A Catalyst for Aligned Action
© Jolie Bain Pillsbury

1. Why Reflective Practice?

Taking aligned action[1] to achieve a common result presents opportunities for awareness and growth. Aligning actions requires an awareness of one's impact on others and a willingness to consider and commit to changes in behavior. Leaders can learn to take the time and space to examine their experience and gain greater awareness of how their actions reflect their:

> Content
> 1. Why reflective practice?
> 2. Practice Method
> 3. Practice Guide

- Values,
- Beliefs, and
- Perceptions of role.

Taking the risk to share these insights with other leaders catalyzes the mutual discovery of what changes in behavior might create the possibility of aligned action and contributions to a common result. This process of examination, insight, and mutual discovery leading to new action is called reflective practice.[2]

2. Practice Method

To begin the practice, stop what you are doing and give your self a moment to breathe, slow down, and pause to reflect on what is happening. Take a few minutes to think and feel more deeply. Write down your reflections and insights– either in a journal or on a piece of paper.

Journaling is not something everyone is comfortable with, however, it is a critical, as it allows you to pause, read what you have written, and then gain insights from your reflections. Journaling becomes easier and more valuable over time.

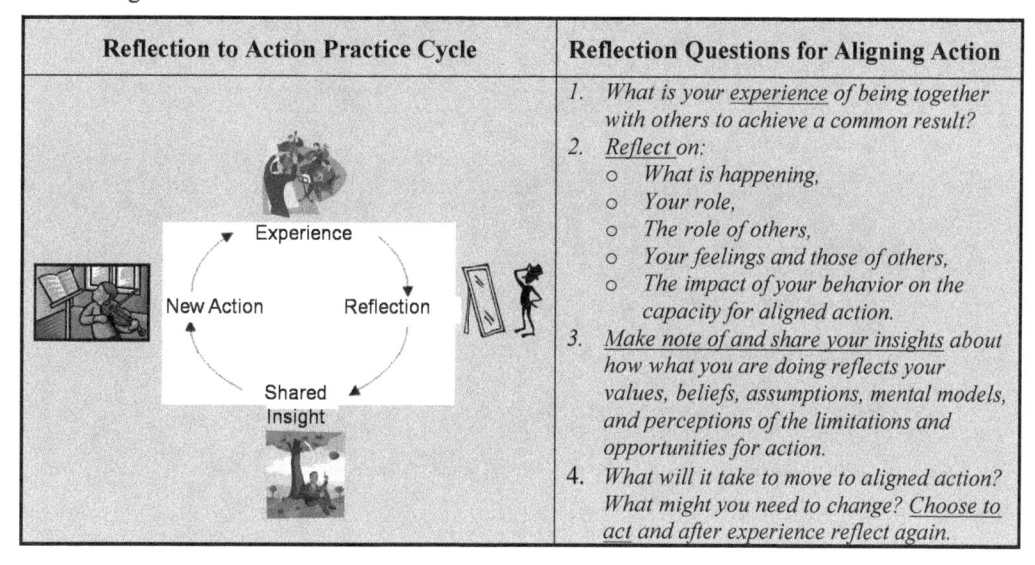

Reflection to Action Practice Cycle	Reflection Questions for Aligning Action

(diagram: Experience → Reflection → Shared Insight → New Action)	1. What is your _experience_ of being together with others to achieve a common result?
	2. _Reflect_ on:
	  o What is happening,
	  o Your role,
	  o The role of others,
	  o Your feelings and those of others,
	  o The impact of your behavior on the capacity for aligned action.
	3. _Make note of and share your insights_ about how what you are doing reflects your values, beliefs, assumptions, mental models, and perceptions of the limitations and opportunities for action.
	4. What will it take to move to aligned action? What might you need to change? _Choose to act and after experience reflect again._

---

[1] Pillsbury, Jolie Bain, *The Theory of Aligned Contributions*, 2008.
[2] Schon, Donald, *Educating the Reflective Practitioner (1987)*

Part 2: Executing to Scope and Scale

3. Practice Guide

- ☑ Carry and use a journal to jot down reflections, insights, and commitments to action
- ☑ Share your insights with other leaders, be curious about their insights
- ☑ Make choices about new actions and give your self permission to be awkward as you try new behaviors
- ☑ Be willing to continue to learn from experience and use the power of reflective practice over time to discover what it will take to move to aligned action
- ☑ Overtime notice what helps you move to aligned action and what blocks movement to aligned action
- ☑ What do these patterns reveal about:
    - Your adaptive leadership [3] challenges?
    - Your MBTI[4] Preferences?
    - Your own assumptions and experiences around race, class, culture, and gender?
    - Your own understanding of the multiple roles you play, the formal and/or informal authority you have in those roles to act and influence others to act?
    - Your orientation toward conflict and the types of conflict that might need to be surfaced and addressed?
    - Your relationships?
    - Your unique strengths and how those unique strengths can be leveraged with other's strengths for aligned action?
    - Your interest and willingness to be accountable for your own choices?
    - Your allies in moving to aligned action?
    - Your competing commitments?
    - Your capacity to manage transitions?
    - Your appetite for risk and your risk management strategies?
    - What you are willing to hold yourself accountable for?
    - Your capacity to change your own behavior in service of a common result?
- ☑ Persist in your practice

---

[3] Heifetz, Ronald *Leadership on the Line*, 2007
[4] Myers-Briggs Type Indicator®

CHAPTER 5

"Me with You"— Work Group Readiness

Courage means to keep working a relationship, to continue seeking solutions to difficult problems, and to stay focused during stressful periods.

– Denis Waitley

Years ago, the Annie E. Casey Foundation experienced success in a results leadership experiment called the Leadership in Action Program (LAP).[1] Following that success, the foundation sought to expand this work by inviting additional facilitators to join in the learning. I was invited to explore LAP in a workshop to see if I was interested in contributing. I recall walking into the meeting room at the University of Maryland and feeling the energy in the room. Colleagues from around the country had gathered, excited about the possibility of engaging in competency-based leadership results work at the community level. Most exciting to me was that LAP was using a results frame in its work (highlighted in Mark Friedman's *Trying Hard is Not Good Enough* cited earlier). That frame focused on the discipline of thinking about and using data and was collaborative in nature. During the course of the day, one core theme emerged: the difficulty of nurturing long-term community collaborative efforts to produce sustainable results. It seems that when the funding faded and the outside experts left, so did the collaboration.

It was then that Jolie Bain Pillsbury, who was the architect of the LAP framework, challenged us all to work *collaboratively* in our own efforts to support local communities. Jolie asked us, "How can we expect others to work collaboratively if we are not willing to do it ourselves?" This challenge led to an in-depth conversation about what could be possible if all of us in that meeting room worked in High Action and High Alignment toward a shared result.

I felt the pull to say, "Of course, I want to work in High Action and High Alignment with all of you," and get on with planning and implementing our work. I also realized that this must happen with many collaborative efforts—people saying yes to working together—without paying much attention to what is actually required to work collaboratively, but also effectively, toward a result.

I told Jolie I didn't know if I wanted to work in High Action and High Alignment with this team, because I didn't know what that concept truly required of me and what I could expect from others. I wanted to be a good team player. However, I knew from experience that wanting to be a good team player is not enough to be successful in working collaboratively. Working collaboratively is difficult: Competing interests, competition for power and status, lack of accountability, avoidance of difficult conversations, and the lack of resilient relationships are all obstacles. For me to work in this way, with this group, would require all of us to have an intentional conversation about reducing those barriers to our success. We had to talk about what working in High Action and High Alignment actually meant.

Moving from the "Me" to the "Me with You"

Working to produce population-level results is a task that requires creating and sustaining a "Me with You" stance. Moving from the "Me" to the "Me with You" is a difficult task—especially when the "You" may be stakeholders who hold different values, beliefs, attitudes, and mental models. To make it even more challenging, this work requires a "You and I"—we must first as individuals be in the right place—who are committed to working in High Action and High Alignment toward a result in the center.

What defines the "right place?" First, leaders have to know what their contribution is to be—the program they run, the policy initiative they advocate, the agency they lead—and how they are to perform in their role. As mentioned in Chapter 3, their contribution should be measurable: how much they are doing, how well they are doing it, and what difference they are making, as gauged by performance measures. This also means that the leader is committed to continuous quality improvement so their performance is at the highest-level possible.

There are many factors that can move a leader from thinking about him- or herself to thinking about engaging with another person. Three elements that can support leaders in operating in High Action and High Alignment with others are:

1. Honoring his or her word: Committing to impeccable discipline in working with others on their contribution to the results work;
2. Honoring his or her role: Holding accountability to the role and tasks; and
3. Honoring his or her relationship: Intentionally building resilient relationships.

With these three elements as a foundation, leaders can more easily undertake the difficult work of achieving results collaboratively. In this chapter, we take a close look at each element, and close with a discussion of how performance can be measured, for quality improvement over time.

Honoring Your Word: Requests, Offers, Promises

In his book *The Four Agreements*[2] Don Miguel Ruiz starts with the first agreement: Be impeccable with your word. He suggests that this agreement is the most important one, and also the most difficult one to honor. Ruiz goes on to explain that the Latin root for impeccability means "without sin," derived from the Latin *pecatus*, or "sin," joined with *im*, meaning "without," thus "without sin." In the context of being a result leader, being impeccable with your word can be interpreted as a commitment to work in High Action and High Alignment with others.

Collaborative work can only go as far as the collective individuals' ability to honor their word—to do what they say they are going to do for the sake of the result.

Work and life are complicated; unexpected circumstances can arise. Honoring your word also means that you acknowledge your failure or inability to keep your word. Results leaders realize that when they are not able to honor their word, they must immediately let others know and renegotiate next steps.

For results leaders to be impeccable with their word, they have to be able to make powerful commitments to action in order to move collaboratively towards results. This involves promises, which consist of requests and offers.

Requests and Offers

In making a request or an offer,[3] a results leader is creating a possibility for something new to occur in the future. It takes two to do this tango:

- A *Requester* is someone who holds a concern about the present and, in making a request, desires something to happen in the future; and
- A *Performer* who, in making an offer (either as part of a specific request or in anticipation of a specific need), acts as a leader who holds the concern of *others*. He or she tries to address those concerns through an *offer* to do something that will support another leader, the collaborative group, or the results process itself.

> See Making Powerful Requests: Generating and Sustaining High Action/High Alignment App at end of this chapter.

The ability of a results leader to make a request or an offer—to be a *requester* or a *performer* who offers to fulfill another's request—is a fundamental building block of all successful results work.

For example, a results leader may need school data on third-grade reading levels from multiple school districts in order to develop a set of coherent, school-based strategies. This leader, motivated by a concern about developing the most effective strategies, could make a *request* to a partner from the school district for the most current data. On the other hand, a school district partner, realizing that many key partners may need the most current data about grade-level reading, may *offer* to provide the data as part of a conversation about strategy development. In both examples, there is a concern about the future being addressed by either a request or an offer.

While making a request or an offer may seem to be a simple act, I have seen numerous breakdowns in communication where someone felt a request made was not honored or an offer made was not accepted. This is more likely to happen when leaders from different systems do not know each other well; use different language (for example health care language v. education language); or have diverse ways of interpreting what they see in front of them. Clarity and precision in making requests and offers can alleviate confusion and miscommunication.

The elements of a powerful request and offer: When someone makes a request in response to some concern that he or she holds, three crucial things happen in the relationship with the person receiving the request:

1. She casts herself in a particular role—the role of customer or *requester*—for this conversation;
2. She casts the other person in the role of the *performer* of that request; and
3. She offers some initial criteria for success in meeting the request, also known as the *conditions of satisfaction*.

With this clarity in mind, the *requester* makes the request in a direct manner to a specific person, and states the reason for the request and connects it to the results work.

The *requester* and *performer* both agree to *conditions of satisfaction,* including:

- A specific time frame for completion of request;
- Standards and criteria for successful completion of the request;
- Agreement that the request role is appropriate; and
- Shared understanding of language and terminology.

For example, Terri, as the leader of a statewide grade-level reading initiative, needs data from Carol, who is the representative from the state Department of Education that would help shape a Teacher Training strategy. Both Terri and Carol understand the "insider" language and terminology within the state Department of Education. Both are clear on the role that Carol plays, as the lead Data Analyst, for the department.

Terri might make a request of Carol as follows:

> Terri: "Carol, I need to get the classroom criteria that the State Department of Education uses to assess teacher performance and how teachers are performing based on your internal assessments. Do you have that?"
>
> Carol: "I can only get you data from the past year. Will that give you what you need?"
>
> Terri: "I think so. I'll use this data to develop our Teacher Training strategy. Can I get that data disaggregated by school district?"
>
> Carol: "I can do that."
>
> Terri: "Great! Can I get it by end of next week? I'd need it no later than noon on Friday so I can review it and get it ready for the strategy development meeting on Monday."
>
> Carol: "Yes."

Both Terri and Carol are interested in creating a Teacher Training strategy that will support teachers in their work with students. Both understood the request and its purpose. They negotiated the criteria by which the outcome for this request will be measured—those *conditions of satisfaction*—for successfully honoring the request. In this example, the conditions of satisfaction for this request included:

1) When the data was needed (the time frame) and 2) The need to disaggregate by school district. Once that was clear, Carol said yes. This agreement transformed the request into an offer—a promise held by Carol.

> **Are you ready to make powerful requests and offers within this framework?**
> Reflect on a recent occasion when you were a requester and/or one when you were a performer. Did you honor these elements that make requests and offers powerful? If not, where did you fall short? This might be a useful conversation to have with others in your collaborative group.

When a Request or Offer Becomes a Promise

A *promise* is a declaration by one person to another that he or she will take some action in the future. In other words, it is the currency that is generated between a "requester" and a "performer." Simple enough, yet this is a place where confusion and breakdown often occur among leaders—especially if they are working across multiple systems, have different interests or pressures, or have differing points of view on a particular subject. I have seen leaders experience breaks in trust or accountability because they thought someone had agreed to take action based on a request they had made but never received adequate follow-through.

A promise is an action that binds people to each other, generates and maintains trust, and is the basis for commitments to action. Making a promise, however, is just the beginning. Someone must take action for that promise to be completed; for instance, Carol in the example above. No matter how well intentioned, not all promises can be met. Remember Carol and her promise to Terri? As Carol attempts to fulfill her promise, she may run into some challenges. For example, she may not be able to fulfill her promise to Terri due to internal disagreements about sharing data or about rules of confidentiality. This circumstance may cause Carol to miss her time frame, to fail to disaggregate the data, or to provide any data at all.

A results leader's public reputation is largely based on his or her ability to make, manage, and keep promises. Human beings base their future behavior on their past experiences. Every time a promise is broken, the future is impacted and the dynamics of relationships may be altered.[4]

When a results leader is able to manage promises well, she enjoys a positive reputation as someone who is trustworthy. When circumstances occur, leaders have to assess the implications of not meeting the promise. At stake is the ability of leaders to take future action with the person who has broken a promise. When leaders do not manage their promises, they can be seen as untrustworthy. They risk having their public identities become negative.

In our Carol and Terri example, let's suppose that all the possible roadblocks keeping Carol from delivering on her promise to deliver data in fact come true. Carol then has to consider the implications of not being able to keep her promise to Terri. Upon realization that she will not be able to keep her promise regarding the data, Carol should let Terri know and renegotiate new conditions of satisfaction to meet the promise (if possible) so that Terri's meeting may move forward as needed.

A results leader must consider three categories of promises: *healthy, shallow,* and *criminal.*[5]

1. Healthy Promise:
    - The promise is kept;
    - The *conditions of satisfaction* are clear and are met; and
    - A promise is made but can't be kept and the performer fulfills the obligation to let the requester know about the inability to keep the promise as soon as possible.

2. Shallow Promise:
    - A promise is made but there is a hidden condition that must be met before it will be kept.

3. Criminal Promise:
    - A promise is made with no intent to keep it.
    - A promise is made with good intent but then broken.
    - A promise is broken, and there is no warning to the requester.

For results leaders and the people we lead, the key to managing promises is to be impeccable with our words and deeds. Refuse to allow or accept shallow promises or what you might suspect to be criminal promises. Once your offers are accepted, do your best to keep them. If you are not able to keep a promise, let the requesters who are counting on you know, and explain why. If possible, renegotiate new conditions of satisfaction for that request.

Public Action Commitments: A Promise Made on Behalf of the Result

Making promises and offers are powerful commitments to create new action in the future. When a leader publicly commits to a promise or an offer, that leader creates an atmosphere of trust and shared accountability. That leader makes it possible for results collaborative work to take place. A public commitment to honor our word makes all the difference. Through this commitment, promises lead to action.

Making and keeping public action commitments is especially important when working with peers, where there is accountability to the result but not to any formal authority. Formally making public action commitments—in writing and based on offers and promises—is a powerful way to build peer accountability. Jolie Bain Pillsbury first introduced me to "action commitment" forms and the impact they have on results work.

When working with a collaborative work group, I will often ask the participants to reflect on the work they just did and identify an action commitment (a promise) they are willing to make. I then ask them to write it on an "action commitment" form. (An example of this form appears in the appendix to this chapter and also below, filled out.) I remind them that the action commitment form is not a to-do list of tasks they would ordinarily do. Rather, it is an intentional action they are going to take after they return to their work; an intentional action with key partners and stakeholders that will help move their results work forward.

I also let them know that the next time they meet as a work group, they should plan to talk about accountability for the action commitments they have made that day. I remind them that results leaders have a bias towards action and are always moving from strategy development, to execution of strategy, to quality improvement in order to make their aligned contributions to the result.

To counter skepticism, I remind them that the power and effectiveness of making public action commitments is supported by research. The University of Maryland's School of Public Policy found that a formal, written process for documenting leaders' commitments can increase accountability by 17 percent for individual commitments and 25 percent for group commitments.[6]

Action commitments outline what actions each person is accountable for and describe the steps, the timeline for the work, and its contribution to the result. The action commitment that Carol—in working with Terri—made on behalf of creating a Teacher Training strategy might look like that shown in Table 5.1. Table 5.2 provides examples of weak and powerful action commitments, drawing on the tool "Are You In High Action And High Alignment," by Vicki Goddard-Truitt and Jolie Bain Pillsbury, which appears in the Apps/Tools section at the end of this chapter.

> See the Aligned Action Commitment form in the apps/tools section at the end of this chapter. It represents a formal process to capture action commitments made by leaders.

> See Are You in High Action and High Alignment? in the apps/tools section at the end of this chapter. It is offered to help make more powerful action commitments.

Table 5.1 **Action Commitment Outline for Creating a Teacher Training Strategy**

Action(s)	With Whom	When	Contribution to the Result	Progress
For each action, write the steps needed to fully implement it.	Who will partner with you?	When will the action be completed?	How will actions contribute to making a measurable difference?	To be completed at the next session.
Get 2016-2017 teacher performance data—disaggregated by school district.	Jim—Lead data analyst for Department of Education	Thursday—next week	Will help develop the key elements and performance measures for the Teacher Training strategy	In process—delayed due to internal data sharing agreement. Will have by end of month

Table 5.2 **Weak and Powerful Action Commitments**

Weak Commitments	Powerful Commitments
At the next staff meeting, I will share what we talked about in the last meeting.	I will meet with my team next week to review our trend line on adoptions and complete a factor analysis. This information will inform the next steps that we will take to meet our targets.
Talk with director about the need to change policy and procedures to improve outcomes.	I will collect information and data to demonstrate what is working and not, and link to best practices. By the end of the month I will make a policy implementation recommendation to the director.
Design job fair	By next month, two key partners and I will attend two job fairs in the tri-state area to gather information. We will present our design recommendations at the next quarterly meeting of the work group.

Through their written action commitments, leaders demonstrate to the group that they are working in role to do the tasks needed to contribute to the program performance measures and population-level result. In fact, research shows that completion rates increase and execution and efficacy improve when action commitments are made in writing, shared publicly with the team or workgroup, and then reviewed and discussed regularly.[7] A practice of regularly using written action commitments and reviewing progress on those actions at meetings helps leaders create the culture of shared accountability discussed in Chapter 2.

The final piece of coaching I offer these leaders is on their ability to make action commitments that are specific, tied to action and time frame, and that have an intentional outcome in mind.

Creating quality improvement. Over time, these two practices—using action commitments, and having conversations about accountability—lead to quality improvement. Leaders overtly see if their actions are creating the desired impact. Is the work moving forward? This analysis of action commitments allows leaders to have systems conversations (and connect to the triple-loop learning discussed in Chapter 4). I will often ask these leaders: What are the barriers, in your system, to making and keeping action commitments? This type of analysis allows leaders to use data from action commitments to improve the quality of their work.

Commitment to Action: A Powerful Way to Move into Collaboration

Fernando Flores, in his book *Conversations For Action and Collected Essays*,[8] states that action occurs *"in the commitments we make to each other, and that we make these commitments in conversations."* I often tell the leaders I work with to have a bias towards action, accepting that that means they will sometimes have to make mid-course corrections, as needed. One way to create this bias is to engage in intentional conversations that stimulate action. Four fundamental conversations for action are those that:[9]

1. Make a request or offer to others;

2. Generate a promise or an acceptance to someone else;

3. Make a declaration of completion by the person who made the offer or promise; and

4. Make a declaration of satisfaction by the person who made the request or accepted the offer.

Reflect on whether as a results leader, you are engaging in these fundamental conversations for action.

Honoring Your Role

When leaders are aligned to the results work, their focus goes towards execution. To be successful in execution, leaders seek to fully honor their role and support others in their roles so highly aligned action can be made towards a population-level result. Honoring role starts with developing a clear understanding of one's role in an organization or a system, as well as the tasks and responsibilities associated with it. Knowing and executing your role allows you to work well with others. *To the extent that people have a clear understanding of each other's roles, they can work together in both High Action and High Alignment and perform work that is complementary, mutually supportive, and designed to make a measurable difference toward results.*

Boundary of Authority

A leader's actions—the tasks they perform in their role—are fundamental to moving results work forward. For results leaders to be effective in their role, they have to know:[10]

- Where and how they get their authority;
- The boundaries of their role—where their authority begins and where it stops;
- The role they are expected to perform—the duties they are to perform and the outcome of their role; and
- The specific tasks they are to perform in their role.

Often, a breakdown occurs when a leader isn't clear on the authority he or she holds or may claim more authority then he or she is authorized to have. Or, there may not be a clear boundary to that authority. For example, a project manager shows up to a crucial meeting of a health collaborative in place of their executive director. This

---

Boundary and Authority

Leaders might reflect on these questions concerning boundaries and authority:

- Who is authorizing me to perform in this role?
- What authority do I have within my role?
- Is my authority sufficient to play my role and deliver the task I am accountable for?
- Are the boundaries of my authority sufficient for me to fulfill my role?

project manager may not have the authority to make a decision on behalf of the organization and yet she chooses to make a decision that goes beyond her authority. This can create confusion within the collaborative work group.

When a leader chooses to take up their authority, they are also choosing to assume the responsibility and accountability to perform in their role and engage in the needed tasks.

Boundary of Role and Task

Misconceptions of role can sometimes be attributed to misconceptions of boundary and authority. With clarity of boundaries and authority, the results leader then is clear on the role they are to perform and the tasks they are to perform in their role.

> The Role Worksheet in the apps/tools section at the end of this chapter is designed to support your work group in achieving role clarity.

Role: Role can be understood as a set of work-related functions and tasks that an individual has the authority to perform. It is through those functions and tasks, in role, that a leader achieves program-level results toward a population-level result. Accountability to role means, most simply, fulfilling the duties of the role you are authorized to play, supporting others to fulfill the duties of their roles, and working together in High Action and High Alignment, as explored later in this section.

For results work to be effective, and to work in High Action and High Alignment, leaders must understand their roles and clearly communicate them to others. This clarity is not only important to the person who takes up the role, but also for the people whose work depends on that person playing their role effectively.

According to Green and Molenkamp:[11] "A formal role is much like a job description. It defines the duties to be performed, the parameters for completing tasks, the people and processes with which interaction must take place, and often the outcomes or deliverables that mark the tangible successful performance of the role. An informal role is one that serves to fill the gaps of authority and tasks abandoned, yielded, or implicitly ceded to them by the organization or group."

Leaders might reflect on these questions concerning role:

- What is the purpose/function of the role in advancing the results work?
- What do I think is required of me to play my role fully in this system for this task (i.e., behavior, presence, self-knowledge, self-awareness and awareness of others)?

- Is there anything missing or needing change from the way my role is currently defined or perceived?
- What areas of role conflict (for example, performing an aspect of a role that is in conflict with a person's values) might there be with those I interact with to achieve my task?
- What informal roles are needed in order to advance the results work?

Task: At its core, a task is the set of activities that produce "something" in the context of the role. A leader seeks to complete a set of tasks that delivers the results necessary to fulfilling the role. A data analyst, for example, may seek to complete a set of tasks that are required to write a report on programmatic performance. These tasks may include data gathering, analysis, vetting, and report writing.

One challenge is that there may be different perceptions of how best to perform those tasks. Each leader brings with them his or her perception of how best to perform their role and execute the tasks. Conflict can arise when leaders' perceptions of performances differ.

Leaders might reflect on these questions concerning task:

- What is the task that I have been given the authority for?
- What is the result that this task is contributing to?
- What data am I using to track the quality of my actions (my "how much" and "how well" performance measures)?
- What data am I using to track the success for the tasks (my "difference made" performance measures)?
- Who do I rely on in order to succeed in my tasks?
- What data am I using to know if I am successful?

Having a clear understanding of your own role as well as the role of others is essential in working in an aligned manner toward results. Connected to role are the tasks that leaders are to perform in their role. In the world of results leadership the primary task can be considered the results work. Everyone is to perform, in their role, to the primary task contributing to results. In addition to the primary task, leaders also have their individual tasks that they are to perform. How do we create momentum towards aligned action? You must know the tasks to perform and the associated performance measures and then be clear on others' tasks and performance measures.

Results Leader: Austin Dickson

When Austin Dickson joined nonprofit Literacy Action in Atlanta, Georgia, as its Executive Director, one of his first tasks was to restore financial stability for an organization whose result is to "make Atlanta more literate." I worked with Austin as part of Annie E Casey's Atlanta Leaders for Results (ALR) Program, leadership program designed to develop a network of results leaders within Atlanta's nonprofit and public sectors. He soon began to see there were deeper issues standing in the way of Literacy Action making progress toward its result. As he said: "There just wasn't much alignment between the mission and what we were doing as an organization, and there was very little accountability, very little sense of our results and how those lined up with what we wanted to achieve."

As he implemented a results frame within his organization, one of his first tasks was to create clarity about individuals' roles and tasks, as well to identify the authority they needed to perform their role. "I realized we needed to get clear on what people's jobs were in the organization," he said, noting that, in the absence of that clarity, Literacy Action had developed a culture of "tension and suspicion."

Consequently, Austin led individual and group processes to clearly identify everyone's role and authority in the organization. As part of the process, the staff inventoried the organization's core strategies and activities and fine-tuned people's roles and job descriptions accordingly. "Basically, we redesigned the organization around the results we wanted to achieve," Austin explained.

"We then came together collectively to look at everyone's job descriptions and roles, and we approved them as a team," Austin said. "This was a way of being crystal-clear as a group on what everyone was expected to do, and making sure we all were doing our part to get to the results we wanted."

Literacy Action has a new and more streamlined mission: "To build better futures for undereducated adults by teaching literacy, life, and work skills that empower them to reach their highest potential." It is increasingly gaining a national reputation for innovation in the field of adult basic education. From 2012 to 2017, the staff grew from 12 to 36, and the budget tripled to $2.4 million. More importantly, due to improved internal clarity, the increased staff and resources allowed the organization to serve hundreds more adult students and open up additional locations throughout the Atlanta region. Literacy Action received the 2017 "Managing for Excellence Award" given by the Community Foundation of Greater Atlanta—further evidence that management excellence goes hand in hand with results.

Most importantly, Literacy Action's programs now are serving a growing number of primarily low-income residents in 16 locations across Atlanta, with a new focus on supporting those students to succeed.

As the example of Austin's work with Literacy Action's programs demonstrates, a clear understanding of roles among members of a collaborative group is essential to working in high action and high alignment. A template designed to help you gain role clarity within groups you lead appears in the apps/tools section of this chapter.

Honoring Relationships: Creating Resilience

I opened this chapter by saying that the difficult work of moving from the "Me" to the "Me with You" in High Action and High Alignment requires three elements:

1. Honoring your word;
2. Honoring your role; and
3. Honoring your relationship.

Having explored the first two elements; it is now time to turn our attention to the third.

When a leader moves from the "Me" to the "Me with You," many conscious and unconscious assessments begin to happen about the "You." Is this someone I can work with? What is their agenda? Are they trustworthy? Can I be vulnerable with them? Can they harm me? Do they have more power and authority than I do? Can I tell them the truth as I see it?

It is no coincidence that these are some of the uncensored thoughts that leaders tell me they have as they start to engage with others as part of a collaborative workgroup. Some leaders will work with others assuming trust and accountability. They seem willing to sustain that assumption until something happens that proves otherwise. Some leaders will step more cautiously into working with others: They need their collaborators to demonstrate trustworthiness first in order to fully engage with them.

Part 2: Executing to Scope and Scale

Coping with a Culture of Politeness

*The safest place for a leader to stand
is on the foundation of results.*

– Raj Chawla

Culture of politeness: A social dynamic that seeks to keep things as they are through passive-aggressive behavior and resistance to change.

Sooner or later challenging moments will arise in every organization—conflict over priorities, power struggles over resources or leadership, a battle over mental models and points of view. When this happens, conflicts or disagreements can go "underground" and remain unresolved. A dysfunctional aspect might seep into the collaborative group. When certain things are said publicly and others are said privately, maintaining resilient relationships becomes difficult.

A group of leaders I work with in Minnesota call this "Minnesota nice." The leaders I work with in Atlanta and other parts of the US South call this "southern gentility." My leaders in Seattle often call this "Seattle freeze." I describe this as a **culture of politeness** that defers to power and prioritizes relationships rather than discussing openly and transparently what is working and what isn't. When I speak to groups of leaders about this notion, they often acknowledge that a culture of politeness exists in their community. Surprisingly, they are often convinced that this only happens in their community or region.

I remind these leaders that the fastest and most direct way to produce results is to *make results the primary task of the work*. The primary task cannot be maintaining relationships, or power, or funding, or control. This means leaders have to be transparent about power dynamics, decisions that are being made, and conflicts that may be arising. Results leadership requires leaders to talk directly about programs that may not be contributing to the results; behavior that may be contradictory to being in High Action and High Alignment; and expectations that everyone involved will be impeccable with their word.

I have seen over the years that my coaching to break this culture of politeness is often met with reluctance, or followed by halfhearted efforts just to please me. Once I leave, the patterns of behavior often quietly revert to their earlier dysfunction. In reflecting on this, I have come to acknowledge that I am not bearing any of the personal risk in an engagement—it is borne solely by the leader I am coaching. While I go off to work with my next leadership group, the good folks

I just left have to hold accountability for figuring out how to work together in perpetuity.

For "Me" to enter into a space of "Me with You" there has to be a common foundation. The safest place for a leader to stand is on the foundation of results. It is on this platform that leaders can speak authentically and transparently about what they feel is happening. They may name the "un-discussables" and build resilient relationships—ones that can withstand conflict and honest feedback, that share a willingness to repair or mend if there is a break. These hard conversations allow leaders to create a results culture.

Resilience and the Collaborative Work Group

While resilience can mean many things depending on the context (i.e., social, behavioral, biological), for results leaders it means the ability of individuals to tolerate change and accept changing roles that require adjustments in their behavior as they move beyond their individual comfort zone and the collaborative work group stretches beyond its collective comfort zone. The pursuit of authentic, resilient relationships may look like:[12]

- A collaborative work group adapting successfully to disturbances that threaten its function, viability, or development;
- A leader and collaborative work group's successful adaptation to an environment of acute stress;
- A leader and collaborative work group ably avoiding harmful and potentially destructive behavior in response to chronic stress;
- A collaborative work group skillfully creating a process to harness resources to sustain wellbeing; and
- A work group resuming its positive functioning following any form of adversity.

To be resilient, therefore, can be defined as the ability of a leader and a collaborative work group to bounce back from adversity and challenge. This adversity may mean enduring a loss of or changes in power, authority, resources, relationship, etc., or working through the potential negative emotions that can emerge from conflict or failure.

Resilience emerges through the social intelligence of the individual and the group. It transforms potentially damaging and toxic stress into something that is tolerable and, ultimately, allows the group to learn, strengthen, and grow. It is through the building of resilient relationships that trust is born and solidified.

Trust: The Fuel for High Action and High Alignment

Trust is the pre-condition for a collaborative work group to be in High Action and High Alignment. With such a crucial role to play, trust deserves a deep understanding.[13]

Alternatives to trust: fear, control, and power. Increasing trust within and among a group of results leaders eases the reins of control. By letting go a bit, groups of leaders can improve efficiency, cooperation, team spirit, morale, and chances for success. Trust, then, is the essential ingredient in the decision-making process that allows the work group to move past authority and competition toward effective collaboration.

At its core, trust involves vulnerability. It is, in many aspects, the opposite of control, which functions to minimize vulnerability. To trust people is to count on their sense of responsibility and integrity. To trust is to take a risk, believing that others will choose to act in an honest and reliable manner, while recognizing the possibility that they may instead choose to betray or break the trust. Taking risks makes us vulnerable.

In my work with leaders, I often ask them to identify a few key stakeholders or partners whom they assess as not being in High Action and/or High Alignment. Frequently, after a few moments of unpacking why they hold this assessment, trust emerges as a key reason. This revelation ignites an inquiry on trust—what is it, how do you maintain it, or how do you repair it?

The first step in building trust: talking about it. The practice of trust starts with the leader who models trustworthiness (comprised of the traits we've been talking about: being impeccable with your word, making and keeping your commitments, and building resilient relationships). Because trust is so integral to working in High Action and High Alignment, a results leader begins with an appreciation and understanding of trust and with the ability to practice the conversations and actions that support it.

These conversations require an understanding of how individuals arrive at an assessment of trust. Trust is not to be confused with familiarity or relationship. For example, someone you have known for many years and are in a good working relationship with may be competent in the area of partner engagement and, therefore, trustworthy to enroll key partners in the results work. However, this same person may not be competent in using data analysis and would, therefore, not be trustworthy in implementing and using a particular data collection methodology. Familiarity and/or relationship are not, in and of themselves, an assurance that the person is trustworthy in all areas of activity. It would not be practical or wise to trust people wholeheartedly in all aspects of the results work.

Assessing trustworthiness. Either consciously or unconsciously, we assess others on their ability to fulfill their promises first by their level of engagement toward the results work itself. This assessment of engagement is based on commitment to make their aligned contribution (High Action) in a collaborative manner (High Alignment) with others.

According to Fernando Flores, whenever we accept a promise, we make a judgment of the other person's sincerity—whether or not the person intends to do what he or she has promised. We also assess the person's competence and reliability to take the actions promised.[14]

Trustworthiness, therefore, relies on these assessments:

- Engagement: Is this person actively involved in the collaborative group?
- Sincerity: Is this person serious about his or her commitment?
- Competence: Is this person capable of following through on his or her commitment?
- Reliability: Is this person able to fulfill his or her commitment in a timely manner?

Generating, maintaining, and repairing trust. Results leaders use the principles above to assess their own and others' trustworthiness regarding acting in High Action and High Alignment toward the result. Because the results work is so important, they are willing to have the necessary conversations to ensure that trust is generated and maintained among the group and, if broken, repaired so the work can continue.

Results leaders might observe some of the behaviors of trustworthiness or their absence described in Table 5.3.

For a variety of reasons, there will be times when your trust is broken. A results leader uses such an opportunity to repair trust. A results leader should be willing to forgive the break and speak to both the learning opportunity that may be present and any future action that might need to happen. The leader should likewise be quick to apologize for his or her own mistakes, inconsistencies, and broken promises. Engaging in a conversation of trust—where trust has been broken and/or needs to be developed—can be difficult. Taking the time to prepare for that conversation can help a results leader connect that conversation to the hard

> See Focusing on Trust: A Prerequisite for Creating Results in the apps/tools section at the end of this chapter. It is offered to help ground leaders in the distinctions of trust.

Table 5.3 **Behaviors of Trustworthiness and Their impact on Results Work**

	Trust	Distrust
How you assess the other person	• This person is committed to the results work • They will do their best to make an aligned contribution and work collaboratively with me	• This person has their own agenda • They are not committed to working in a collaborative manner with me
Behavior you might notice	• Sharing of information • Willingness to cooperate and collaborate towards the result • Offering ideas freely and openly • Openness to learning and quality improvement • Willingness to give and get feedback and examine own behavior	• Withholding information and ideas • Not sharing openly, exploring differences, or holding a stance of a learner, • Defending actions and complaining about others • Blaming others
Impact on Results Work	• Being in quality improvement • Using data to assess all the work • Problem solving	• Defending work or programs that are not contributing to results • Becoming fragmented

See Preparing for a Trust Conversation Worksheet in the apps/tools section at the end of this chapter. It is offered to help leaders prepare for trust conversations to support working in High Action/High Alignment.

work of producing results. This preparation helps to frame the conversation; the requests you may be making; and the condition of satisfaction you are seeking as you work to develop trust. At the end of this chapter you will find a worksheet that can help prepare for this conversation.

Recall Jim Czarniak and his work with Onondaga County's Juvenile Justice System from Chapter 2. Part of the initial work the cross-sector stakeholders had to do was to build trust among each other so they could work together toward a shared result. Jim understood that all the stakeholders (including the Juvenile Justice system) would have to work hard in order to create the resilient relationships needed to generate population-level results. As he said:

"Trust was the biggest part of it. There had to be a lot of honesty in the room. It was not about me convincing them to do it in a different way. They understood why we were doing what we were doing. In order to move from finger-pointing to owning the result we had to have several trust conversations. Where in our past work had we lost trust with one another? Was it a break in sincerity, was it a lack of reliability, or was it due to a lack of competence in what we were tasked to do? We had to talk about what was happening in our systems that created breaks in trust and about what we were expecting from each other. It was from this hard work that we were able to gradually repair and build trust among each other. This intentionality towards resilient relationships is something we pay ongoing attention to. Without trust we could not work in High Action or High Alignment with each other."

To summarize: A results leader knows that trust is the fuel that allows a group to move forward with others toward a result. Trust is at the heart of any progress they may make. Resilient relationships are needed to ensure trust is maintained. Finally, a results leader knows that social intelligence is needed to make sure that all individuals are in High Action and High Alignment.

Generating and Maintaining Trust

In order to generate and maintain trust, results leaders should learn to use the following tactics:

1. Have open conversations about trust, which builds the capacity of the results work group to talk about trust.

2. Tell the truth about actions and events.

3. Know the difference between your unexpressed expectations and someone's promises. An expectation becomes a promise when the other person says yes to a clear expectation you hold *and express.*

4. Overtly thank and give positive feedback to those who fulfill their promises to you and provide constructive feedback to those who do not.

5. Support others, if possible, in keeping their promises. This might mean giving additional information, connecting to other resources, renegotiating deadlines, and taking on additional responsibilities from the other so they have time to fulfill the promise.

6. Be clear on your assessments of others' sincerity, competence, and reliability, as well as your own.

Reflect on whether, as a results leader, you are using these techniques to generate and maintain trust in your collaborative work group.

Chapter 5 Summary

You should now be feeling more familiar with how results leaders move from the "Me" of leadership to the "Me with You" of collaborative work in High Action and High Alignment to a population-level result.

We have discussed three elements essential in this transformation, elements that require the leader to model specific behavior and expect it of others. These are: being impeccable in one's word, holding accountability through public action commitments, and building resilient relationships on a foundation of trustworthiness. These elements support collaborative work groups in making progress toward a population-level result in the center.

After a deep dive into each of these three elements, I discussed the role performance measures play in assessing program performance. Measures are how we know how far we've come, how well, and with what impact.

Chapter 5 Applications: Tools and Worksheets

1. Making Powerful Requests: Generating and Sustaining High Action and High Alignment 172
2. Sample Aligned Action Commitments Form 174
3. Are You In High Action and High Alignment? 175
4. Role Worksheet 177
5. Focusing on Trust: A Prerequisite for Creating Results...179
6. Preparing for a Trust Conversation..................181

To download these apps, visit the book's online resources:
http://ChooseResultsBook.com/resources.html

Part 2: Executing to Scope and Scale

Making Powerful Requests:
Generating and Sustaining High Action and High Alignment
© Raj Chawla

Results leaders choose to work together in both high action and high alignment[1] out of a shared commitment to create a future that benefits people. In other words, results leaders come together to make their aligned contributions towards a shared population level result. They choose to be in resilient and trusting[2] relationships and do the hard work of staying in high action and high alignment.

When a leader assesses that a partner is not in high action/high alignment, that leader has an obligation to have an authentic conversation[3] to support that partner in getting to or returning to high action/high alignment. Sometimes these conversations will require making a "Powerful Request".

Contents
1. Results partners can fall out of working in high action/high alignment
2. Powerful requests can help generate and sustain High Action/High Alignment
3. Sincere foundation for a powerful request
4. Key elements of a powerful request
5. Responsibilities of

1. Establishing a sincere foundation for the powerful request
Establishing a sincere foundation for the powerful request sets the stage for a successful exchange, and allows the requestor to gather information helpful for understanding the situation. This foundation should include:

Genuinely wanting assistance at the time of asking.	➔	And anticipating that the assistance will be needed until the point of "delivery."
Using data and/or shared criteria to make your assessment.	➔	This grounds your assessment in a shared reality.
Asking others if they share your assessment, based on the available data and/or criteria.	➔	This can help eliminate any blind spots or misinterpretations.
Making hypotheses about the reasons your partner(s) might have for not working in High Action/High Alignment, including issues of potential loss, lack of trust, work avoidance, and/or lack of clarity in role.	➔	This helps shape the kind of request you may make.
Identifying the impact of not working in High Action/High Alignment, including meeting population level results and related performance measures.	➔	This highlights the concern or the "for the sake of what" for which you are making the request.

2. Integrating key elements of a powerful request
The desired outcome of making a powerful request is to have the recipient of the request say "yes," which converts the request made by the requestor into a promise made by the recipient. However, if requests are vague or sloppy, then this exchange can actually set the stage for additional breakdowns in high action/high alignment. To create a precise request and set the stage for renewed work in high action/high alignment, make sure these key elements of a powerful request are in place:

---
[1] See High Action High Alignment App, Pillsbury and Chawla
[2] See Trust App, Chawla
[3] See Ten Conversations App, Chawla

Chapter 5: Apps/Tools

- **Make the request in a direct manner to a specific person.**
  This means it is spoken directly to the person of whom the request is being made and identifies who is actually expected to complete the task. Plus, it is not disguised in other statements. "Raj, please submit the latest version of the report to me," is far more powerful than, "It's been a while since I've seen that report, will someone submit it?"

- **State the reason for the request and connect it to meeting results.**
  The receiver of the request will more likely respond if they see the impact of not working in High Action/High Alignment and how that connects to meeting (or not meeting) population level results. It can be helpful to also link the request to meeting (or not) the partners' individual performance measures and related strategies as a way of galvanizing a response.

- **Specify a timeframe for completing the request.**
  Creating clarity about the timeframe for completion allows the person to know if the request is urgent and trumps existing work, or can be met within the frame of ongoing work. Being clear on the timeframe enables someone to determine whether they can meet your expectation, whether they need to decline or delegate the task to someone else, or negotiate a different timeframe.

- **Make explicit the standards and criteria for successful completion of the request.**
  This is the place of greatest likelihood for a breakdown to occur. Clarity of standards and criteria (sometimes referred to as "Conditions of Satisfaction") allows the person to know what exactly is required for the request to be successfully fulfilled. Having a conversation about standards and criteria can reveal priorities and intent at a person, role, and system level. This conversation provides an opportunity for someone to say "no" to the request if they are not able to meet the desired standards and criteria. And, it also allows for negotiations to co-create mutually agreeable standards and criteria for success.

- **Ensure the request is role appropriate.**
  This means knowing if you are the right person, in role, to be making the request, and if the person receiving the request is the right person, in role, to be fulfilling the request.

- **Create a shared understanding of language and terminology.**
  Pay attention to any jargon used in making the request and check in to make sure that the person fulfilling the request understands what is being asked of him/her.

3. Establishing the responsibilities of both the requestor and receiver of the request

Responsibilities of the Requester:	Responsibilities of person receiving request:
Support the person receiving the request	Be genuine in agreeing to undertake the request
Share any new information that may impact the request and its fulfillment	Be competent to perform the required action
Declare satisfaction when the conditions of satisfaction and timeframes of the request have been met	Analyze and agree on the data and criteria about not being in High Action/High Alignment and upon which the request is based
Declare dissatisfaction if the request has not been met and negotiate next steps	Inform the requester if circumstances interfere with fulfilling the request and renegotiate

Part 2: Executing to Scope and Scale

Aligned Action Commitments

■ To be filled in next session

Name: _____

DATE: _____

What priority action(s) will you take to accelerate the result?

Action(s) *For each action, write the steps needed to fully implement it.*	With Whom *Who will partner with you?*	When *When will the action be completed?*	Contribution to the Result *How will actions contribute to making a measurable difference?*	Progress *To be completed at the next session.*

174

Chapter 5: Apps/Tools

Are You In High Action and High Alignment?
© Victoria Goddard-Truitt and Jolie Pillsbury

Data Drives Leadership Efficacy

While an action commitment can be written to be powerful, this power is only realized when implemented. Developing a practice of accountability is essential. Leaders who hold themselves accountable for performance are more likely to complete action commitments.[1,2] Completion rates increase when action commitments are committed to in writing, shared publicly with the team or workgroup and then reviewed and discussed regularly to improve execution and efficacy.[3]

Action commitments are assessed along a continuum of action and alignment. Collaborative groups spend a great deal of time collecting information and planning, but often lose momentum and fail to execute at a scope and scale that will make a difference. The following assessment tool allows leaders to assess whether they are in high action and high alignment. By knowing where they stand individually and as a team, leaders can make decisions about the likelihood of effecting positive change and how to strengthen actions to accelerate results.

Rating the Level of Action

No Action (0)	Assessing/Pre-Planning (1)	Planning/Preparing (2)	Execution (3)	Increasing Scope/Scale (4)
No action commitment is made that focuses on: • Outcomes, benchmarks • Actors (direct reports or peers, program recipients, superiors, or external partners) • Personal leadership development	The action commitment focuses on the collection or sharing of information. It might include: • Collecting baseline information and data • Understanding underlying issues and factors • Sharing general information to increase awareness of the problem, but without the expectation of influencing the outcomes/result • Developing personal leadership skills	The action commitment focuses on the preparatory phase required for successful execution. This commitment might include: • Developing strategies or structured activities • Preparing people, materials or products required for execution • Meeting with others to leverage contributions to achieving results • Joining strategic partners who will make a direct contribution • Collecting information or data to assess the needs of a population or to strengthen strategies	The action commitment focuses on implementation of strategies/activities/tactics. This involves action that has a direct impact such as: • Implementing activities to improve the well-being of a population • Preparing strategic partners to make a direct contribution • Using information to assess effectiveness of strategies • Providing information to target populations for their use	The action commitment is focused on strengthening actions or taking actions to scale. These commitments might include: • Restructuring strategies for better impact • Expanding the scope or scale within the group, agency or community • Expanding the scope or scale to broaden reach across agencies or communities

---

[1] Littlefield, J. & O'Brien, J. *Policymaking through Collaborative Networks: Issues of Accountability and Performance.* Poster presented at the annual conference for the Association for Public Policy Analysis and Management, Boston, Massachusetts, November 4-6, 2010.

[2] Pillsbury, J., Goddard-Truitt, V. & Littlefield, J. *Cross-Sector Performance Accountability: Making Aligned Contributions to Improve Community Well-Being.* Panel presentation at the American Society for Public Administration Conference, Miami, FL, 2009.

[3] O'Brien, J., Littlefield, J. & Goddard-Truitt (2013). *A Matter of Leadership: Connecting a Grantmaker's Investments in Collaborative Leadership Development to Community Results.* Foundation Review, V5: 1, 26-42.

Part 2: Executing to Scope and Scale

Rating the Level of Alignment

In collaborations, strategies and activities are lined up in such a way that they bridge, leverage and support each other for greater impact. Imagine a rowing team with each member rowing in a different direction—lots of action but no forward movement! When in high alignment, collaborative groups are linking goals and objectives to focus on a common result, with each leader making a contribution.

No Alignment (0)	Low Alignment (1)	Moderate Alignment (2)	High Alignment (3)	Alignment with Others Outside of Original Scope (4)
Actions are not connected to: • Results • Goals • Strategies • Interests of other leaders • Development needs of leaders	Actions aligned with • Development needs of leaders • Supporting the structure of a team • Building basic understanding of agreed-upon results • Connecting with individuals to build familiarity • Joining new people without specifying role and contributions • Deeper understanding of other leaders' perspectives, values, resources and interests	Actions aligned with • Broad vision and strategic direction • Needs to build capacity in self and others • Agreed-upon preliminary actions • Strengthening relationships and resolving conflicts • Accepting the distribution of work to accomplish strategies based on common agreements	Actions aligned with • Agreed-upon strategies and actions • Assessment of the impact of actions and performance to inform decisions and accelerate results • Leveraging relationships on behalf of results, strategy or performance • Leaders holding self and others accountable for commitments • Actions are based on holding a part/whole perspective	Actions taken to link and connect • Actions with positive outcomes for greater impact • Leaders trusting the resilience of relationships to take risks and make the changes necessary to execute effective strategies

Getting and Staying in High Alignment and High Action

Once leaders have used the above rating tools to self-assess their own level of action and alignment, and give feedback to other leaders, the information can be displayed to show progress over time and identify opportunities for moving to higher action and higher alignment. The visual display of ratings supports problem solving, accountability and increases collaborative leadership efficacy.

Chapter 5: Apps/Tools

Role Worksheet
Raj Chawla

Formal Role: _____

A leader's actions—the tasks they perform in their role—are fundamental to moving results work forward. For results leaders to be effective in their role, they have to know

- Where and how they get their authority;
- The boundaries of their role—where their authority begins and where it stops;
- The role they are expected to perform—the duties they are to perform and the outcome of their role; and
- The specific tasks they are to perform in their role.

Authority: I am authorized to perform my role by:

Questions for consideration:

- Who is authorizing me to perform in this role?
- What authority do I have within my role?
- Is my authority sufficient to play my role and deliver the task I am accountable for?
- Are the boundaries of my authority sufficient for me to fulfill my role?
- In what ways do I "take up" my authority, i.e., my personal authority?

Role: In my role, I am held accountable for:

Questions for consideration:

- What is the purpose/function of the role in advancing the results work?
- What do I think is required of me to play my role fully in this system for this task (i.e., behavior, presence, self-knowledge, self-awareness and awareness of others)?
- Is there anything missing or needing change from the way my role is currently defined or perceived?
- What areas of role conflict (for example, performing an aspect of a role that is in conflict with a person's values) might there be with those I interact with to achieve my task?
- What informal roles are needed in order to advance the results work?

Part 2: Executing to Scope and Scale

Tasks: In my role, my key tasks are:

Questions for consideration:

- What are the tasks that I have been authorized to complete?
- What are the results that these tasks contribute to?
- What data am I using to track the quality of my actions (my "how much" and "how well" performance measures)?
- What data am I using to track the success for the tasks (my "difference made" performance measures)?

Boundaries: With whom do I need to engage so I can be successful in my role?

Questions for consideration:

- What are my expectations of them?
- How do I assess if they are successful? What data am I using?
- What conversation(s) do I need to have with them?

Reflection: What are my improvement and learning practices?

Questions for consideration:

- How do I assess if my contribution (as measured by my performance measures) is successfully impacting the strategies I am executing?
- How do I share if I am successful or not with my colleagues?
- What difficult conversations do I need to have with others in order to improve performance
- What are my quality improvement practices?

Focusing on Trust: A Prerequisite for Creating Results[1]
© Raj Chawla

Work is about creating results together. It can be a very complex challenge (both technical and adaptive) to align everyone's contribution so that the work creates the agreed upon result. There are many elements required to create success towards a result. One element – trust – is often overlooked until it is broken or shaken. To be effective at creating results a leader has to have the ability to generate, maintain, and repair trust. *This is because trust is the necessary predisposition for coordinated action.* In other words, trust is required for there to be high alignment among and between groups of people committed to creating a result together.

Contents
I. How Do I Trust?
II. Trust as a Choice
III. Trust Breakdowns
IV. Trust Repair Strategies

I. How Do I Trust?
Trust can be understood as believing others to be:
- Sincere – what is said matches what is thought
- Reliable – what is done is dependable and consistent
- Competent – what is delivered reflects the ability and capacity to perform what is promised

If you assess someone to be sincere, reliable, and competent in a <u>particular aspect of work</u>, you deem him or her to be trustworthy in that area of work. If one of these three assessments is missing then there is cause not to trust someone enough to be in high alignment in that area of work.

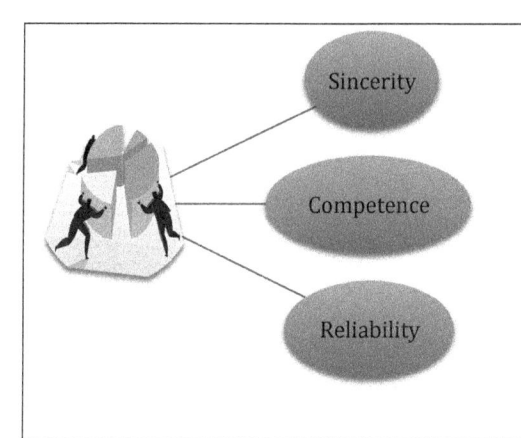

Sincerity / Competence / Reliability	Assessing someone to be sincere, competent and reliable means that you trust that person – in that particular domain of work – to be trustworthy.
	If you do not trust that person ask yourself:
	• Are they sincere in what they are saying?
	• Are they reliable in what they are offering?
	• Are they competent to perform what is asked of them?
	Then ask what you and the other person can do to build trust

II. Trust as a Choice

To engage in a trusting relationship with someone, therefore, requires a commitment to the agreed upon result and then reflection, scrutiny, and engagement. Without this you risk either being in simple or blind trust (or mistrust). Trust means choosing to trust knowing that there could be a break in that trust. It is, therefore, a bold act of leadership. This type of trust is based on

---
[1] Based on ideas from **Building Trust: In Business, Politics, Relationships, and Life** by Solomon and Flores

judgment, constantly nurtured in interactions and words, and is particular to each relationship and situation. For example, I may assess someone to be trustworthy in dealing with finances but not competent in working complex negotiations between two adversaries. Or, I may assess someone to be trustworthy in responding to my emails within 24 hours but not reliable in attending 8am meetings.

In any instance where I choose not to trust someone, I have the opportunity to discuss with that person why I don't trust him or her – in that specific area of work. If, for example, I choose not to trust someone to be competent in a particular area I have a choice of offering training or some support to build his or her competence or not looking to him or her for a contribution in that area.

III. Trust Breakdowns

There are many reasons trust can breakdown on an individual level. For example, breaking a promise or someone unreliable in actions or insincere in words can break trust. Broadly speaking the following are major contributors to organization and/or team breaks in trust.

- Team members and/or leaders do not have a distinction between unfulfilled promises and unfulfilled expectations.
- Leaders spread their assessments of distrust to a whole class of people instead of distinguishing specific individuals.
- Team members and/or leaders acting unpredictably in their moods and behavior
- "Cordial hypocrisy" – stating publicly there is trust and knowing there is none -is accepted as an organizational practice.
- Those suffering the impact of unfulfilled promises are not allowed to provide any feedback.

IV. Strategies to Generate, Maintain, and Repair Trust

With the result in mind, a powerful leadership move occurs when a leader chooses to act on this issue of trust. Here are a few strategies to inform your actions – what might you choose do?

1. Actions that Generate Trust
    - Have open conversations *about* trust.
    - Tell the truth about actions and events.
    - Know the difference between *promises* and *expectations*.
    - Thank and give positive feedback to those who fulfill their promises to you.
    - Provide constructive feedback to those who do not fulfill their promises to you.
2. Actions that Maintain Trust
    - Support people to *help them* fulfill their promises to you.
    - Be clear on your assessments of others' sincerity, competence, and reliability.
    - Hold yourself to be sincere, reliable and consistent.
    - Solicit feedback on your impact on others.
3. Actions that Repair Trust
    - Apologize for your mistakes, inconsistencies and broken promises.
    - Learn to forgive the person who caused the break.
    - Have conversations about the impact of a break in trust on team alignment and the ability to achieve results together.
    - Move to take actions to repair trust with regular check-ins on progress.

Preparing For A Trust Conversation
Raj Chawla

1. **Determine your readiness for talking to the person or stakeholder about the trust issue by addressing the following questions:**
   - What is the impact on the results work by not having trust with this person or stakeholder? In what ways does the lack of trust influence or impact being in high action and high alignment?
   - What might you lose by having the conversation (e.g., relationship, status)? What might you lose by continuing to distrust this person (e.g., not meeting performance targets)?
   - How will it benefit the results work - being in high action and high alignment - by trusting this person?

   If this trust conversation does not benefit your results work or move you into high action and high alignment then you may not need or be ready to have this conversation. Therefore, examine what issues (other than trust) might be present that are impacting the results work.

2. **Identify the trust assessment(s) you are concerned with: sincerity, competence, and/or reliability - be clear on your standards for sincerity, competence, and reliability.**

   If you are not able to name your assessments or identify your standards you may need to gather more data, gain greater clarity on your criteria or definition, and/or re-examine the issue of a break in trust

3. **Identify the specific actions or behaviors that have led to your assessment of distrust.**
   - Name, as specifically as possible, what the person did and/ or said (or don't do/ say) in order to help the person understand what happened and the impact of what happened.

   If you are not able to identify specific behaviors or actions you may need to gather more data and/or re-examine the issue of a break in trust

4. **Determine what you need from them in order for them to regain your trust.**
   - Be specific about your "conditions of satisfaction" – **your "how much" "how well" and "difference made" performance measures** – that you will be looking for to demonstrate a regaining or rebuilding of trust?
   - Determine if there is a timeframe involved.
   - Ensure there is alignment or agreement on these conditions of satisfaction.

   If you are not able to be specific about your conditions of satisfaction you may need to re-examine your criteria for working in high action and high alignment and/or re-examine the results work and the aligned contributions needed to make progress on the result itself.

CHAPTER 6

"Us"—Creating a Results Culture

You can always tell when the groove is working or not.

– Prince

Several years ago I was asked to work with a group of about a dozen policymakers who had spent a year exploring issues of race, class, and culture dynamics impacting their constituents. After a year of exploring these important issues, they developed into a strong, caring, and committed group. They knew each other's stories and how they had suffered or seen the effects of race, class, and/or culture dynamics.

They now wanted to use their insights and reflections to think about on-the-ground applications in their role as policymakers. They were interested in exploring how the elements of results leadership could support them.

I was invited to lead this group in a two-day results leadership session and provide an overview of this process. My first request of these policymakers and their staff was for them to bring the data they use to make decisions and assess progress—data about their constituents and key indicators of education, health, and community that were important to them. This request was met with some reluctance from a few of them and embraced by others.

The day of our gathering, all the policymakers brought with them data—of varying quality and focus. I asked them to place their data on the wall next to some relevant national and state data I had prepared, and then engaged them in a data conversation by initiating a process called a "data walk."[1] In this instance, I asked the policymakers to "walk" the room in pairs and assess the data. What was it saying about

Part 2: Executing to Scope and Scale

key issues they were concerned with? (I define and explain the data walk later in this chapter.)

The conversation that ensued was very interesting. Most of the policymakers shared that the data told a powerful story about poverty, education, health, and community. They also noticed that key pieces were missing, and this left open quite a few questions about the factors and causes that created or contributed to these circumstances. Finally, they noticed that some systems in their communities were not willing to share data, which presented a big challenge to them as policymakers. One policymaker even stated that at times making policy was like shooting in the dark.

This conversation felt familiar and appropriate. I had heard similar conversations from leaders likewise stepping into results leadership and engaging in their first data walk. There was another reaction that was also familiar to me—a general mistrust of the data. There were one or two policymakers who had been hostile to bringing in the data; then to engaging in a data walk; and then to using that data as part of the upcoming work. They shared their deep convictions that this kind of data had, historically, been used against poor and disenfranchised people to justify policies and legislation ill-adapted to their constituents, with negative effects on people's lives.

This competing perspective regarding data started to create a split within the group. Again, this was familiar to me. I kept asking the group how they wanted to work together—with the best available data they had? The group, after exploring its differences and points of view about the usefulness of the data, decided to continue to use it to deepen their understanding of what was happening in their community and to help inform their legislative, judicial, and administrative policy decisions.

As the two days with this group continued, I started to notice some disruptive dynamics among the few policymakers who resisted and mistrusted the data. They became the "naysayers" of the group. They seemed to be actively pushing back on the strategies that were being developed and openly questioning some of the choices that were being made. It got to a point where these few individuals sat with their backs to me during the whole group session while others made it a point to say that for the first time—as part of this group—they felt as if they were doing real work (they had been working together for over a year.)

As I reflect back on this, I recognize many complex and competing dynamics at play. One that needs to be highlighted for this chapter is how they acted in the context of group-as-a-whole. These policymakers had spent a year together as a close-knit group that cared about each other and were deeply connected to their shared experiences. They were now—perhaps for the first time as a group—exploring real differences that existed between group leaders present the whole time. This split felt threatening to the group. Some blamed me for causing the rift or for not smoothing over the differences; while others enjoyed the differences and being separate from the group. The group was unable to contain or confront the tension and anxiety of disagreement and had thus split into factions to feel safe.

As the story illustrates, moving as a group of leaders in an aligned manner toward a shared result is a difficult task. The work is fraught with tension, anxiety, and resistance to change. This is to be expected given that the work of results leaders is to address problems that are connected to multiple sectors, multiple stakeholders, and multiple points of view, all of which are needed to make contributions. Results leaders must be aware that collaborative groups will—consciously or unconsciously—move away from their primary task of engaging in results work when asked to address unproductive behavior, examine dysfunctional norms, or endure some real or perceived loss.

This group of policymakers had to decide how best they were going to work together in the future. They had to have a series of difficult conversations about how they would hold and examine the differences of opinion within their group so they could work together effectively. Some members of the group realigned their efforts to put results in the center, others engaged as needed while maintaining relationships, and some dropped out of the group all together.

Collaborative Work Cycle

When results leaders choose to join together in a collaborative group and work toward a population-level result, they engage in a collaborative work cycle.[2] It is in the collaborative work cycle that leaders use data to develop their strategies, name their baselines, declare their targets, and develop their results action plan. It is in the collaborative work cycle where midcourse corrections are identified and implemented; where different mental models, perspectives, and interests are revealed; where adaptive challenges are named; and where the stresses and anxieties of execution are experienced. It is through the collaborative work cycle that leaders do the work to get to both scope and scale of their work (this will be discussed in Chapter 7).

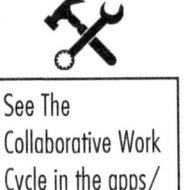

Part 2: Executing to Scope and Scale

> See The Collaborative Work Cycle in the apps/tools section at the end of this chapter.

The four steps of the collaborative work cycle are:

1. Enter a meeting with a focus on results. The purpose and work of the meeting is directly connected to the results work occurring outside of the meeting.
2. During the meeting, engage in conversations that move the work from talk (information sharing, idea generation) to solving problems and resolving conflict in order to execute strategies that contribute to the population-level result.
3. Exit the meeting having made commitments to action.
4. Create accountability for keeping commitments to action between meetings.

Figure 6.1 summarizes these four steps.

Figure 6.1 The Four Steps of the Collaborative Work Cycle

POPULATION RESULT

PROGRAM RESULT

BE ACCOUNTABLE
4
Progress
Work occurs when people are accountable for keeping commitments

Check in with results

BEGIN WITH RESULTS
1
Meeting Purpose
Calls people to action and defines and aligns meeting results

3
Collaborative Work
Occurs when people work together to take aligned action
ALIGNED ACTION

Check out with commitments

2
Meeting Results
Are accomplished when people move from talk to action commitments
END WITH COMMITMENTS

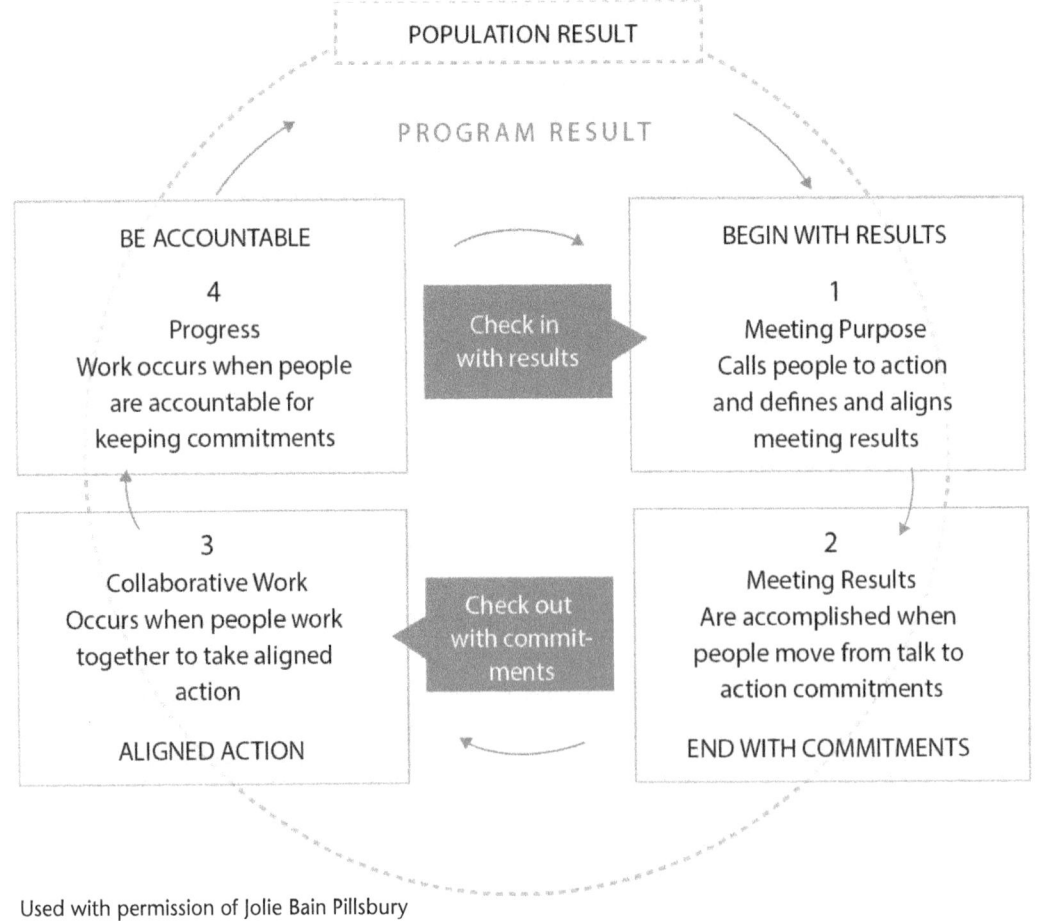

Used with permission of Jolie Bain Pillsbury

Given the challenges of engaging in results work, collaborative work groups engaged in the collaborative work cycle will:

- Encounter work avoidance; and, thus,
- Need to develop a robust results culture to help circumvent it.

In this chapter, we go deep into understanding work avoidance as a coping strategy, and how you as results leaders can create a robust results culture that will keep the group focused on its primary task, instead. I conclude with the results leadership mandate to have intentional conversations that bring to life the results culture you've created in the world.

Work v. Survival: What is the Primary Task?

I remind the leaders I work with that groups have their own "inner" life that must be understood and addressed or else there is a chance that the results work can be derailed. Often leaders see a group as a collection of individuals who have their own unique gifts and challenges. While this is true, these individuals also form into a "Group with a capital G" when they start to interact and put energy into their shared identity as a group and agree to work towards a common result. In other words, they focus on a common task.

When a group of leaders become a "Group" they not only become a collective entity—with a work task comprised of shared activities, functions, and purpose—they also become a "System." A primary focus of any system is survival. As such, every group has both a work task and a survival task.[3] When a group shifts to survival mode, it can quickly derail the work the group is tasked to do. I have seen many collaborative work groups disband because they were in survival mode and could not do the work to confront their dysfunctional circumstances. My example group of policymakers was in survival mode when they faced conflict and disharmony for the first time as they shifted the focus of their work from exploring issues of race to using data to explore results. Attacking me—as some did—was easier than fighting with each other. Aligning with me—as some did—was easier than publicly stating their differences and seeing how they could best work together.

When a group shifts from work task to survival task mode, its behavior can be connected to conscious or unconscious fears of group disintegration or destruction. A certain level of prestige, power, accountability, and/or responsibility can accompany being part of a certain group and its leaders. With a lot at stake, survival can easily take over as the primary task of the group. Therefore, we must acknowledge simultaneously that when a results work group comes together, its primary task is to be a work group; yet, it will be confronted with a basic instinct of any system—survival. The work of a results leader is to support the group in working towards population-level results while dealing with the stresses and anxieties inherent in group work.

> ### Types of Survival Modes
>
> **Dependence:** The group is over-reliant on one person for security and protection of the group. This over-authorization of one leader leads the group to abdicate its own intelligence and authority.
>
> **Fight/Flight**: The group is engaging in destructive fighting behavior (blaming or scapegoating others) or in flight behavior (withdrawing or becoming passive) in order to avoid addressing the real issues.
>
> **Pairing:** A pair from within the group forms a special bond and does the work of the group while the rest wait passively.
>
> **Oneness:** the group merges and commits itself to a task that supports survival. The group may become a support or friend group instead of a work group.

Knowing what behaviors to look for may help leaders understand what is happening and how best to support the group. Table 6.1 compares behaviors of a work group and a survival group.[4]

When challenges emerge, as they will in any group engaged in results work, leaders may find it difficult to recognize whether these obstacles are par for the course for a well-functioning work group (i.e., conflict over strategy or accountability) or evidence of a group engaged in survival. As we saw in Chapter 1, one fundamental aspect of complex public problems is that all stakeholders have a contribution to the way things currently are and a contribution to the solution. Addressing one's own contribution to the way things are, as well as the need to change or modify values, beliefs, and behaviors, can create both stress and anxiety, both of which will pull the group towards survival. Results leaders are aware that the group must confront these issues in a productive way—perhaps taking on new learning or enduring some loss— and that the confrontation will likely be met with resistance—otherwise known as work avoidance.

Table 6.1 **Behaviors of Work Groups v. Survival Groups**

Behavior regarding...	**Behaviors of a Work Group**	**Behaviors of a Survival Group**
Focus	Leaders focus on the results work and build relationships that serve to support the work of the group.	Leaders lose sight of the results work and engage in other—often competing—interests and use their relationships to serve those competing interests.
Action	Leaders take action to support working in both High Action and High Alignment in order to make progress on the result.	Leaders deny or avoid the real issues that confront them by: • Either fighting against or taking flight from working on the task • Engaging in fighting among themselves • Challenging the leader • Addressing matters irrelevant to the work.
Culture	Leaders develop resilient relationships based on authentic trust. As such, they build a work environment where leaders take risks with each other, engage in difficult conversations and expect everyone to be accountable to their role.	Leaders have limited trust of each other and continuously feel vulnerable to possible threat or danger in the group. This may cause survival behavior such as denial ("we're not a group") or "fight/flight." Group members struggle and seem unable to resolve differences.
Resilience	The group has a fierce commitment to the results work—one that recognizes that different perspectives and mental models are needed to confront the complexity of the challenges faced. Therefore, leaders will work with conflicts that surface in the group. These conflicts may result from the stresses and/or different perspectives are discussed and accepted by leaders.	Leaders form subgroups based on professional, educational, ideological, and social identities, where allegiance to subgroup is stronger than that to the group and its primary work task. This may mean: • Blaming and scapegoating occur • A sense of dependency on the leaders of the sub-group to make others feel included.

continued

Table 6.1 *continued*

| Relationships | Recognition and acknowledgment of differences and similarities among leaders and a willingness to work with rather than against their existence in the group. This could be a healthy sense of dependency and interdependency on the talents of the diverse leaders in the group. | Leaders deny the importance of differences in the group. There is a pull for a oneness in the group. |

Work Avoidance: A Coping Strategy

Work avoidance can be seen as a coping strategy to resist addressing the challenging dynamics that may surface within the group.[5] This resistance can be directly connected to:

1. The losses (i.e., power, status, relationships, or competence) that stakeholders may have to face if things change; and
2. The "forced" gains—for example, taking on the new learning that will be required (such as having to work toward results with less formal authority or control) or having to meet the transaction costs that come with collaborative strategies.

Resistance to these losses and difficult "gains" creates a conscious or unconscious desire for a less painful way to achieve results. This desire may evoke a shift to survival task for the group. Work avoidance can feel less painful, at least for a while. These behaviors are sometimes deliberate and protective against the forces of change, but sometimes they are simply unplanned or reflexive reactions.

I often tell the leaders I work with that the presence of work avoidance behavior might mean that the group is doing hard and real work. Although they may not feel like celebrating, I will congratulate them on good work done as evidenced by that work avoidance. I remind them that work avoidance may signal that a system is on the verge of learning to do something new and/or different—perhaps the very behaviors that are needed to effect the changes required to meet population-level results. Work avoidance, in this regard, signals that an opportunity might be at hand.

I also remind them that if work avoidance is not addressed, the population-level results may be derailed. This derailment can (and often will) lead to cynicism and/or hopelessness that changing or adapting their behaviors could be different.

> See Countering Work Avoidance: What is the Primary Task? in the apps/tools section at the end of this chapter. It is offered to help leaders address issues of work avoidance that leaders may confront.

Chapter 6: "Us"—Creating a Results Culture

©Glasbergen
glasbergen.com

"I want you to find a bold and innovative new way to do everything exactly the same way we've been doing it for 25 years."

Used with permission.

Supporting the group as they address these deeper issues is a leadership task. Table 6.2 lists examples of possible questions a leader can use to engage in this process.

Table 6.2 **Countering Work Avoidance: A Framework for Leaders' Actions**[6]

Leadership Task	Key Questions
Focus everyone on the population and program level results	*What result are we trying to accomplish?* *Based on the data, how well are we doing to achieve the result?*
Identify execution challenges and possible causes	*What isn't working and why? What data are we using to make this assessment?* *What are "our" individual and collective contributions to these execution challenges?* *What are the systems conflicts or competing agendas that are contributing to these challenges?* *What existing policies or procedures are inhibiting execution? What new policies or procedures might be needed to support successful execution?* *What systems dynamics are contributing to execution challenges?*

continued

Part 2: Executing to Scope and Scale

Table 6.2 *continued*

Leadership Task	Key Questions
Address the "deeper" issues	*What power dynamics are at play?* *Who might have to confront losses if the work is successful?* *What kinds of losses would that be (i.e., resources, relationships, loyalties, power, etc.)?* *What can be done to address these losses?*
Develop and/or modify strategies	*What do we need to do differently and why?* *Who will be aligned with these new efforts and who will be adversarial towards them? Why?*
Identify or re-examine resources	*What resources do we need to implement, repurpose, or shift for these strategies to be successful?* *Who will benefit from this? Who will lose?*
Identify what is working and what we are learning	*What does the data reveal about who is succeeding and about what we are learning actually works?* *How will we implement what we are learning?* *What anecdotes can help us understand what is working?*
Establish responsibility and accountability	*Who should do what by when?* *Who is not holding responsibility for execution and why?*
Have difficult conversations about accountability	*Whom should we confront for indifference, incompetence, or sabotage? What data are we using to justify that?* *If needed, how do we ask these stakeholders to leave the group? What will be the impact?*

What does work avoidance look like in your group?

Work avoidance behaviors can include:[7]

- Avoiding the real conflict by creating a proxy fight, such as a personality conflict;
- Discounting solutions that threaten legacy behaviors and relationships;
- Offering fake, pretend, or marginal solutions;
- Marginalizing or attacking the person trying to raise the difficult issues;
- Attacking or blaming formal authority; and
- Delegating the hard work to those who can't do anything about it—like taskforces or consultants.

Reflect on whether, as a results leader, you are seeing these behaviors in your work group.

It should now be clear: Developing a results culture is foundational so that the group can move back to its primary task of engaging in the results work.

Example: Offloading Accountability

Several years ago I was part of a team working in a relatively large city in the Midwest on a complex public problem related to public safety. A group of leaders convened to work together on a problem that had both social and political complexities. Data seemed to indicate that the situation was not getting any better, and they decided to work toward a population-level result by engaging multiple stakeholders and partners.

Linda, as the point person from the city, declared to the other leaders in the room, "The Mayor has told me that I am to wake up thinking about this issue and go to sleep thinking about this issue." It was with this declaration that Linda claimed her authority in the room.

The work was not going well. Because Linda held her formal authority for this result so forcefully, the other leaders felt they were in the room in roles of either support or opposition. Everyone had his or her opinion as to why the effort was going so poorly. Some felt the mayor's office was incompetent, so they had to create a workaround. Others felt there was something to be gained professionally by working with the mayor's office, so they persevered. Still others felt the government services (state and local) were to be ignored; that the best way to mobilize was by engaging the community and/or the private sector.

Given that their work was to address a complex social problem, it was an adaptive challenge for everyone in the community. The group experienced itself going into survival mode of fight/flight, pair bonding, and dependence. Ironically, having the mayor's office hold all authority on this issue gave the other stakeholders a way to get out of their accountability to finding a result. When the group of stakeholders and partners experienced limited progress and failed attempts, it was easy blame the mayor's office for incompetence. The mayor's office was willing to blame others for their lack of support. Because that office held responsibility for the result through formal authority, it was unwilling to share responsibility and accountability with others. As the difficulties continued, this group of leaders engaged in work avoidance—blaming of others, avoiding the structural and systems conflicts, and making the problem focus on personalities.

Part 2: Executing to Scope and Scale

The path to shared accountability required that they acknowledge the complexity of the problem; the reality that all stakeholders had a contribution to the current circumstances; and the need to address the systems challenges. They needed to engage in new learning and practices on order to make progress.

I wish I could report that that is exactly what happened. In a very roundabout way (that proves the resilience of results leadership), it did. Linda ended up leaving her position. Those partners who were putting all the blame and expectation on Linda and the mayor's office withdrew from the collaboration. A new person was assigned to Linda's role, some new partners joined the collaborative, and the work started anew. They eventually made demonstrable progress toward a result at the end.

This concludes my discussion of the individual and very human behaviors results leaders are likely to see when the "Me with You" discussed in Chapter 5 begins to work in shared accountability. Yes, you will lead groups that frustrate you with their focus on survival task and their work avoidance. But with what you've now learned, you are prepared to lead them toward more productive behaviors. Let's shift our focus to the technical tools and "soft skills" required to bring a group to working in shared accountability.

Creating a Robust Results Culture

The challenges that may present themselves when engaging in a collaborative work cycle with others can create chaos and stress. As the story above illustrates, this may reveal itself as a variety of behaviors—work avoidance, survival, pretense of cohesion, and/or dissolution of the group itself. This ever-present threat of chaos and stress requires leaders to intentionally create practices, establish norms, and develop workspaces that support the group to focus on the results work.

We call this process developing a **results culture**. A results culture helps support groups in navigating the tension, the anxiety, the chaos and stress, to create a new order. A results culture becomes crucial in helping a group engage with its primary work task and not becoming "stuck" in survival task. A robust results culture allows the group to address its issues of work avoidance, support individuals in new learning or behavior, and in enduring any potential losses.

An organization's culture can be defined as its collective values, beliefs, and principles, including the organization's vision, values, norms, systems, symbols, language, assumptions, beliefs, and habits. A results culture, then, is one all of these things support the group to hold results in the center of the work. A results culture supports a group so it can work in both High Action and High Alignment. This culture is intentionally developed by:

- Creating a "container" for the work:
  - A physical container where the work is done;
  - A metaphorical container—a "holding" environment[8]—to contain the work;
- Holding results meetings and;
- Engaging in intentional conversations that create and reinforce a results culture.

Together, these factors contribute to supporting "us" working in shared accountability. Let me explain what I mean by these phrases before we dive deeper into the work of creating a robust results culture.

Containers: Holding the Work

The word "container" takes on two different meanings in the context of results work: literally, a *physical container* that provides the infrastructure needed to hold results meetings, and metaphorically, a *holding environment,* a concept from psychology that, in results meetings, creates a place where individuals feel safe to be uncomfortable, as is required to do hard work.

Physical container: As Patton Stephens states in her booklet *Creating a Container to Achieve Results,*[9] the container is the sum total of all the infrastructure-related elements that go together to support a group as they meet to achieve designated results. Without an adequate container, groups do not have the preparation, structure, support, or resources to get their important work done. Even with talented professionals leading the meeting and committed participants, a porous container leads to less-than-optimal meeting results, which, in turn, impact the achievement of targeted results. Figure 6.2 illustrates this physical container.

When I work with leaders, I encourage them to focus on the physical container for their collaborative meetings as well as a container in their home organizations. *I know a results culture is alive when I see a population-level results statement prominently placed in the meeting space and key data points displayed, with trend lines, targets, and a timeline.*

A key component of a physical container is data. Results leaders understand that a deeper understanding of data will help them in decision-making, as well as in navigating the complicated dynamics that can pull the group off its primary task. In a data-rich environment, leaders can quickly make decisions that impact or influence action or

---

Results culture: A work culture where the values, norms, language, assumptions, beliefs, and habits all support the group to hold results in the center and to work in both High Action and High Alignment. A results culture supports leaders in their primary task of working towards a shared result.

Physical container: This infrastructure-related element can be understood as a visual display of a results culture that supports a group, a team, and an individual to address the work at hand and maintain the focus on results.

Part 2: Executing to Scope and Scale

Figure 6.2 **A container provides a seamless infrastructure that supports the hard work of making progress on complex public problems.**

© Sherbrooke Consulting

execution of strategies and programs. As mentioned above, a physical container has key data elements of the results action on the wall or otherwise displayed. These include:

- Population-level result and indicator(s)
- Whole population analysis
- Baseline and target tied to measurement cycle
- Factor analysis
- Strategies
- Strategy work plans
- Results timeline

This type of data allows leaders to know how they are progressing in the work. As we learned earlier, one way the urgency of results work manifests is through targets—indicators, strategies, programs—mapped in time. A timeline allows leaders to know if they are progressing or if something needs to change.

The data should be updated on a regular basis—especially the timeline data—so that leaders can track their progress. The purpose of having a data-rich environment is to put the results work in the center of the conversation, to assess the progress of the shared work, and to make visible where there may be a need for changes and/or quality improvement.

One of the most powerful things that Jim Czarniak does in his work with stakeholders is to create a powerful container. He makes sure that the voices of young people are represented in the room where leaders have their meetings. For example, he works with Poetry Behind the Walls,[10] an ongoing journal dedicated to writings from incarcerated youth, to make sure the stakeholders can hear those voices when they make their choices. He will have poetry written by children who are incarcerated hung on the walls and incorporate this as part of regular data walks. For example, leaders might find this poem on their wall:

A Life in Hillbrook

By Ronnie

I wake up in the night,
Thinking I'm doing everything right
I drifted back to sleep, only to hear a knock at my door
1:00 AM, my life in hell started
By the end of the day, I had been told what to do at least 30 times
I have no time alone
The staff thinks I'm one of "them" _
It makes me want to give up on life
Here in Hillbrook,

Poetry Behind Walls (PBW)

All the stakeholders are given a copy of the book in which this poem appears as part of a reminder that their actions impact real children.

Metaphorical "holding" environment: As results leaders engage in the hard work of solving complex public problems, they use their results culture to create a "holding environment"[11]—*an environment that is both safe and uncomfortable.* A holding environment is safe due to the relationships leaders have to the results work as well as to each other. This holding environment is uncomfortable in that it allows the leaders to engage in difficult conversations, explore new learning, and

> A **holding environment** is a sense of space formed by a network of relationships within which people can tackle tough, sometimes divisive questions without flying apart.[12]

develop new behaviors that will be needed as they tackle their tough public problem. A holding environment comes alive when leaders use data to engage in conversations of accountability, conflict, systems challenges, or any other needed conversations. It is the work that is done within a holding environment that supports a group to stay on task and confront its survival instincts.

Results work is difficult because of the marked uncertainty individuals must confront, as well as the potential losses they may have to endure. Results leaders seek to create a holding space that is safe for leaders to engage in new practices and behaviors and uncomfortable enough that the difficult work may be confronted. There are many requirements for creating an authentic holding space, and it could look different depending on the people, the context, and the work. However, there are a few key elements that seem to be present in all holding spaces. These include:

- A shared language rooted in the Results Playbook;
- Alignment on the data and the analysis used to create the results action plan;
- Agreement on what it means to work together in High Action and High Alignment;
- Connection to individual and to collective values and purpose; and
- An ongoing culture of resilient relationships rooted in conversations of trust, commitment, and accountability.

A results culture helps shape the collective values, beliefs, and principles of its members with a focus on staying on task to create results. The artifacts and symbols (the physical container, the data) support that culture. The holding environment, uncomfortable as some of its elements can sometimes be, is also necessary to support a robust results culture.

Results Meetings: Doing the Work

You will recall that at the heart of the collaborative work cycle are meetings. Leaders enter meetings with a focus on results and ready to engage in the needed conversations that create action towards the result. They leave the meetings having received action commitments.

As results leaders join in the execution of their strategies and programs, their ability to leverage resources becomes essential. Results meetings offer the possibility to create that leverage. For example, a network representing pediatricians might engage with a network focusing

Chapter 6: "Us"—Creating a Results Culture

on early learning and offer children's books to their young patients and their families as part of every health and wellness check-up.

In a robust results culture, leaders hold their meetings in data-rich environments that are both safe and uncomfortable so that they can do the difficult task of working together across sectors and systems. Some suggest that there are four phases in this type of engagement:[13]

- Talking nice (concern for how the self is perceived by others);
- Talking tough (focus on expressing one's self);
- Reflective dialogue (understanding others' views); and
- Generative dialogue (co-creating something new).

For these four phases of engagement to occur, I encourage results leaders to develop the skills and practices embodied in Results Based Facilitation (RBF)—a specific, hands-on method developed by Jolie Bain Pillsbury that enables people to practice the skills for getting different and better results in their meetings and conversations.[14] RBF is a competency-based approach to participating in and facilitating meetings in order to get results. Through the practices highlighted in Results Based Facilitation, leaders engage in its three working hypotheses.[15]

See Elements of a Results Meeting in the apps/tools section at the end of this chapter. It is offered to help identify what leaders might see and experience in a results meeting.

1. The work of meetings occurs through conversations. Meetings are a series of conversations that can create meaning and movement toward action and results.
2. Group conversations can be designed, prepared for, and flexibly supported by someone with a set of listening and speaking skills.
3. A facilitator working in support of the group while holding a neutral role can accelerate the work of the group.

Therefore, in a results culture, leaders can expect their meetings to have a:

- Strong physical container in a data rich environment that:
    - Holds the conversation,
    - Focuses on the work, and
    - Uses data to inform decisions.
- Strong holding environment that:
    - Allows for difficult conversations to occur;
    - Holds and facilitates the conflicts that may occur; and
    - Creates accountability to the work within and between meetings.

199

Part 2: Executing to Scope and Scale

One key purpose of creating this kind of meeting space for a group of leaders is to prepare for the difficult work that is sure to reveal itself as well as to keep the focus on their primary task. Participants and facilitators both use their competency in RBF to move groups from talk to action in order to produce results within programs, organizations, and communities. There already exists a robust body of work on Results Based Facilitation so I won't go into the details here, but recommend you add study of RBF to your lifelong learning goals.

Are You Leading with High Action and High Alignment?

Results leaders are—at all times—held accountable for actions contributing to particular results, and this can be uncomfortable when outcomes are uncertain and depend on the necessary contributions of others. As you learned in Chapter 2, such "discomfort" is an essential prerequisite of working in High Action and High Alignment. As a leader...

- What is your orientation toward being accountable for action?

- Does accountability support you in moving to action?

- How does your orientation toward accountability for action influence how you participate in meetings?

- How does your approach to accountability for action inform how you facilitate meetings?

Engaging in Intentional Conversations: How the Results Culture Comes to Life

> *An organization's results are determined through webs of huma commitments, born in webs of human conversations.*
>
> *– Fernando Flores*

Consider all the ways conversations take place in and around results work, as work groups collaborate within and across the boundaries to achieve results in the center. What could be cacophony becomes productive when we pay attention to the kinds of conversations that:

Chapter 6: "Us"—Creating a Results Culture

1. Use data to illuminate the work at hand;
2. Support working in High Action and High Alignment;
3. Tell results stories; and
4. Create public accountability to the results work.

Each has its own characteristics and purposes, so let's examine them.

Data Conversations

Data conversations are valued and expected in a results culture. Throughout this book, data has been highlighted as central to the work of producing results. Results leaders create a culture that is data-rich and create conversations that use that data to inform decisions on how best to execute their results work. Therefore, results leaders know the importance of data in their work and will act accordingly. One way that data conversations are emphasized is through **data walks**.[16]

As illustrated by my earlier example at the start of this chapter, results leaders will create a data walk as a physical way to engage in a data conversation. Data walks can happen—and should happen—throughout the group's work. I often invite leaders to walk in pairs or trios and have a data walk where they will review the data on the wall and have a conversation based on a set of questions.

Data walk: An intentional data conversation among partners and stakeholders that fosters shared understanding and alignment towards the results work. It is often conducted as an actual "walk" around a meeting room where data is displayed according to the practices of results meetings.

Leaders in Appalachia report back after their Data Walk. A conference meting space has been transformed into a physical container and holding environment for their work.

201

Part 2: Executing to Scope and Scale

> See the Data Walk App and the Guidance for Data Walk document in the apps/tools section at the end of this chapter. Both can help create an intentional data conversation among the partners and stakeholders.

As a result of using data in this way, results leaders can expect to:

- Gain awareness about themselves;
- Build relationships with their colleagues by understanding similarities and differences in perceptions, experiences, and interpretations, and acknowledge the emotional impact of the information;
- Learn about the conditions of wellbeing of children and families and other possible stakeholder groups through pictures, data charts and stories;
- Better understand the use of data to connect the targeted result with the specific populations;
- Identify what data is needed and not yet available;
- Learn about resources available within the group through the relationship connection.
- Experience the reality of having the best available data (B.A.D.); and
- Affirm or adopt the population, result, and indicator.

Results Leader: David Newell

In supporting the work of PromiseShip—a public-private partnership tasked with building effective systems of care for at-risk children and parents in the eastern part of Nebraska—David Newell decided to use data as an initial way to build trust among PromiseShip's partners and community stakeholders. I first met David when he was fellow in the Annie E. Casey's Children and Family Fellowship[17] and I was one of four people serving as faculty to support the fellowship. As the CEO for PromiseShip, David was keen on implementing a results frame for his organization, Not only was it clear that his organization could not do it alone, they would also need the authentic engagement of their partners and stakeholders to do this work.

In meetings with the community and their stakeholders, David walked people through the data showing where PromiseShip was making progress in improving outcomes, and, also, where it was not. "Some people didn't want me to do this, and there was definitely risk involved in opening ourselves up to the community in that way, but my response was that we had to build confidence and trust. We also had to show people that we cared, first and foremost, about results, and that we had plans and a strategy to do better," David said. "No matter how much you personally believe in what you are doing, you have to let the facts speak for themselves. You can't be defensive when things aren't going well. You look at the data, and if the data says there is a problem, you work together to turn things around."

Conversations for High Action and High Alignment

The resilient relationships that leaders forge through intentional conversations of trust (discussed in Chapter 5) are a prerequisite for any work group to function in High Action and High Alignment. Since trust comes from conversations, intentional conversations where we avoid pretense (and the other behaviors of survival task and work avoidance) are foundational to group work. This includes the difficult conversations that must occur to address those issues that may block the group from doing its work and thus cause it to shift into work avoidance behavior.

Once results leaders create their criteria for working in High Action and High Alignment and assess where they are in those quadrants, the work begins to move all the individuals involved towards higher action and alignment. There are many factors that may impact how stakeholders work together towards a result; or, accordingly, how results leaders develop hypotheses and take the needed action based on their assessment of those factors.

These types of intentional conversations are more likely to occur within the workgroup than in a public setting:

- **One-to-ones:** Often what is required is a direct conversation with an individual about his or her work and the need for being in greater action and alignment. Leaders I've worked with have had to identify the kind of conversation they need to have (for example, a conversation of possibility or accountability), prepare for the conversation, and then do the hard work of engaging in the conversation. Sometimes, the conversation is welcomed, sometimes it is met with resistance or avoidance. Regardless, the conversation is the start of the work to get all to work towards High Action and High Alignment.
- **Group conversations:** Sometimes there is a conflict present within the group of leaders that needs to be addressed so the group can work in High Action and High Alignment. Knowing what kind of conflict is present and having a willingness to be open and direct is a powerful practice to break a culture of politeness or issues of work avoidance. Group conversations that openly address conflict make it easier to make progress towards a population-level result.

I recall an example of productive intentional group conversations from my initial work with Josh Davis and the Indianola Promise

> See Ten Conversations App and Ten Conversations To Have At Work in the apps/tools section at the end of this chapter. These are offered to help results leaders engage in intentional conversations that support the primary task of the work group.

Neighborhood team. When I first met the team, they were focused on the technical aspects of the work as well as the technical aspects of their individual roles. For example, they were trying to get service providers to expand the number of slots available to pre-school and early learning sites. They were using their funding to purchase additional slots and then to convince parents to bring their children to their early learning centers. The technical aspects of their work included presenting information, creating working agreements with service providers, transferring funds, reaching out to parents, and presenting data to their funders.

When they focused on population-level results and creating a shared results action plan with partners and stakeholders—including addressing issues of disparities, root causes to the issues they were concerned with, and the larger systems work—they had to confront their own dynamics as a team. Some members were frustrated that the work they were doing was not bold enough, others felt the pressures of meeting the expectations of funders, and still others felt a reluctance to take the necessary risks in an organization culture that was risk-averse.

This group had several rounds of intense conversations exploring their different points of view. I believe these early—very intense—group conversations allowed the Indianola team to become a very effective work team.

Conversations That Tell Results Stories

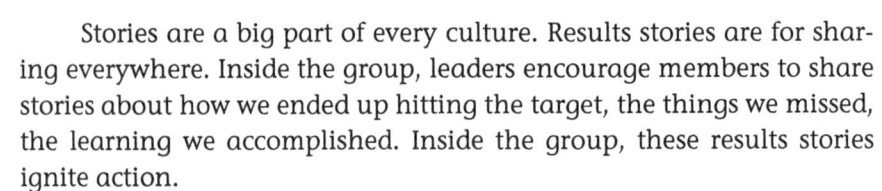

Stories are a big part of every culture. Results stories are for sharing everywhere. Inside the group, leaders encourage members to share stories about how we ended up hitting the target, the things we missed, the learning we accomplished. Inside the group, these results stories ignite action.

Outside the group—in conversations with potential funders, potential partners, and other stakeholders—do share the stories of "how well, how much, and difference made." **Storytelling** impacts your results work and generates resonant emotional connections. The Results Playbook helps us tell these true stories outside in the world.

The way leaders tell stories defines the culture they value. The stories they share offer metaphors, as well as concrete examples that explain how people should behave, what they should value, and how they should engage with each other. These stories help to educate new stakeholders and partners so they learn the language, the rules, and the focus of the culture. Chip and Dan Heath, in their book *Made to Stick*, offer six guidelines on the qualities of stories that stick in people's mind: Make them simple, unexpected, concrete, credible, emotional, and action-oriented.[18]

> **Storytelling** is the sociocultural activity of sharing narratives, often with elements of improvisation, theatrics, or embellishment. Stories have been used in every culture as a means of entertainment, education, cultural preservation and imparting moral values.

Fortunately, results leaders can use the work highlighted in their results action plan to create and share results stories about their work. Depending on the audience (i.e., board of directors, legislators, potential partners, etc.) and purpose (i.e., engagement, growth, enrollment of others, etc.), leaders can highlight any of the key story elements of the playbook to make their point.

Jim Czarniak is a master at using results stories to enroll and engage partners from the different sectors needed to make progress towards the population-level result. Earlier in this chapter, we saw that he places the words of young people in the juvenile justice system in the physical container. He will leverage those words in the container and use the various elements of his results action plan to create results stories that will invite others to join the work. I have heard him speak to the population-level result and connect that directly to the kids in the "system." He'll speak to the factors in the community that contribute to things being the way they are. He'll use data to describe the current state of affairs, and targets to create a sense of urgency for the work. He'll speak to the success of the strategies implemented and the quality improvement efforts implemented. He'll then invite other stakeholders to make their contribution by showing what is needed and how it benefits the work.

> See Elements of a Results Story in the apps/tools section at the end of this chapter offered to help results leaders create stories targeted to their audience.

Public Conversations: Accountability to Declared Targets

The key purpose in creating a results culture is to foster an environment that supports the primary task of the work. In this sprit, results leaders publicly declare targets on a timeline, both at a program level and at a population level. After such a declaration, all the work that leaders do is geared to achieve or surpass their targets.

In a results culture, leaders use each target and time milestone to engage in a public and transparent conversation of accountability. Leaders speak outside the group to stakeholders, authorizing bodies, the media, and others to carry their "result in the center" out into the world. These conversations are often about accountability and accomplishments: "We said we would hit this target by [date], here's the data, here's what happened."

Accountability to Targets: The purpose of this type of public accountability conversation is to widely share whether a leader, or a group of leaders collectively, is achieving their stated target or not. In addition, this conversation is designed to highlight any learning that emerged during work toward the target. This display increases the group's ability to move forward with greater insight and to achieve subsequent targets as they gain experience.

This public conversation of accountability is not meant to be a "show and tell" or an "inquisition" about the work that was done. This process is designed to reinforce the ownership of the commitment to the population-level result and to clarify and explain the learning and reflection about the work that was done. This public conversation invites colleagues and stakeholders to be thought-partners in the results work that has been executed, as well as in finding ways to implement quality improvement measures in the next round of work. This conversation has both quantitative and qualitative elements: Quantitative in that the data illuminates measurable impact of the work and qualitative in that the conversation reveals to what degree the leaders have been working in High Action and High Alignment.

There are many ways that a group of results leaders can structure this type of conversation. There are, however, at least two components of this: **Data** and **Reflection**.

Data: The results data shows whether the target was hit or not. Included in this data in a concise way are the following:

- The population-level result and indicator targets for work;
- The target in context of performance measures answering the questions: What kind of a target was it—the "how well" and "difference made" measures? And, How is it connected to an indicator target
- What it took to hit, or make progress toward, the target;
- Strategies developed and lessons learned in execution, including what it took to gather performance measure trend data; and
- Partners engaged and in what role, with what contributions.

Reflection: The conversation should include a concise overview of the following themes:

- Learning and reflecting about the results work itself—what worked and what didn't;
- Learning and reflecting about being a results leader—places for growth and exploration of blind spots;

- Quality improvement measures needed for future target work; and
- Quality improvement measures needed as a results leader.

This public conversation of accountability has a quantitative component (review of the data) and a qualitative component (thematic reflection on what was learned). A final qualitative element of this conversation is the telling of results stories. Through this process, the group comes to "know what it knows" and, ideally, becomes energized (or re-energized) to continue working in High Action and High Alignment.

Engagement in a public conversation of accountability is not easy. It requires results leaders to become comfortable with vulnerability in order to be able to share the work done, to name victories and failures, to highlight any new learning, and to declare a new target.

Recall Terri Clark (from Chapter 1) and her work in Arizona on grade-level reading. We arranged to have a data walk and a public conversation of accountability that included both the work her team did at the state level and the work of the city-level team in Phoenix. In getting ready for this conversation, I reminded the two groups that this conversation was not just a long "show and tell," but also a place to engage in a learning inquiry with their colleagues. I encouraged them to invite guests who were important to their work and who had a contribution to make. I encouraged them to take a risk and invite those who may not have been aligned to the work that was being done. The Arizona and Phoenix teams took the challenge and invited a large group of outside guests—some of whom were aligned with the work and some of whom they expected to hold different points of view.

At first, everyone was nervous. Leaders asked themselves: "Do I have the right data?" or "Am I telling the right story?" and "We didn't hit our target, what will they think? Yet, things calmed down when the guests came into the room and engaged in the data walk. It was powerful for these guests to see the data about their community and the work their colleagues were doing. As the accountability conversation unfolded, there was a general acknowledgment of the work done as well as the system's challenges that existed across the various sectors represented in the room.

At the end of this conversation, no one was engaged in a "blame game." Rather, participants worked together to identify lessons Terri and the other leaders could learn based on insights gained from this round of working to a target goal and apply them to the next target. There was also a conversation about new partners, new contributions, and additional resources that needed to move the work forward.

> See Engaging in a Public Accountability Conversation in the apps/tools section at the end of this chapter. It is offered to help results leaders engage in intentional conversation of accountability to the primary task of the work group.

How a Robust Results Culture Supports Aligned Action

Finally it all comes together: Attention to the technical aspects of results meetings, and their physical and psychological containers, creates a robust results culture supported and enhanced by various uses of intentional conversations that bring the results culture to life. Let's pause to reflect on the road we've traveled.

In Part 1, we determined that we're here because we understand the nature of complex public problems, discussed in Chapter 1. We are ready to put the results in the center, as described in Chapter 2. We're capable of executing to a results plan that creates accountability to tasks and timelines, as discussed in Chapter 3. The results action plan establishes the foundation of the culture.

Now the four perspectives of Part 2: "Moving from Fragmentation to Shared Accountability," start coming into play. In Chapter 4, you learned about "I"—leader readiness, working on yourself, knowing your values and mental models, and committing to being a lifelong learner. In Chapter 5 you got to know "Me with You"—preparing a collaborative group to work with integrity, commitment, and resilience in support of a robust results culture. In this chapter you've been learning how to hold results meetings, tell results stories, and have public conversations around accountability. Intentional conversations are the medium through which the results culture flows.

Creating a robust results culture is about much more than countering work avoidance. It is what leads to the crescendo coming in Chapter 7—"Us in the World," where results leaders work across programs, strategies, and roles to create scope and scale.

See Checklist for a Results Culture in the apps/tools section at the end of this chapter.

Your work, as a results leader, is to pay attention to creating a culture that reinforces and supports the hard work needed to make progress towards a population-level result. You'll have to put results in the center of the work and notice the impact that it has on others. I recall a leader I worked with who put a "results in the center" map in her office. I coached her not to waste time trying to convince others to build a results culture, but to start one on her own and see what happened. She started to hold meetings that focused on the collaborative work cycle—making action commitments, having difficult conversations. She also started to use data to highlight what was working and what wasn't. At first, she received push-back. After she asked, *why?* (She initially thought everyone would be interested in the results work and happy to do what was needed to move forward) she had a powerful insight. What was really in the center was not results but rather "no conflict, no tension, no bad feeling." With this newfound clarity, she had choices to make about how she engaged with her boss and her team. I wish I could say that she transformed her entire organization but that's not what happened. She ended up leaving her organization and joining one that she felt could hold her interest in putting the results in center. I can report she is quite happy with her new role and the change she is helping to create in the world.

The following story of the results work done in Berea, Kentucky, drives home this point. You will notice the hard work the Berea team put into creating a results culture and the engagement with others it required to make progress toward a population-level result.

Results Leader: Dreama Gentry

Dreama Gentry, executive director for Partners for Education at Berea College, is creating a results culture in Appalachia. She is one of my favorite results leaders. Dreama is so committed to the people of Appalachia that she has devoted her career to improving educational outcomes for all young people who live and go to school there. She was born and raised near Berea, Kentucky, and was the first in her family to graduate from college. After she received her law degree, she could have gone anywhere in the country to work. Dreama chose to stay in Kentucky to support the families and all the young people who live there.

When I met Dreama, her organization was one year into a five-year implementation grant through the Department of Education's Promise Neighborhoods initiative[19] and I was part of the team supporting that work. Her organization had been awarded many other federal and state grants and, as a result, was providing much-needed assistance to the young people in the counties it serviced.

When I introduced the Results Playbook to her team and challenged them to move towards population-level work, she had two reactions. The first was: How come the major funding organization under whose auspices I was working hadn't introduced the results leadership program to the group during the planning year? The second was: There was no way the Berea team would have enough resources to achieve a population-level result! My response to her and her team was that it is never too late to pivot your work toward that end, and that you cannot program your way to such a result, either. I challenged her to shift her organization away from a grants culture and toward a results culture by putting results in the center, creating a shared Results Playbook, and working in High Action and High Alignment with partners and stakeholders. Notice how many of the elements of creating a results culture I've discussed in this chapter are present in the story Dreama shares below.

Results Leader

"I had to change how I led. With a smaller organization that existed primarily through grants, I found myself leading primarily based on relationships. It was possible to focus on the specific outcomes of a grant through relationships. But as the work started to grow, and I started to hold more of a results orientation, I had to change.

I was introduced to the results frame through the Promise Neighborhoods work, [and] the ah-ha for me was that the results were at the middle. When we became a larger organization, the results had to be in the center. While relationships are a key way to move the dial, they have to be strategic and in service to the results.

To create a results culture that worked for us meant we had to change the language we used, how we did our work, and the identity we had with the work. My first task was to change my language—the way I talk about the work—from programmatic language to results language. This meant using the language of the Result Playbook (population-level results, indicators, strategies) and aligned contributions.

I recall hiring a new communications director and talking about results and results language. He told me that when we present our work—on our website, on our promotional material, in the way we talk to the community—we connect it to programs and grants. He told me that the team leaders go back to naming things by their programmatic or funding streams. I realized that creating a results culture was more than my insisting that we use the results frame and results concepts. We had to change the way we run our meetings, the way we engage with our partners, the incentives we use. This was going to be difficult, but it was essential for us to become a results organization. It is easier when you get a new program to just add it there. It is harder to show how the new program connects to the results and strategies and to communicate the impact. It is a more difficult message and it requires more intentional thinking.

One reason it was difficult was that our program managers' identities were tied to their program. We had to make some hard calls. We had to redefine and redesign programs, because they were not pulling toward the result. It is difficult to focus an organization on the result. Funders want to segregate. They want to see the program named. Even in community work, we have to push the program. We cannot get away from the program.

With our internal team there was a focus and emphasis on compliance and details [and] a fear because we knew we needed to segregate the dollars due to the rules and regulations connected to our funding. There was fear that we would be breaking the rules. We have about 20 federal programs that we tie together. All need separate grants. It is a technical challenge that derails leaders from becoming results leaders. Shifting to a results orientation helps us hold the grant and requirements in context of the results we are trying to accomplish.

Creating our results culture is not easy. We are still struggling with that. When we say how to move the dial, it is not 'implement a grant such as Promise Neighborhoods or Gear Up.' We say, 'We lift educational aspirations. We build skills. We connect to college and career and engage families in the process.' Those four things will move the dial. And then we talk about how to make them happen, about how results are in the center of the work, that all partners have an aligned contribution to make toward that result, and that our contribution is to help frame the work in a results way and to bring in needed programs—that is when we talk about Promise, Gear Up, and Upward Bound. That is the level of refinement I am working on.

As we work with our external partners, we try to hold the concept of the Theory of Aligned Contributions. Going to scope and scale in Appalachia is going to require our partners joining in a shared result. Again, I had to change my thinking and start believing that others could do the work as well as we could and that we needed partners to own pieces of the work and get them to trust us as well. Using the Results Playbook was foundational for our work with partners. We asked them the join us in the population-level result and commit to making progress on a set of education indicators.

One key piece for us in creating our results culture was to define, with our partners and stakeholders, the overarching strategies that will move our shared result. This allowed our partners to see their contribution and how we can make progress towards the result. It allowed all of us to create a shared results culture.

The good news is that we are seeing progress. We are having an impact in our community and, therefore, more willingness to work toward shared results. One example of this is through our using performance measures and shared performance measures

Part 2: Executing to Scope and Scale

One of the things we created was a "result room" where our results banner is displayed: "All Appalachian Kentucky youth succeed in school." We have data on the wall that shows the progress of our kids. We put the results and data in front of partners and community members. When people asked me to come and make a presentation, I started by naming the results statement. The results were the foundation of all of our work.

All photos by Raj Chawla.

to track progress and accountability to the results work. This is hard to do, but we are starting to do this.

For example, we are working with a credit union. They are at the table and they are bringing dollars to the target result of "all kids being successful." They get that. But, there was a disconnect in how we do the work. We saw success differently than they did. They saw success as how many people were signed up for a program. We had not talked with them about shared performance measures. We agreed on population-level results, but when we met, I introduced the "how much are you doing, how well are you doing it, and is any one better off?" questions. Then it was easy to come up with shared measures. The president of the credit union thought it was ingenious. We were not selling him on a results frame or methodology, but, rather, saying, "Let's look at it this way." This is a bright guy. The results frame has an intuitive appeal. We did not have to sell him on philosophy, but instead get him to start adopting it. Our results culture was the basis to have this kind of conversation and this kind of engagement.

Recently, I was talking to Dreama about her work and the progress that was being made in the 25 Kentucky counties where Partners for Education was engaged. She informed me that she was raising the stakes of the results work. She, with her team, decided that they needed to hold a population-level result for all people in this region of Appalachia—not just those in Kentucky. This meant that the focus on the results work needed to encompass 54 counties spreading over to Virginia, West Virginia, and Tennessee, as well as Kentucky.

Chapter 6 Summary

Work group behavior, tools, and processes have been my focus in this chapter on "Us" and how we work in shared accountability. You should now be able to recognize when a work group is slipping from its results focus into survival task, and when its members are getting in the habit of work avoidance instead of making their aligned contributions.

You should now be familiar with the technical tools of a results culture and how to use the results meeting methodology and have intentional conversations for High Action and High Alignment. It should be evident how to create a robust results culture, a checklist for which appears in the appendix to this chapter.

I hope the path from the way your work group, stakeholders, and partners work today to the place of collaboration in shared accountability is now clear. I also hope it feels achievable—in spite of conflicts over power and control, and the work avoidance so frequently encountered when individuals have not fully bought into the need to work in High Action and High Alignment.

Chapter 6 Applications: Tools and Worksheets

1. The Collaborative Work Cycle 216
2. Countering Work Avoidance: A Key Tool For Executing Toward Results. 218
3. Elements of a Results Meeting. 222
4. Engaging in a Data Walk: A Prerequisite for Action 223
5. Guidance for a Data Walk 225
6. Ten Conversations: Creating Alignment and Action 227
7. Ten Conversations to Have at Work 229
8. Elements of a Results Story 232
9. Engaging in a Public Accountability Conversation 234
10. Checklist for Creating a Results Culture. 235

To download these apps, visit the book's online resources:
http://ChooseResultsBook.com/resources.html

Part 2: Executing to Scope and Scale

The Collaborative Work Cycle
© Jolie Bain Pillsbury

The Collaborative Work Cycle (CWC) is a foundational Results Based Facilitation (RBF) mental model.[1] The four steps of the CWC provide a frame for moving to aligned action and achieving desired results. The figure below illustrates the four steps of the cycle.

Contents
Contents
1. Collaborative Work Cycle
2. The Four Steps
3. Repeat Until Successful

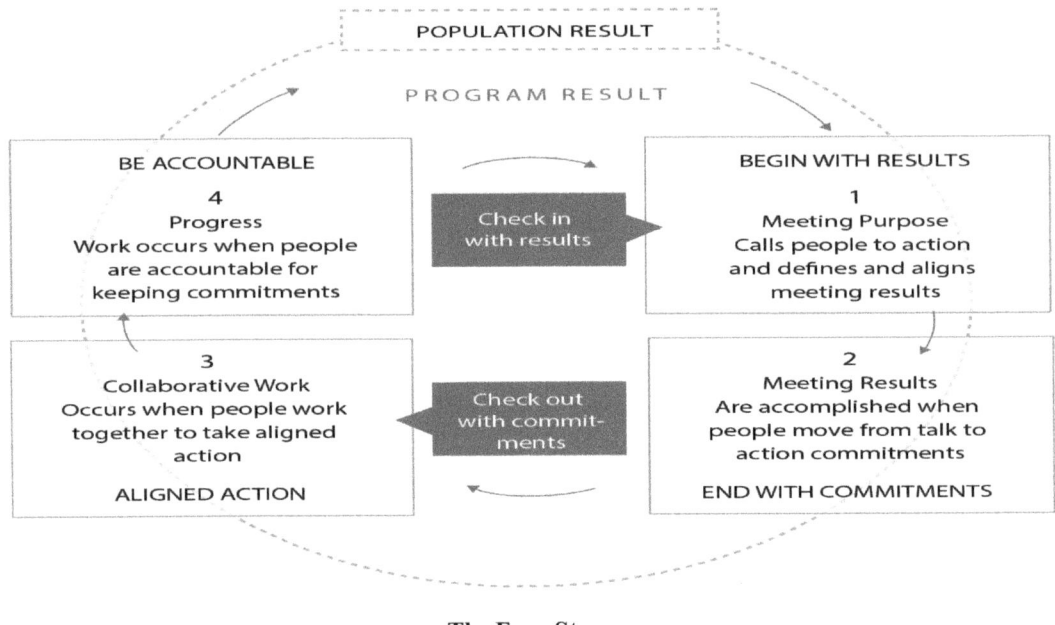

POPULATION RESULT

PROGRAM RESULT

BE ACCOUNTABLE
4
Progress
Work occurs when people are accountable for keeping commitments

Check in with results

BEGIN WITH RESULTS
1
Meeting Purpose
Calls people to action and defines and aligns meeting results

3
Collaborative Work
Occurs when people work together to take aligned action
ALIGNED ACTION

Check out with commit-ments

2
Meeting Results
Are accomplished when people move from talk to action commitments
END WITH COMMITMENTS

The Four Steps

1. Begin with Results

The first step in the Collaborative Work Cycle is to define the results that you and your team want to produce and for which you will hold yourselves accountable. These results must be measurable and observable.

2. End with Commitments

Results maybe be for a meeting, a project (requiring multiple meetings), or a collaboration requiring multiple workgroups and meetings. Results for each meeting can be scaffolded into project or collaboration results. There is an additional app, *The All-in-One 3R Agenda*[2], which can help you organize the meeting results.

---

[1] Results Based Facilitation: Book 2 – Advanced Skills – 2nd Edition, Jolie Bain Pillsbury, Sherbrooke Consulting Press. 2015

[2] Ibid

Participants leave *effective meetings* with *action commitments* in hand. These commitments have a *What I will do; By when; and with Whom*. In multiple meeting projects, subsequent meetings can start with an self- and group assessment of progress made towards meeting these action commitments. There is an app, *The Action Commitment Analyzer*, which can be used to enter, assess and display action commitments
across time.

3. Aligned Action

Aligned action occurs when individuals come together around a common result and align their efforts to have the maximum impact on achieving those results. The *Theory of Aligned Contributions*[3] is the foundation for Results Based Leadership. The booklet can be downloaded from RBL-APPS.

In addition to the theory booklet, to apps, *High Action/High Alignment and the HAHA Assessment Tool* help people understand and assess the two dimensions of the action commitment.

4. Be Accountable

Action commitments without personal accountability are meaningless. Accountability is the ability to make commitments to action, then keep those commitments, or acknowledge that you haven't and figure out what you need to do to move to action.

Many people's experience with accountability conversations is negative and often associated with punishment or shame rather than learning or celebration.

The App, *Accountability Pathway*[4] can be used to create conversations about keeping commitments that are interesting, meaningful, engaging and lead to more effective action.

Repeat Until Successful

In a multiple meeting context, the cycle is repeated with the individual meeting results building toward the program or population level results. Accountability for prior meeting action commitments fold into the agenda for the next meeting and into the new action commitments made.

Success will occur when meeting participants align their commitments to actions that produce results

---

[3] The Theory of Aligned Contributions, Jolie Bain Pillsbury, Sherbrooke Consulting Press, 2007.
[4] Additional "apps" and tools can be found at rbl-apps.com

Part 2: Executing to Scope and Scale

Countering Work Avoidance: A Key Tool for Executing Towards Results

By Raj Chawla

> *It ought to be remembered that there is nothing more difficult...than to take the lead in the introduction of a new order of things. Because the innovator has for enemies all those who have done well under the old conditions, and lukewarm defenders in those who may do well under the new.* - Niccolò Machiavelli

The primary work of Results Based Leadership is to make progress towards a desired population level result for a given group of people and/or a specific place. However, as stakeholders and partners move into execution to achieve the result, organizational and systems barriers will have to be confronted. These organizational and systems barriers might look like:

- **An unwillingness to name dysfunctional behaviors or practices that are impeding the results work**. For example, people won't name the "undiscussibles" in a public meeting but rather discuss them in quiet corners or backrooms.
- **A lack of accountability on promises and commitments that are made**. For example, people agree to take steps to move into execution and yet there seems to be no follow-up.
- **An over-commitment on activities that may not contribute to achieving the desired result**. For example, people are very busy with competing commitments and to-do lists, and yet no progress is made towards desired result.
- **An ongoing and persistent gap between what is wanted and what is actually happening**. For example, stakeholders remain unwilling or unable to change, modify, and/or implement policies, procedures and requirements needed to meet the desired result.

There comes a time when results leaders have to acknowledge that "every system is designed perfectly to produce the results that are currently being produced" and that, in fact, the current habits, beliefs, attitudes, and behaviors of the involved partners and stakeholders is contributing to things being—and staying—the way they are.

With this awareness, results leaders have to take the bold step to shake up the status quo and disrupt systems by asking their stakeholders (including themselves) to do the hard work needed to see the ways they have contributed to (and perhaps benefitted from) things staying the way they are. And, in doing this, they have to be ready for the inevitable resistance to this disruption that stakeholders will feel.

This resistance is directly connected to the losses (for example, of power, status, relationships, or competence) that stakeholders may have to face if things change and to taking on the new learning that will be required (such as having to work towards results with less formal authority or control). The resistance to these losses and difficult learning, and a conscious or unconscious desire for a less "painful" solution or way to achieve results, can lead to "work avoidance."

> *Countering work avoidance is a powerful leadership skill.*

Work avoidance behaviors are sometimes deliberate and protective against the forces of systems change, but sometimes they are unplanned and/or reflexive reactions. Keeping this in mind can help leaders identify and address work avoidance without taking a judgmental or blaming stance towards workers who are caught up in it.

To help spot work avoidance, watch for two common forms of it: **Diversion of Attention and Displacement of Responsibility.**[1]

What Diverting Attention Might Look Like:

- Defining the problem to fit current knowledge and expertise – for example, remaining blind to the new learning and practice that may be required.
- Denying the problem exists – for example, being unwilling to use or believe the data that might point the real problem
- Avoiding the conflict – for example, continuously using jokes and humor to avoid conflict or hurt feelings.
- Creating a proxy fight, such as a personality conflict, to avoid addressing the real problem.
- Discounting solutions that threaten legacy behaviors and relationships.
- Offering fake, pretend, or marginal solutions.

What Displacing Responsibility Might Look Like:

- Marginalizing or attacking the person trying to raise the difficult issues.
- Scapegoating someone or externalizing the "enemy" – placing a systems blame solely on a person or a group of people or stakeholders
- Attacking or blaming formal authority – waiting for formal authority to fix the systems problems
- Delegating the hard work to those who can't do anything about it, for example, consultants, committees, and task forces.

While achieving desired results is the primary reason for countering work avoidance, there are two other related factors that are important to consider. First, work avoidance signals

---

[1] Heifetz, Ronald A.; Linsky, Marty (2002-08-09). Leadership on the Line: Staying Alive Through the Dangers of Leading. Perseus Books Group.

Part 2: Executing to Scope and Scale

that a system is on the verge of learning to do something new and/or different, perhaps the very things that are needed to effect the changes required to meet population level results. Work avoidance, in this regard, signals an opportunity is at hand. Second, if work avoidance is not addressed, systems changes will almost certainly be derailed, leading to cynicism and/or hopelessness that anything could be different.

Using Data to Address Work Avoidance

Once work avoidance is identified, the best line of defense against it is to place the attention back on the work designed to produce the population level result. Bring every discussion back to the data at hand, including data that tracks the implementation of programs, achievement of performance measures, progress of strategies, meeting of targets, and changes in the population level result.

> The safest place for a leader to stand is on the foundation of results - Raj Chawla

By putting results and data back at the heart of the work, leaders are willing to risk relationships, reframe loyalties, and confront their own losses. They are also asking their stakeholders and partners to do the same. With so much at stake, use the framework below to help develop a solid plan for countering work avoidance.

Countering Work Avoidance: A Framework for Leaders' Actions[2]

Leadership Approach	Key Questions
First focus is on self	• What is the data telling me about achieving the result? • What is my contribution to challenges of execution? What are my values, beliefs, attitudes, and/or behaviors that I might have to examine? • What is my new learning? What might I have to lose if the work is successful? How do I benefit with things remaining the way they are? • Are my relationships with others resilient enough to address the issues of work avoidance? If not, how do I strengthen them?
Focus everyone on the population and program level results	• What result are we trying to accomplish? • Based on the data, how well are we doing in achieving the result?
Provide regular updates on work done thus far	• What are the work groups or strategy groups doing and accomplishing? • Is their work robust enough to meet performance targets? How do we know? What data are we using?
Follow up on prior commitments	• Were the previously agreed-upon actions taken? If so, what happened? In what ways did these actions impact the result? • Are the actions still important?

---

[2] Modified from the work of Behn, Robert D. (2014-06-18). The PerformanceStat Potential: A Leadership Strategy for Producing Results (Brookings / Ash Center Series, "Innovative Governance in the 21st Century")

Chapter 6: Apps/Tools

Leadership Approach	Key Questions
Identify execution challenges and possible causes	• What isn't working and why? What data are we using to make this assessment? • What are "our" individual and collective contributions to these execution challenges? • What are the systems conflicts or competing agendas that are contributing to these challenges? • What existing policies or procedures are inhibiting execution? What new policies or procedures might be needed to support successful execution? • What systems dynamics are contributing to execution challenges?
Address the "deeper" issues	• What power dynamics are at play? • Who might have to confront losses if the work is successful? • What kinds of losses would that be (i.e., resources, relationships, loyalties, power, etc.)? • What can be done to address theses losses?
Track or re-examine population and performance targets	• Who should achieve what result by when? • Are we on track to hit our performance targets? • Will these performance targets allow us to hit our population-level targets? If not, why?
Develop and/or modify strategies	• What do we need to do differently and why? • Who will be aligned with these new efforts and who will be adversarial towards these efforts? Why?
Identify or re-examine resources	• What resources do we need to implement, repurpose, or shift for these strategies to be successful? • Who will benefit from this? Who will lose?
Identify what is working and what we are learning	• What does the data reveal about who is succeeding and about what we are learning about what works? • How will we implement what we are learning? • What anecdotes can help us understand what is working?
Establish responsibility and accountability	• Who should do what by when? • Who is not holding responsibility for execution and why?
Recognize accomplishment	• Who deserves thanks for significant improvements? • What can we learn and apply from these accomplishments?
Have difficult conversations about accountability	• Whom should we confront for indifference, incompetence, or sabotage? What data are we using? • If needed, how do we ask these stakeholders to leave? • What will be the impact?
Tell results stories	• What bright spots can be highlighted? • How do we use results stories to share our work and to enroll others?

Elements of a Results Meeting

- ✓ Container with Data
    - Holds the conversation
    - Focuses on the work
    - Have a meeting agenda focused on results and action
- ✓ Check-in – joins people to the work
- ✓ Accountability Conversation
    - Work done/to be done
    - Progress/Learning/QI
- ✓ Key Work of Meeting
- ✓ Action Commitments
- ✓ Check-out

Chapter 6: Apps/Tools

Engaging in a Data Walk: A Prerequisite for Action
© Jolie Bain Pillsbury, Raj Chawla

A data walk creates an intentional conversation among and between results leaders who have a shared commitment towards a population level result. The physical act of walking with other leaders around a room set up with relevant data on the wall—in contrast to just sitting and looking at the data on a handout—promotes more authentic conversations about the current circumstances and the work to be done. The group walks and talks in pairs and trios, exploring,

Contents
I. Set up the Space for the Walk
II. Select the Data to Display
III. Frame the Conversation
IV. Ignite the Conversation
V. Debrief the Conversation

discussing, and reacting to the data. That animated dialogue will form the foundation for the decisions made during that and subsequent meetings, including strategies to be taken, programs to be implemented, and targets and timelines to evoke urgency and accountability. Depending on the robustness of the data, the data walk usually lasts between 15-30 minutes.

I. Set up the Space for the Walk
The set-up of the room in which the leaders engage in the data walk is important to the walk's success. Print the data on poster-size paper for easy viewing, and display it on either easels or adhered to the wall. Space the posters at intervals that allow walkers to stop in small groups in front of each poster without crowding those at the next poster. In addition, the data can be grouped by category, i.e., national, local, issue-oriented, etc.

11. Select the Data to Display
Always include a banner near the center of the data walk that displays the population level result the group is working to achieve. "All children enter school ready to learn," for example, is the population level result in the sample data walk pictured below. For other data to display, consider including:
 1. Population level data, disaggregated by race, gender, geography, etc., to illuminate possible disparities and the possible impact of interventions;
 2. Indicator data, reflected as a baseline and trend line;
 3. Additional disaggregated socio-economic data, if available, such as, education, employment, health, and community data; and
 4. Other data that will inform the conversation about the work.

Sample Data Walk Space with Posted Data and Population Level Result:

(Copyright 2015 Sherbrooke Consulting, Inc.)

III. Frame the Conversation using a Data Walk Guide
Provide a helpful frame for the conversations about the data by developing some guiding questions in either a handout given to participants or on posters placed at the start of the walk. These questions are designed to allow results leaders to explore the current condition of well being for people in their

community as well as explore why things may be the way they are. They may also allow the leaders to experience the data from their own lived or work experience and from the systems they represent.

Consider these items as you develop your guiding questions:
- Who are the participants in the walk? What sectors do they represent, what contributions can they make towards the result, and what potential conflicts or different points of view might they have on the current circumstances?
- Try to illuminate the perspectives of the multiple stakeholders who are impacted by the results work.
- Highlight the multiple contributing factors to the current situation.

For the population level result in the sample above, "All children enter school ready to learn," some illustrative guiding questions are:
- What is the current state of school-readiness in this community? Who is doing well and who isn't? Why?
- How does this compare to other communities?
- What do you notice about the connections between school readiness and:
    a. Race/ethnicity, age, gender, and/or language?
    b. Demographics of the footprint?
    c. Rates of formal and informal care?
- Was there specific data that you found interesting or compelling and, if so, why?
- What data is missing? What additional information would help you better understand school readiness in this community? From what sectors?
- What works to support school readiness? What, from your experience, is important to support school readiness for all children?

III. Ignite the Conversation

As the results leaders enter the room, invite them to get settled and then find a partner(s) from a different agency, unit, or organization and engage in the data walk. Offer the leaders the data walk handout or point them to the posted guide, and give them large post-its on which they can write comments, observations, and/or questions and stick directly on the associated data poster. Encourage them to reflect with their partners on what they see and what data is missing. Missing data can evolve into a data development agenda for the leaders to create.

During the walk, notice who is talking to whom, any differing points of view, or places where participants are aligned. These observations will inform you in the next step in the process – debriefing the data walk conversation.

IV. Debrief the Conversation

Once the data walk is finished, invite the leaders to come back and have a conversation with their tablemates about the data. This allows the leaders to integrate the experience and hear from voices other than their partner(s) in the walk. This small-group conversation serves as a springboard for the next large group conversation. Sometimes the larger group also needs to discuss the data, or they may be ready to move on to the next conversation on strategy, accountability, or any other topic that moves their results work forward and aligns with the meeting agenda.

Chapter 6: Apps/Tools

Guidance for Data Walk
Raj Chawla

Use the following to create the data slides that you want to share as part of a whole group data walk

POPULATION LEVEL RESULT AND INDICATOR(s)
Remember, a whole population level result should include:
- The population with number for the people (e.g., All 32,000 children age birth to six in Baltimore) and
- A clearly stated condition of well-being (e.g., are healthy; are educated; etc.).

Remember, an indicator(s) should include:
Trend over time with sub-population data disaggregated by at least two (2) key variables that may include:
- Race
- Ethnicity
- Gender
- Geography
- Social economic status

> Something to Consider
> At a minimum, indicator(s) should be correlated with the condition of well-being for the population with at least one data point and the commitment to produce a second data point within what will become the measurement period. Think of it as a projection of trend "if nothing changes".

WHOLE POPULATION ANALYSIS
Analysis should:
- Include additional disaggregation to illuminate possible disparities and impact of interventions; and
- Surface disparities in sub-populations (e.g., in MD "all children are healthy" began to see data disaggregated by development milestones, access to quality health insurance, etc.).

BASELINE AND TARGET TIED TO MEASUREMENT CYCLE
Consider and name your target(s) for your work as part the Children Health Leadership Network (e.g., CHIP target, network adequacy target, etc.).
- Remember, baseline should include:
    - A number (#) and percent (%) that shows current condition of problem over past few years, etc. disaggregated by sub-populations.
- Remember, a target should include:
    - A number (#) and percent (%) of improvement to be achieved by when (declare date, one measurement cycle); and
    - Something that would not happen if nothing was done differently.

Part 2: Executing to Scope and Scale

> Something to Consider
> Remember that a change in the slope of a negative or positive trend is acceptable.

FACTOR ANALYSIS
Remember, root cause factor analysis should:
- Identify the priority factors for the target population to "turn the curve"; and
- Show the contributing and constraining factors that will help refine, validate and confirm your strategies.

> Something to Consider
> If applicable, name data development agenda needed to bring in local data, community voice, field level research, etc.

STRATEGIES
When naming strategies, remember:
- That strategies should address priority factors defined; and
- To include difference made measures developed for each strategy and how the strategy will contribute to the result.

> Something to Consider
> Strategies are NOT activities.

STRATEGY WORK PLANS
For each strategy, name:
- WHO: Your contribution and your aligned partners and their contribution(s);
- WHAT: Sequenced work plan with major activities and next steps to move the strategy forward over next 30-45 days; and
- HOW: Your initial performance measures and the shared performance measures of your partners.

RESULTS TIMELINE
Create a time horizon, segmented in relevant time periods (e.g., months, quarters, etc.) that show from now until end of your measurement cycle:
- Completion of major tasks/milestones;
- Public conversations/major events to keep on the radar; and
- When strategy performance measures should be met.

> Something to Consider
> Timeline should show strategy implementation/execution.

Chapter 6: Apps/Tools

Ten Conversations: Creating Alignment and Action
© Raj Chawla, Jolie Bain Pillsbury

"An organization's results are determined through webs of human commitments, born in webs of human conversations." Fernando Flores

At the heart of leadership is the capacity to create results that matter to the people you work with and the people you serve. When you and those you work with have a common understanding and a shared commitment to achieve measurable results that matter to you all, then acting together effectively can become your daily practice. Having the ability to know the kind of conversation that is required in a particular situation to be in alignment and action together is a powerful leadership skill.

Contents
I. Conversations for High Alignment, High Action
II. Starting the 10 Conversations
III. Practice

I. Conversations for High Action, High Alignment
The first step is to notice the current level of alignment and action for yourself and those you work with. Once you know the situation you are in, the second step is to choose a powerful conversation that will move you to or sustain you in high action and high alignment.

High action, low alignment	High action, high alignment
A leader working actively and independently to contribute to the result, but not reaching out to build relationships with others to achieve complementary efforts. **Conversations that forge alignment: Meaning, Relationship, Possibility, Success, Results**	A leader with resilient relationships acting on collaborative decisions and being accountable for measurably improving results. **Conversation that sustain high action, high alignment: Reflection/Learning, Results**
Low action, low alignment	**Low action, high alignment**
A leader observing what is going and not engaging in either relationship building or taking action that can contribute to result. **Conversation that forge alignment and ignite action: Meaning, Personal Power, Results**	A leader joining with others and fostering relationships, but not using the relationships to leverage contributions to the result. **Conversations that ignite action: Accountability, Commitments/Promises, Action, Results**

II. Ways to Start the Ten Conversations
Moving Towards High Alignment
Leaders engaging people to work together for a common result requires connecting different interests, commitments, and perspectives in a new way so everyone has a relationship to each other and a shared result. Low alignment is a symptom of undeveloped relatedness. The four conversations of meaning, relationship, possibility and success move you and others out of low alignment by fostering aligned connections to shared results.

Conversation	Possible ways to start the conversation
Meaning	This is what is important to me and what I want to do with you...What is important to you? What matters to you? What do you want to do together?
Relationship	I'm not satisfied with our level of commitment and I'd like us to talk about it. I'd like to hear what you value about our working together? How can we build a cohesive working relationship
Success	What a successful outcome for each of us? What are our conditions of satisfaction for our work together?
Possibility	What can we create together? What is possible? What are the different options? What is open to us? What is our true potential? What haven't we considered?

Part 2: Executing to Scope and Scale

Moving Towards High Action

Mobilizing action requires addressing issues of pace, capacity, competency, and peer accountability. Intentional conversations of accountability, commitments/promises, action, and results can support moving a group to action.

Conversation	Possible ways to start the conversation
Accountability	This is what I am contributing…In what ways are you willing to contribute towards our success? When are you willing to make the contribution? What are you willing to say yes to? What do you say no to? What are the consequences for each of us of taking this action? What's required of us that no one has yet taken responsibility for?
Commitment and Promises	What is your commitment to the results and the work so that we can meet our goals? What is your commitment to me so that I can be successful? What commitment do you need from me so you can be successful? What has each of us promised to?
Action	Lets coordinate the timing and communication of our tasks in order to get this work done in time. This is how I am progressing on my commitments…How are you progressing on your commitments? Do you want my input? Do you have any input for me? What proposals do you have for who needs to do what when?
Results	What outcome do we want to see? How important is that result? What are we willing to do, stop doing, not do or change to achieve that result? Is this bottom line reasonable? What do others expect of us? What do you expect as a result of our working together? What do you expect that our work will produce? Who will benefit from achieving the result? How will we know if we have achieved the result? Who are partners who can contribute?

Conversation to Move Out of Low Action Low Alignment

The cornerstone conversation to move out of a place of both low alignment and low action is one that allows you or those you work with to reflect on their own personal power – the power to act and the power to forge relationships.

Conversation	Possible ways to start the conversation
Personal Power	If you could move forward on your own, what would you do? What prevents you from exercising your power? What are your sources of power -- From your own unique gifts, talents and experience? In your roles of both formal and informal authority? In the systems you are part of? If there were no constraints how might you approach this? What do you need from us to support you? What can you give yourself permission to do? Is there risk you need to mitigate? If this is not a place you want to be what can you do to make it meaningful? What do you need to do to leave?

Conversation to Sustain High Action and High Alignment

Once you are in a place of high action and high alignment there are conversations of reflection and learning that can sustain this high level of engagement until the program results are achieved.

Conversation	Possible ways to start the conversation
Reflection	What just happened? What did we learn? What should we do next time? Were our working assumptions accurate when we started? Isn't it time to stop and reflect? What of the conversations that got us here do we need to have again?

III. Practice

Identify what conversation you need to have with whom. What do you hope to achieve with this conversation? What was the impact of the conversation – what happened? Journal…keep practicing.

Ten Conversations To Have At Work
Raj Chawla

Conversation	What this creates	What to expect	What happens if it is missing	Ways to start the conversation
Meaning	Creates a shared context for our working together. It allows people to show their values and principles; it reveals intention.	A connection with others; grounding for coordinated action; insight into our beliefs and values.	Our understanding of our work together remains superficial and our commitment to doing the work together is ambivalent. It is often evidenced by lack of action, motivation, energy	Why is this important to you? Why does this matter? What are we supposed to be doing?
Personal Power	Generates the awareness of inner knowledge. Validates personal wisdom and experience as sources for addressing complex problems.	A sense of purpose, energy and drive that create trust, responsibility and a willingness to see new possibilities and make new offers.	There is an over-reliance on rules, compliance and positional power to generate strategy and take action.	If you could move forward on your own, what would you do? What prevents you from exercising your power? If there were no constraints how might you approach this? What do you need from us to support you?
Relationship	Creates commitment, accountability, trust, and responsibility	This conversation results in moving into action with a shared purpose and ownership	Without conversations of relationship the possibility for effective coordinated action is compromised. We lose our cohesiveness, potential, the ability to have a meeting of minds, etc.	I'm not satisfied with our level of commitment and I'd like us to talk about it. I'd like to hear what you value about our working together? How can we build a cohesive working relationship
Success	Conversations of success allow us to understand our client and each other's conditions of satisfaction around outcomes.	This conversation enables us to align different needs and wants for effective action.	Without this conversations, we are may go off in different directions with our own ideas of success and thus fail to deliver satisfactory product or service. Even if the work is satisfied we could experience personal disappointment and alienation.	What would constitute a successful outcome for each of us? What are the client's conditions of satisfaction for this project?

Part 2: Executing to Scope and Scale

Conversation	What this creates	What to expect	What happens if it is missing	Ways to start the conversation
Possibility	Creates new futures and potentials for action. It calls forth the creative artist in all of us.	This conversation brings new ideas, directions, or opportunities to our organizing. Possibility allows discovery of new terrains/ horizons.	Without conversations of possibility, new ideas would be limited; we may rely too much on existing frameworks and established ways of doing things.	What can we create together? What is possible? What are the different options? What is open to us? What is our true potential? What haven't we considered?
Accountability	Conversations of accountability generate publicly our intentions for the things for which we want to be responsible.	Individual promises and commitments and the personal responsibility for their fulfillment.	Possibilities for coordinated action are unknown and group members operate on ungrounded assumptions and expectations. With continued breakdowns the trend is to go towards compliance.	In what ways are you willing to contribute towards our success? What are you willing to say yes to? What do you say no to? What are the consequences for each of us of taking this action? What's required of us that no one has yet taken responsibility for?
Commitment and Promises	Future action. Conversations of commitments and promises are linked to accountability. These conversations tell others what I am willing to do and what others can expect from us.	All the elements for coordinated action are in place.	Without conversations of commitments and promises the possibilities for coordinated action remain vague. May contribute to a culture of blame and recrimination.	What is your commitment to the project so that we can meet our goals? What is your commitment to me so that I can be successful? What has each of us promised to?
Action	Conversations for action generates the doing that allow fulfill our intentions and achieve our desired outcomes.	Activities consistent with promises and commitments that we have agreed are needed for success.	Without conversations of action, there is likely to be confusion and conflict about what to do next. Without this conversation, we could be stuck in speculation.	Lets coordinate our tasks in order to get this work done. How are you progressing on your section of the report? Do you want my input?

Chapter 6: Apps/Tools

Conversation	What this creates	What to expect	What happens if it is missing	Ways to start the conversation
Possibility	Creates new futures and potentials for action. It calls forth the creative artist in all of us.	This conversation brings new ideas, directions, or opportunities to our organizing. Possibility allows discovery of new terrains/ horizons.	Without conversations of possibility, new ideas would be limited; we may rely too much on existing frameworks and established ways of doing things.	What can we create together? What is possible? What are the different options? What is open to us? What is our true potential? What haven't we considered?
Accountability	Conversations of accountability generate publicly our intentions for the things for which we want to be responsible.	Individual promises and commitments and the personal responsibility for their fulfillment.	Possibilities for coordinated action are unknown and group members operate on ungrounded assumptions and expectations. With continued breakdowns the trend is to go towards compliance.	In what ways are you willing to contribute towards our success? What are you willing to say yes to? What do you say no to? What are the consequences for each of us of taking this action? What's required of us that no one has yet taken responsibility for?
Commitment and Promises	Future action. Conversations of commitments and promises are linked to accountability. These conversations tell others what I am willing to do and what others can expect from us.	All the elements for coordinated action are in place.	Without conversations of commitments and promises the possibilities for coordinated action remain vague. May contribute to a culture of blame and recrimination.	What is your commitment to the project so that we can meet our goals? What is your commitment to me so that I can be successful? What has each of us promised to?
Action	Conversations for action generates the doing that allow fulfill our intentions and achieve our desired outcomes.	Activities consistent with promises and commitments that we have agreed are needed for success.	Without conversations of action, there is likely to be confusion and conflict about what to do next. Without this conversation, we could be stuck in speculation.	Lets coordinate our tasks in order to get this work done. How are you progressing on your section of the report? Do you want my input?

Elements of a Results Story
Raj Chawla

Leaders can use the results action plan as a frame to tell results stories. Depending on audience, it might be more helpful to talk about the impact the work is having on people, what the data is revealing, or contributions of partners. The table below offers how some parts of the results action plan can contribute to a results story.

Focus or Element of a Story	Results Action Plan	Sample Language
Impact on People and/or communities • Current status of people or circumstances • Disparities	Results Statement Disaggregated populations and program populations	*"Youth of color are over represented in our juvenile justice system. Black youth represent 6 percent of our state population and 24 percent of the young people in facilities."*
Data • Progress on targets—expressed in whole numbers and percentages	Indicators Baseline and Targets Performance measures	*"We know that young people are leaving our system better than when they came in, as 95 percent of our provider partners are making a measurable contribution to positive youth outcomes."*
Theory of change • The overarching strategies that move the indicator that demonstrates an improved condition of well-being	Strategies Root Cause Analysis	*"Investing in a community based continuum of care provides critical opportunities for young people to receive support and accountability in the most cost effective way."*

Chapter 6: Apps/Tools

Focus or Element of a Story	Results Action Plan	Sample Language
Individual and Partner contributions • Actions by leaders, partners, and/or stakeholders who are impacted by or supporting the work • Personal connection to the work	Programs Performance Measures Targets	*"To achieve results, we cannot do this alone. Our partnerships with non-profits are essential in providing community based alternatives to confinement."* *"I believe that all youth deserve fair and equitable opportunities that I would want for my own children"*
On-the-ground work • Key activities and particular programs	Programs Performance measures	*"We are engaging with parents and community members to actively include their perspectives in policy and program development."*
People who make a difference • Individuals who are working in communities to make progress to the result	Performance measures Programs	*"Providers in our school based health centers are providing essential health care to our most vulnerable youth who may otherwise not have health care access."*
Return on investment • Data showing progress • Budget and costs	Indicator and performance measure data Disparity data	*"For every dollar invested in diverting youth from the juvenile justice system, we are able to return four dollars to the tax payers without compromising pubic safety."*
Achievements and Milestones • Performance relative to targets and timeline data	Target and timeline data	*"Over the past year, we have reduced the number of youth confinements by 55%."*

233

Part 2: Executing to Scope and Scale

Engaging in a Public Accountability Conversation
Raj Chawla

The purpose of this public accountability conversation is to share publically whether you achieved your target or not, learn from the experience and move forward with greater insight to achieve subssequent targets. It is not a "show and tell" or "inquisition" about your work. **This process is designed to reinforce the ownership of the commitment to the population result – as represented by perforamance level target - and illuminate learning and reflection about the work you have done**.

It invites your colleagues to be both accountability and thought partners on the work and what you plan on doing in the future within the context of your results work. It has both quantitative and qualitative elements.

Getting Ready:

Prepare the data needed to engage in the conversation of accountability and then consider how you will share briefly and concisely whether you have hit your target and what your insights are going forward. Data that is important to share includes:

- Target data – population and/or program level
- Strategy data
- Performance measure data

Sequence

1. Declare whether you hit the target or not. Then use your data to give a 3-5 minute overview of the following:
   - Name population-level result and targets for work
   - Put your target in context: What kind of a target was it – "how well" and "difference made" measures? And how was it connected to a population target.
   - What did it take to hit (or make progress towards) your target
   - Strategies developed and lessons learned through execution, including what it took to gather performance measure trend data.
   - Partners engaged and in what role, with what contributions.

2. If appropriate, be willing to discuss:
   - What you are learning about being a results leader?
   - How will this learning impact how you will move forward to your next target?

3. After the 3-5 minute overview your colleagues are invited to continue the conversation by:
   - Asking questions, making comments, and observations about your work and your data?
   - Offering hypotheses about your work
   - Supporting your thinking about executing to your next target.

Checklist for Creating a Results Culture
Raj Chawla

A results culture helps supports groups to navigate the tension, the anxiety, the chaos and stress, to create a new order. A results culture becomes crucial in helping a group hold its primary work task and not become "stuck" in survival task. A robust results culture allows the group to address its issues of work avoidance, support individuals in new learning or behavior, and to endure any potential losses.

Norms: The expected behaviors that are adopted as part of being part of a culture. Some norms are enforced formally – such as updating action commitment forms at the beginning of every meeting. Some norms are displayed informally – such as doing work within a results container. In a results culture norms are tied to working with the results in the center, having the discipline of data, and engaging in the collaborative work cycle.

Values and Beliefs: Influenced by norms, beliefs are the assumptions that are made about the world and the values that stem from those beliefs. In a results culture, values are things that are deemed important and can include concepts like accountability, honesty and directness, equity and equality, transparency, and aligned actions.

Artifacts: The physical things that are found that have particular symbolism for a culture. The main thing is that they have special meaning for the people of a particular culture – they remind people of what is deemed as important, as valuable, as treasured, etc. In a results culture these could be the objects in a results meeting room such as an accountability pathway, action commitment forms, data on the wall, results banners, etc.

Language: It is generally agreed that language and culture are closely related. Language can be viewed as a verbal expression of culture. It is used to maintain and convey culture and cultural ties. Language in a results culture is designed to focus on the result work, the building of resilient relationships, and working in high action and high alignment.

The following table offers a possible checklist that can be used to create a results culture in your organization. This is not a definitive list and should be adapted to meet your unique organizational culture.

Part 2: Executing to Scope and Scale

Elements of a Results Culture	Complete	In Process	Not Started	Next Steps/Resource
Creating a "Container"				
• Population Level Results Declaration (i.e., Results Banner)				
• Data prominently displayed – indicator, trend line, targets				
• Materials to engage in work (i.e., flip charts, tables and seating positioned for engaged conversations)				
• Other?				
Results Meetings				
• "Normalized" conversations of accountability (i.e., accountability pathway)				
• Using skills identified in Results Based Facilitation				
• Public declarations of future action (i.e., action commitments)				
• Data as central focus				
• Other?				
Intentional Focus on Working in High Action and High Alignment				
• Using a common/shared "results playbook"				
• Identifying and working with shared performance measures				
• Criteria for working in High Action and High Alignment identified				
• Using intentional conversations to support group to be in high action and high alignment (i.e., trust)				
• Using results "stories" to reinforce results culture				
• Other?				
Conversations of Public Accountability				
• Targets and Timelines displayed in meeting room				
• Collecting qualitative and quantitative data for public accountability meeting				
• Engaging in public accountability meetings with key stakeholders and partners				
• Other?				

CHAPTER 7

"Us in the World"—Working Toward Scope and Scale

The name of our proper connection to the earth is "good work," for good work involves much giving of honor.

— Wendell Berry

When results leaders come together to execute their shared results action plan, they are working towards both scope and scale of their work. They work to create robust, interlocking strategies that move the needle on the indicator. They also work to create shared performance measures that allow partners and stakeholders to leverage each other's work to impact larger and larger numbers of people. Finally, they engage in quality improvement efforts in order to make adjustments quickly. The following example highlights how a group of leaders moved to scope and scale in their work. (Note, this engagement is drawn from my actual experience, but the numbers cited are for illustrative purposes only.)

Ex-Offenders Successfully Reintegrate Into Their Community

Many years ago I was working with a group of community leaders in Marion County, Indiana, who were addressing a complex public problem: helping ex-offenders successfully re-enter their community. The population result they held at the center of their work was: *All adult offenders in the county successfully reintegrate into the community.* This work was done through the Leadership In Action (LAP) program sponsored by the Annie E. Casey Foundation.[1] I had the honor of being part of an implementation team (that included Jolie Pillsbury—the primary architect of LAP) and Donna Stark of the Annie E Casey Foundation.

Based on their data and factor analysis, they chose several important strategies to develop and implement, including efforts focused on policy, education/training, and employment. Each strategy had its own team whose preliminary concern was to define the focus of the work and identify the key partners and stakeholders necessary for success. They recognized that these strategies were interconnected and interdependent. They also knew that the people these results work sought to impact would be affected by all the strategies.

One example of this interrelationship was between the employment and the education/training strategies. They knew that if ex-offenders found employment, the likelihood of returning to prison decreased. They also knew, based on research and evidence-based practices, that if ex-offenders had a job that paid a living wage on re-entry and held that job for at least six months, the likelihood of recidivism (repetition of criminal behavior) dropped dramatically.

These community leaders discovered that there were many conditions required for ex-offenders to get hired—among them, ex-offenders needed skills and employers willing to hire them. As a result of these insights, their employment strategy included these key elements:

- **Specific skills and apprenticeships** aligned with the jobs available in their community;
- **Formal education** of ex-offenders in order to qualify for jobs;
- **Job search and interviewing skills** training for the ex-offenders; and
- **Employee recruitment** and development by local employers.

This working group included members who could help with each element for the ex-offenders—partners who offered job training; partners who provided formal education needed for diplomas (i.e., high school, associate, and four-year college level); partners who provided job search and interview training; and partners who could work with local employers on recruitment and development strategies.

This group used the power of performance measures—including the three questions "how much are we doing," "how well are we doing it," and "what difference are we making"—to create urgency for action, accountability to the strategy, and as the basis for quality improvement.

Their goals were 1) to have ex-offenders employed in jobs paying a living wage within six to nine months of their release, and 2) six months after being hired, the ex-offenders would still hold these jobs. To use performance measure language, these were their "difference made" measures.

They also realized that if this were to happen, the work to match ex-offenders to employers (the interview process) would need to take place three to six months after release. In the language of performance measurement, this was their "how well" measure.

They realized that to reach their goal, the group would have to start preparing the ex-offenders and employers up to three months prior to the interviews. This meant teaching job search and interviewing skills to the ex-offenders. It also meant preparing the employers to identify the skills needed and develop any appropriate infrastructure necessary to support ex-offenders. In performance measure language, this was their "how much" measure.

As the timetable became clearer, the working group realized that to get ex-offenders ready for the interviews, they needed to offer the "soon-to-be" ex-offenders the requisite formal education and job-specific skills training before their release. This was also part of their "how much" measure.

Table 7.1 shows this working group's performance measures regarding their employment strategy to reduce likelihood of recidivism among ex-offenders.

These leaders used targets and timelines to create accountability to move the strategy forward. For their "difference made" measure they chose an employment target of 50 ex-offenders to be hired by mid-November—six to nine months after their release.

They then worked backwards from that mid-November date to identify when they wanted to hit their "how well" measure. They estimated that one out of two ex-offenders who reached their second interview would get hired. They also realized that a certain number of ex-offenders who reached the first interview would not reach the second interview. Their goal was to have 150 ex-offenders be selected for a first interview and then, out of that pool, 100 to reach the second interview. They chose September/October as their target date for these "how well" measures.

They realized that to have 150 ex-offenders selected for initial interviews meant they needed to have a larger pool of people submit their resumes and be ready for those interviews. Their goal was

Part 2: Executing to Scope and Scale

Table 7.1 **Performance Measures Regarding Goal to Reduce Ex-offender Recidivism**

Employment Strategy Performance Measures	
How Much	**How Well**
• The number (and percentage) of ex-offenders who have the needed formal and job specific skills necessary to gain employment with a livable wage • The number (and percentage) of employers who have jobs that pay a livable wage and can support ex-offender employees • The number (and percentage) of ex-offenders who send out resumes and have appropriate job interview skills • The number (and percentage) of employers who receive resumes and agree to interview	• The number (and percentage) of first interviews that take place • The number (and percentage) of second interviews that take place
Difference Made Measures (count)	**Difference Made Measures (percentage)**
• The number of ex-offenders who are hired at a livable wage • The number of ex-offenders who are still hired after 6 months	• The percentage of ex-offenders who are hired at a livable wage • The percentage of ex-offenders who are still hired after 6 months

to have 175 ex-offenders submit their resumes by early April. This allowed the group of leaders a window from January to March to work with ex-offenders to get ready for the interview process. This work connected to their "how much" measures.

Finally, they realized that the ex-offenders needed to have the required job and education skills to be able to take advantage of potential employment opportunities. This required offering GED and training programs for the ex-offenders prior to their release.

On the employer side of the equation, the work of the employment strategy was to identify a pool of employers, make them aware of the strategy, and prepare them to potentially hire ex-offenders. To accomplish this, employers would need to determine which jobs were appropriate and what special supports (if any) the ex-offenders might need. Equally as important, they would need to recognize and believe in the benefits of engaging in this process.

Chapter 7: "Us in the World"—Working Toward Scope and Scale

Using the same time frame used with the ex-offenders, the leaders in this working group decided to target 25 to 30 employers who would be willing to be part of the employment strategy. These employers would have to be ready to accept resumes and then set up interviews, and this would have to done by early April (matching the ex-offender time frame of submitting resumes by early April).

The working group also recognized that not every employer would agree to this strategy; they would need to reach out to a larger pool of potential employers to get to their targeted number of participants. They defined January to March as their outreach time and chose to target 50 to 60 employers to meet with individually and in groups. Again, by working backwards, they used October through December to research potential employers, and to create and refine their message. They chose to launch this process by scheduling a series of public service announcements to air on local TV and radio networks and by holding a large employer fair with guest speakers, and more, followed by individual outreach. Figure 7.1 shows the timelines for employer readiness and preparing ex-offenders for employment.

Figure 7.1 **Timelines for Ex-offender Employment and Employer Readiness**

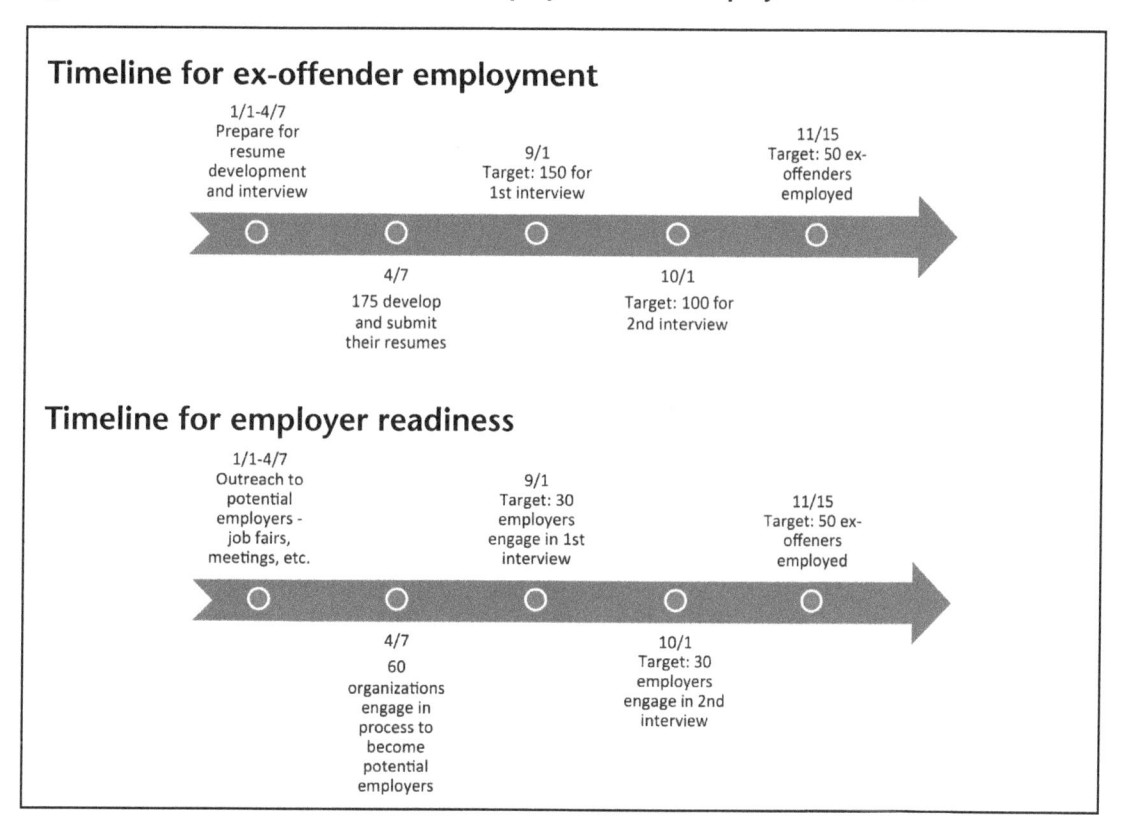

Timeline for ex-offender employment

- 1/1-4/7: Prepare for resume development and interview
- 4/7: 175 develop and submit their resumes
- 9/1: Target: 150 for 1st interview
- 10/1: Target: 100 for 2nd interview
- 11/15: Target: 50 ex-offenders employed

Timeline for employer readiness

- 1/1-4/7: Outreach to potential employers - job fairs, meetings, etc.
- 4/7: 60 organizations engage in process to become potential employers
- 9/1: Target: 30 employers engage in 1st interview
- 10/1: Target: 30 employers engage in 2nd interview
- 11/15: Target: 50 ex-offenders employed

Ensuring Successful Re-entry into the Community

When ex-offenders were hired, the work of these leaders did not stop. They knew that job retention was as important as job placement to their "difference made" performance measures. These leaders kept engaged with the employers and the ex-offenders to offer any support needed post-hiring so both groups would have resources, if necessary.

They soon discovered that there were two unforeseen barriers to the ex-offenders keeping their jobs. First was the ability to get to and from their place of work. Most of these ex-offenders relied on public transportation or their family networks for rides, which left them dependent on other people's schedules. Second, these ex-offenders were required to meet with their parole officers during the workday. Both transportation barriers and parole requirements created an issue of unreliability. As much as the ex-offenders wanted to engage fully in their work, they were coming to work late or having to leave early because of transportation needs. Additionally, they were being pulled off the job in order to meet the demands of their parole officer.

Given that complex public problems inherently cross boundaries and connect to multiple systems, it was not a surprise that unplanned obstacles would come to light. The task then became how to surmount them.

To lower the transportation barrier, these leaders worked with their Department of Motor Vehicles to improve access to securing driver's licenses and state identifications for ex-offenders. They also identified transportation options such as expanding public transportation and car donation programs. To minimize time off work to meet parole requirements, they worked with the Department of Corrections to have parole meetings scheduled after work hours or on weekends. The modification to the Department of Corrections' administrative policy worked for the employers and the ex-offenders while honoring the state's requirements for the ex-offenders' release.

Let me share a final thought about the work of these leaders. Their employment strategy connected with their transportation strategy as well as their policy strategy. They also implemented a health strategy and a community strategy. All the strategies were needed for these leaders to make progress on their result: *All adult offenders in their county successfully reintegrate into the community.* Although these leaders did not hit their target of 50 ex-offenders successfully obtaining and retaining their jobs, they came close. Importantly, they did engage employers, service providers, and government agencies in this comprehensive strategy. The considerable success they did achieve (45 ex-offenders retained employment) allowed these leaders to focus on the next cohort of ex-offenders to be released and determine how best to engage in quality improvement, set new targets, and go to scale with their work.

This story illustrates how leaders use the power of a results action plan to engage the various systems that impact the results work. It also shows how they developed a set of robust strategies guiding how they made their aligned contributions. In addition, it shows the power of targets, timelines, and performance measures to create the urgency to do their work. Finally, it shows that the work does not end when a target is achieved (or comes close). It shows that leaders apply their new learning and insights from their initial work to then set a new target connected to a timeline. This continued focus on the incremental progress towards population-level results is the basis for "scope"(a variety of leaders working together to become more efficient in their work) and "scale" (leaders working together to impact larger numbers of people).

The story of these results leaders working collaboratively to reduce recidivism gives us the framework for the final set of relationships that must be understood to make progress toward a result: the relationships within and across systems that must interconnect to achieve scope and scale.

Working Toward Scope and Scale

Collaborative results work is ultimately defined by what leaders produce together in the world. All the work needed to create a results action plan—engaging the needed partners and stakeholders, defining the baseline and targets of the work, mapping their work to a timeline—is designed to produce measurable results in the world in a way that is more effective and efficient than doing the work in a siloed or fragmented manner.

As the opening story reveals, results leaders choose to work in such a comprehensive and multifaceted manner because it allows them to respond more holistically to the complex public problem at hand. They want to achieve success in their own work, and they realize that together they have capacity to go "broad" and "deep" in the results work in a way they cannot achieve by themselves. After all, this isn't about any individual leader's success in his or her silo: It is about the result in the center. The work is about going to **scope** and **scale**.

Going to Scope

Results action plans are designed to go "broad" in the work—in other words, to engage a variety of stakeholders across sectors who are ready to work together to produce a desired result in **one measurement cycle** (defined by the target set to a timeline). In developing the scope of the work,[2] results leaders seek to create the greater efficiencies that are formed by engaging with multiple stakeholders and partners.

Scope is about achieving more impact because of *who* becomes involved, not *how many* become involved. For results leaders, creating "actionable" scope means that any group of stakeholders who hold themselves in High Action and High Alignment can move into action together. As the work progresses (and strategies are further defined or quality improvement measures are implemented) additional stakeholders are recruited to contribute to the defined scope of the strategy.

For each results collaborative, what scope means, what is deemed "comprehensive" or appropriate, depends on multiple factors:

- The interests of the communities;
- The priorities of the partners and stakeholders;
- The desired results; and
- The existing capacities of the individuals, organizations, and communities involved.

Usually, the group selects a target and the time frame in which they intend to achieve it, and then determines a scope of work that can be accomplished within those parameters. (Remember, targets pose the question, "Where do we want to be?") The scope takes into account conditions on the ground in the targeted communities, the priorities of the partners and stakeholders, the desired results, who is or can be engaged now, and the capacity of the partners in the working group. In other words, scope is directly related to the cumulative efforts and aligned contributions of stakeholders and partners for a stated indicator or performance measure.

Defining an appropriate scope to generate meaningful results can be a challenge given the urgency of the work at hand and the need for the individuals involved to master the tools of results work: putting results at the center, reaching work group readiness, and learning to work in shared accountability. We must rise to that challenge.

Going to Scale

With a focus always towards the next target, the next timeline, and the next measurement cycle, results leaders generally work to

---

Scope refers to the conditions of the targeted communities, the priorities of the partners and stakeholders, the desired results, and the existing capacity of the partners involved. It means engaging a variety of stakeholders across sectors to work together to produce a desired result in **one measurement cycle** defined by the target set to a timeline.

affect more people through the repeated execution of their strategies. Results action plans are designed to go "deep" into the work—in other words, to impact larger numbers of people and, ultimately, the entire targeted population. This is known as *creating economies of scale,* or doing things more efficiently by increasing the size and/or speed of the work. For example, once a program had been designed and implemented to have cars donated to ex-offenders in the Marion County community, it could be applied to other counties or cities in Indiana. Those other venues won't have to reinvent the wheel because Marion has already identified the root problem and one workable fix. Going deeper comes about through the learnings gleaned from first going to scope. Results leaders start the work of going to **scale** as they create the next target for their shared work.

For each results collaborative, determining an appropriate scale depends on context. What extent must the work reach to achieve its greatest impact? Scaling up from the small to the large is often accompanied by an evolution from simplicity to complexity while maintaining basic elements or building blocks of the system unchanged or conserved.[3]

In the context of working to targets and timelines, leaders focus on iterative cycles that step up the scale of the work, while engaging in continuous improvement. For example, in Marion County, the leaders working to bring employers into their strategy quickly realized they had to increase their outreach with so few positive responses to their requests. In addition, they realized they would need to work closely with leaders to prepare the ex-offenders for their interviews. They provided feedback and other information to their colleagues about the kinds of skills employers were looking for. This allowed the education and training group to incorporate the appropriate job training and education to match the employers' needs. With each cycle of work—setting a target with timeline, doing the collaborative work to achieve the target to the timeline, engaging in a quality improvement process, and setting new targets and timeframes—the group increases its capacity for going to scale.

As results leaders work to scope and scale, they start to see the interconnected and interdependent nature of their strategies. They see how one strategy impacts or influences another. They notice that the people affected by one strategy are the same people affected by others. In the Marion County example, results leaders used their work in their employment strategy to connect education, employment, transportation, and policy sectors to make progress towards their result.

> **Scale** refers to the extent the work must reach in order to achieve greatest impact. It is the bonus that is achieved by going from small to large. Economies of scale are the efficiencies created by increasing the size and speed of the work.

To achieve scope and scale for a population-level result, then, requires results leaders to execute at a systems level by:

- Developing and executing a set of robust, interconnected population-level strategies;
- Leveraging shared performance measures in order to impact larger numbers of people; and
- Implementing rapid-cycle quality improvement processes along the way.

Executing at a Systems Level

In the most basic sense, a system is any group of interacting, interrelated, and/or interdependent parts that make up a whole. A toaster, for example, is a system made up of interacting, interrelated and interdependent parts all designed to produce toast. A school system has a host of interacting, interrelated, and interdependent parts designed to produce results for students, just as a health care system has for patients. The same is true for any system that results leaders are interested in addressing.

As I often tell the leaders I work with, everything is currently working as it is designed to and "all systems are designed perfectly to produce the results they are currently producing."[4] This largely invisible factor becomes obvious if you pause to consider it: The system, (e.g., the way the various parts of a system engage with each other and the way the collaborators execute their work) is currently producing today's results. To achieve a different result, the current system must change.

Therefore, as results leaders first develop their overarching strategies and then execute their shared results action plan, they have to engage in systems thinking. A systems-thinking approach supports the development and implementation of a set of interacting, interrelated, and/or interdependent strategies that influence the systems currently in place.

Systems thinking means that results leaders use the work of the population-level result to see:

- Interactions between parts, not the parts themselves;
- Reoccurring patterns rather than just individual events; and
- Change over time.

Chapter 7: "Us in the World"—Working Toward Scope and Scale

The "Systems Iceberg" frame can help leaders move from the events that are there for all to see to the structures that are below the surface. This metaphor supports results leaders to:

- Notice and interpret day-to-day events as data about larger systems dynamics;
- See events as part of larger patterns of behavior or trends and explore why these trends are taking place; and
- Examine the structures that are in place that may be influencing or shaping the behaviors or trends.

Figure 7.2 depicts this frame.[5]

Figure 7.2 **The Systems Iceberg Frame: Events, Patterns, Structures**

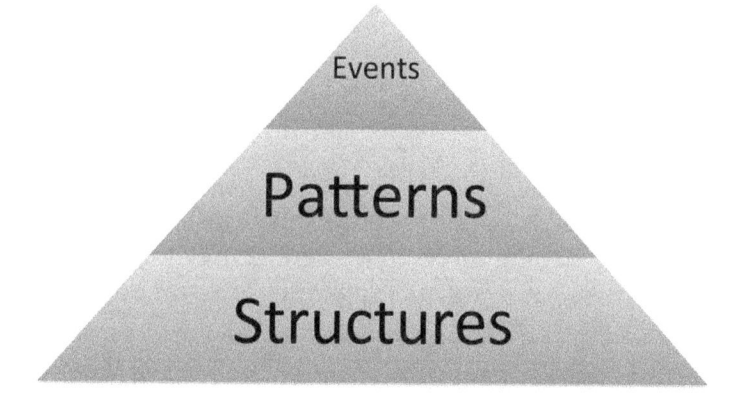

As events unfold, leaders have an opportunity to connect their work to larger systems work by noticing the patterns or trends those events reveal and examining the root causes (see Chapter 3) of those patterns. They can also identify the structures in place, which can include the physical location and/or allocation of resources; the requirements and regulations that organizations currently operate under; the data systems that influence decisions; the incentives that influence staff behavior; and the policies and rules with which communities must comply.

Working at the structures level of the Systems Iceberg requires leaders to explore the interactions and interdependencies among and between systems partners. As the story about recidivism illustrates, understanding the norms, regulations, and operations of a system's components, and understanding the interdependencies between those components, may help create leverage points that can shift the way an entire system operates.

Leaders who engage in systems thinking focus on "leverage points." These are places within a complex system where a small shift in one thing can produce big changes in everything.[6] I sometimes describe it as rotating a small wheel in a watch that in turn rotates the larger wheels in the watch. An example which we'll explore in some detail below, drawn again from Marion County, would be a single high-level corrections department policy change that permitted parolees to meet their parole officers at pre-determined after-hours meetings to avoid missing too much work.

In identifying potential points for leverage, systems leaders explore:

- Existing norms and behaviors of systems partners;
- Existing or current resources, regulations, and operations of systems partners; and
- Feedback loops and "relational" dynamics between system partners.

Executing at a systems level, therefore, depends on the partners and the focus of the results work. At different points in the timeline it might look like:

- Working across multiple sectors that are engaged together towards a common result (i.e., education, housing, health, and community sectors working towards an academic result);
- Working with multiple "elements" within one sector: schools, pre-schools, before- and after-school programs as part of the education sector, for example; and
- Working within one organization and its multiple parts, say, a high school with its components—classrooms, counseling, administration, etc.—all working toward academic success.

Regardless of focus, most system-change endeavors will address the underlying structures and supporting mechanisms that operate within that system (which is why Structures is depicted as the base of the Systems Iceberg). These mechanisms might include policies, routines, relationships, resources, power structures, and values. To execute at a systems level, results leaders focus on the leverage points to influence those structures that determine behaviors and decision-making.

An example addressing both the underlying structures and supporting mechanisms of a system can be seen in the earlier story about the work of results leaders engaged in with ex-offender reentry. As we saw, the result in the center for these leaders was the statement, "all

Chapter 7: "Us in the World"—Working Toward Scope and Scale

ex-offenders successfully re-enter into their community." This meant that these leaders worked with the education, employment, health, housing, and policy sectors to ensure that ex-offenders would not return to the prison system.

In executing their strategies, they discovered that due to technical rule violations, many ex-offenders were back in the court system and some risked ending up back in prison. In examining both the boundary and interrelationship between the parole, transportation, and employment systems, they identified minor changes to the system that could create a reduction of technical rule violations and allow more ex-offenders to keep their new jobs. This systems change contributed to the overall decrease in recidivism.

What changed? The leaders in the employment group discovered that the parole officers working for the Department of Corrections were asking the ex-offenders to meet with them during work hours. This left the ex-offenders with only two choices: either miss work regularly to meet the parole officer or miss the parole meeting to go to work. This reinforcing behavior between two of the elements of this system was creating worse outcomes for ex-offenders.

In addition, these leaders discovered that the existing rules for parole violation—rules originally designed to support the community in feeling safe and to help guide the ex-offender—were, in fact, sending ex-offenders back to prison for technical rule violations, such as not completing drug treatment, not holding a job, and missing appointments with parole staff. In balancing the interdependencies between community needs and ex-offender accountability, this group worked to change the rules for these types of violations so the ex-offenders could avoid going back to prison (and instead get other supports) and the community could feel safe.

For these leaders working towards reducing ex-offender recidivism, and any leaders working to address complex public problems, leveraging system change is a priority. These leaders recognize that systems are resistant to change. They have learned that the first leverage points to move toward systems change are often those external elements that generate pressure. If parole officers can increase compliance by accommodating ex-offenders in terms of *when* to meet, what other impediments might be embedded in the system that actually encourage the negative result of recidivism?

Executing at a systems level—by using leverage points, exploring the interactions and interdependencies among partners, and using the Systems Iceberg Frame to identify structures that operate below the surface—allows results leaders to move toward scope and scale

> See Systems Leverage Points in the apps/tools section at the end of this chapter. It is offered to help results leaders identify points of leverage in their results work. When you try to identify and use leverage points to create systems change, you can expect resistance by partners who are impacted by the change. This tool will help.

249

by developing robust strategies and identifying shared performance measures.

Interconnected Strategies: The Roadmap to Scope and Scale

Achieving the scope that makes a difference is usually a case of strategically integrating potentially synergistic programs and activities. That's a mouthful, so let's break it down.

By "synergistic programs and activities," I mean the structures that comprise the systems level in this work. By calling for "strategically integrating" those structures, I'm saying that we must intentionally connect the dots between various efforts capable of addressing the root causes of a problem. This is more likely to create a lasting solution than simply doing various, different, unrelated things and hoping they add up.

The ability of results leaders to create interconnected strategies—to connect the dots—is the basis for executing collaboratively toward results. The ability to execute collaboratively, in the shape of programs and activities, is where synergy comes from. To achieve a scope that makes a difference, results leaders need strategies that fuel synergies. For example, leaders who are interested in the result of school readiness know there will need to be a set of robust, interconnected strategies that focus on early learning, teacher development, health and wellness, parent engagement, and community safety. When these strategies are directly impacting the children and families, larger systems, and communities, in an aligned and complementary manner, there is greater likelihood of making progress at scope and scale. The work of ThinkSmall provides an example.

ThinkSmall is a wonderful organization located in Minneapolis. They hold as their result in the center that "all children in Minnesota enter school ready to learn." ThinkSmall focuses its efforts primarily in the seven counties in and around Minneapolis. Their contribution to the result is to create high-quality learning centers where they offer evidence-based curriculum designed for early learners, and provide professional development to support teachers. They realize that there are many factors that impact young children's kindergarten readiness, such as transportation, health, and community. As such, they are working with their partners to create a set of robust, integrated strategies that address systems and structures affecting those factors, while they focus their work on what happens in early learning centers.

Strategies play a central role in the work toward both scope and scale. In Chapter 2, we learned that strategies can be considered the "game play" that allows leaders to work together in High Action and High Alignment. Strategies reflect the best thinking from results leaders

Chapter 7: "Us in the World"—Working Toward Scope and Scale

on what it takes to move an indicator in the desired direction. As Chapter 3 explored, they are developed by leaders who first engage in a root cause/factor analysis, identify the key priority factors they believe are impacting the way things currently are, and then develop a set of coordinated actions to make progress on those high-priority factors. These coordinated actions—or strategies—are founded in the theory of change leaders hold regarding their population-level work: e.g., "If strategies A, B, and C are implemented, then there will be progress toward the indicator."

Once strategies have been identified and implemented, it becomes of importance to capture and leverage the interconnections that may exist. This can be supported by:

1. Prescribing strategy work plans to insure the integration and execution of the work; and
2. Placing these strategies to a shared matrix and timeline.

This is an iterative sequence that generates an ability to work within a system, in coordinated efforts that put results in the center across programs and stakeholders.

A strategy is simply "the how." The plan, means, method, or series of maneuvers for obtaining a specific goal or result. Strategies are specific and actionable. In the context of results work, strategies require identifying what works to improve the condition of people's wellbeing—what actions have the power to improve the indicator and achieve set targets. Results leaders develop strategies by identifying the priority factors that are increasing and/or decreasing the indicator trend line.

Strategy Work Plans

Once strategies are identified, results leaders move into execution by creating *strategy work plans*. These plans identify the targets, the actions, the specific contributions, and the accountability needed for execution. You may find the strategy work plan template shown in Table 7.2 and filled-in example in Table 7.3 helpful. You will also find a template in the apps/tools section.

To fully create a strategy work plan, it is important to be explicit about the work. Specifically, define the what, who, how, when, and with whom (partners) for initial strategies. Work plans should have explicit next steps that move some tasks to accomplishment within 30 to 45 days. Content should reflect initial factor analysis. Typically some but not all partners will be engaged. Establishing initial performance measure targets helps place the strategy work on an overt timeline.

Part 2: Executing to Scope and Scale

Table 7.2 **Strategy Work Plan Template**

Strategy Name:

Strategy Result:
Key members of strategy:

Activities	Who	When	Impact	Performance Measures

Table 7.3 **Strategy Work Plan Example: Early Care Education**

Strategy Work Plan: Early Care Education
Increase the # and % of entering kindergartners who participate in high quality early care and education.
Result: Children in the school footprint will meet their developmental milestones. *Strategy members:*

Activities	Who	When	Impact	Performance Measures
Obtain data from school footprint—generally as well as specifically from programs and providers (high quality early care, early care, home based, licensed and unlicensed, clinical settings, parenting education, etc.)—DATA DEVELOPMENT • How many children age 0-5 are in the footprint? • How many children are engaged with/in footprint programs and providers? • How many of these children are being assessed on their developmental milestones?		ASAP	Provide measurable baseline and asset map.	Quality and quantity of data, written report

continued

Table 7.3 *continued*

Activities	Who	When	Impact	Performance Measures
DATA DEVELOPMENT *continued* • How are these assessments or screenings being administered, by whom, with what tool, and how frequently? • What are the aggregate results of these assessments/screenings? Is it possible to identify any unmet milestones at a population level?				
Convene meeting of school footprint high quality early care, early care, home-based, licensed and unlicensed, clinical, etc. and parenting education providers—everyone: • Share data and identify opportunities to improve and align practices re: developmental milestone screenings • http://www.acf.hhs.gov/programs/ecd/child-health-development/watch-me-thrive		October and ongoing	Increase in the number of providers assessing developmental milestones and sharing info with parents	# of providers who measure developmental milestones # of providers who align practices regarding developmental milestone screening
Open an additional Public Pre-K classroom in the school footprint • Identify the partner • Write the proposal		Fall 2017	Increase in the number of children in Pre-K	# of students
Increase the number of families/children receiving in-home supports. • Identify in-home supports, create info packet for providers • Attend provider meetings to increase outreach and thus number of referrals (See strategy #1)		ASAP	Increase the number of families/children receiving in-home supports	# of referrals from families

Table 7.3 shows an example of a strategy work plan developed by a group interested in the population-level result that "all children in their school system enter kindergarten ready to learn." One important strategy was one that focused on children participating in high quality early learning.

Strategy Matrix and Timelines

Managing the complexity of multiple strategies requires knowing and leveraging the work of all strategies. (That is how the "strategically integrating potentially synergistic programs and activities" discussed earlier gets done.)

As results leaders execute their strategies, they develop a matrix that can capture the key elements of the strategies. The team interested in kindergarten readiness (from the strategy work plan example in Table 7.3) identified four overarching strategies they believed, if executed, would support the work of local partners to meet grade-level reading targets. These strategies were:

1. Integrate community supports;
2. Ensure high-quality early care and education;
3. Use family engagement; and
4. Support families' basic needs.

They created a strategy matrix (Table 7.4) and a timeline (Table 7.5) that allowed them to track progress over time to ensure that they were executing their work towards their target mapped to a timeline.

Based on the performance measures for these strategies, the kindergarten-readiness team leaders could create a shared timeline that would allow them to track progress, share data, leverage resources and relationships, and create accountability for their work.

The documented strategy work plans, accompanied by a matrix and timeline for each and taken in sum, create an overarching strategy that integrates everyone's execution for impact on the overall target.

This concludes our examination of executing at a systems level—specifically, the use of strategies, work plans, matrices, and timelines as a method by which results leaders move toward scope and scale. However, it is impossible to judge strategies without metrics; thus, our discussion moves to shared performance measures.

> You will find the Strategy Matrix and Strategy Template in the apps/tools section at the end of this chapter. They are offered to help results leaders develop effective strategy work plans.

Chapter 7: "Us in the World"—Working Toward Scope and Scale

Table 7.4 **Strategy Matrix**

Strategy Matrix				
Strategy:	Integrate Community Supports	High quality early care and education	Family Engagement	Support families basic needs
Strategy Result:				
Strategy Target:				
Strategy Performance Measure:				
Strategy Partners:				

Table 7.5 **Strategy Timeline**

Strategy Timeline				
Strategy Workgroup	Summer Targets: Performance Measures and Milestones	September Targets: Performance Measures and Milestones	October Targets: Performance Measures and Milestones	Winter/Spring Targets: Performance Measures and Milestones
Integrate Community Supports				
Quality Care and Education				
Support/Engage Families				
Basic Needs				

Part 2: Executing to Scope and Scale

Shared Performance Measures: The Pathway to Scope and Scale

Recall the "Results in the Center" frame from Chapter 2: Its premise is that placing a result in the center allows multiple stakeholders, even those with very different perspectives, to join in making progress toward a population-level result. The Results in the Center diagram (page 30) allows leaders to consider key questions:

- Who can contribute?
- What is their contribution?
- What strategy will leverage that contribution?

The visual representation of the Theory of Aligned Contributions (see Figure 2.1, page 30) supports a group of leaders to move toward population-level results and helps individuals see their contribution to that result. The work of alignment starts when each partner noted in the Results in the Center frame can identify a quantifiable number of defined individuals (such as "children and families in Indianapolis") impacted by their contribution. These numbers, when added together, create a contribution to the scope and scale of the work.

> A **shared performance measure** is designed to gauge the effectiveness of aligned actions taken by two or more stakeholders and partners. Results leaders monitor performance data to assess the effectiveness of strategies, programs, and individual actions—what is working, what needs to be improved, and what needs to be changed.

Leaders must engage in the difficult work that makes these aligned contributions possible. As highlighted in Chapter 3, it is by taking the time to do the data analysis that aligning actions toward a result becomes possible. The data—through the hard work of population-level analysis, root cause analysis, and defining baseline and target measures—turns the Results Playbook into something that compels leaders to move into action. It is the measures—specifically performance measures—that make the alignment actionable.

Performance measures, as you recall, allow results leaders to answer a set of three questions—How much are we doing? How well are we doing it? What difference are we making?—in assessing their work at both a program and strategy level. *Although leaders make separate contributions, they all hold themselves accountable for all strategies identified in their results action plan.* One way accountability is demonstrated is when leaders identify and work towards their **shared performance measures.** This is a common "how well" or "difference made" measure between two or more partners or stakeholders. For our kindergarten-readiness group, such a shared measure might be reaching goals in the number and percentage of providers administering the same assessment measures at the same intervals throughout the identified area.

Performance measures are the most powerful way to create aligned action among partners and stakeholders. For example, when partners

Chapter 7: "Us in the World"—Working Toward Scope and Scale

and stakeholders identify their shared performance measures, this creates an incentive for them to share data, and generate greater understanding and transparency as to how they engage with their customers; how best they can support each other,; and how best to improve their interactions. Take the leaders working on the various strategies impacting the ex-offenders. There may be several partners working to increase skills that transfer directly to employment. They have worked on different programs—education skills, technical skills, interview skills—that may share the same "how well" measure of job interview and the same "difference made" measure of job placement and retention. A success for one is a success for all, and a motivating one at that.

Once partners and stakeholders are identified, contributions named, strategies declared, and shared performance measures highlighted, it is important to put the information on a mapping template. Mapping shared performance measures to strategies and partners is a necessary process for creating aligned action in order to move to scope and scale. Table 7.6 offers a template for this mapping.

> See Shared Performance Measure Worksheet in the apps/tools section at the end of this chapter to help results leaders identify their shared performance measures with other partners.

Through this mapping process, results leaders are able to identify partners and actions that can help create scope and scale toward that result in the center. It makes clear how they and others can contribute to a population-level result. With the actions mapped, leaders may select appropriate performance measures to track progress and shared performance measures that will leverage the work toward both scope and scale.

Table 7.6 **Template for Mapping to Shared Performance Measures**

Who can contribute?	What is their contribution? Their performance measures?	What strategy will leverage their contribution?	What performance measures can be shared to create aligned action?

Part 2: Executing to Scope and Scale

Scenario: "All Babies Born Healthy"

Consider, for example, a group of leaders who share a concern for the health of newborn babies in their region. They join together to work toward a result that "all babies are born healthy." They select infant mortality as one of their indicators. Through a factor analysis of the situation in their community, they realize that there are a few key factors contributing to infant mortality. These include high rates of teen pregnancy; chronic health issues such as diabetes, lack of proper nutrition, smoking, alcohol use; and lack of stable and safe housing. As a result of this factor analysis, the group creates a set of overarching strategies that flow directly from their findings. They choose to create a teen pregnancy strategy, a smoking cessation strategy, a housing strategy, and a nutrition strategy.

Each strategy in this set has its own set of performance measures and targets. For example, the smoking cessation strategy could target reducing smoking by 50% in the first trimester of pregnancy. Each partner who contributes to these strategies—government-led quit line services, tobacco replacement therapy, home health care providers, outreach to expectant mothers and pediatricians who provide health screens—will have its own set of performance measures.

Together, these partners also have a set of shared performance measures that all contribute to the target of a 50% reduction in smoking within the first trimester of pregnancy. For example, pediatricians and community outreach workers have a shared performance measure of expectant mothers obtaining information about the risks of smoking and numbers enrolling in smoking cessation programs or availing themselves of quit line services. As these partners work together to hit their targets for this smoking cessation strategy, they go to scale by reaching for higher numbers at both a program and strategy level, learning through each iteration so they may adjust their strategies according to feedback. Working with shared performance measures becomes the pathway for partners to go to scale with their work. Table 7.7 shows a strategy matrix that allows this group to see how their strategies integrate to achieve the targeted result.

Part of the strategy implementation includes the partners sharing performance measures (for example, the number and percentage of women participating and completing a smoking cessation program and/or using a quit line service and the percentage and number of women who stop smoking). Partners also agree on how to collect and use the performance information to align their efforts; how to ensure ongoing quality improvement for effectiveness in service delivery to

Chapter 7: "Us in the World"—Working Toward Scope and Scale

Table 7.7 **Strategy Example: Smoking Cessation**

Strategy: Smoking Cessation			
Who can contribute?	What is their contribution?	What strategy will leverage their contribution?	What performance measures can be shared to create aligned action?
Pediatricians and health providers	Health screenings, education, linking to support programs	Smoking cessation education	• How much: # of mothers engaged in smoking cessation program and/or use a quit line service • How well: # of mothers complete smoking cessation program and/or engage in the quit line services • Difference made: % and # of mothers who stop smoking
Department of Health Services	Quit Line Services	Smoking cessation education	• How much: # of mothers engaged in smoking cessation program and/or using a quit line service • How well: # of mothers complete smoking cessation program and/or engage in the quit line services • Difference made: % and # of mothers who stop smoking
Community Health Organizations	Outreach, education, enrollment in health programs	Smoking cessation education	• How much: # of mothers engaged in smoking cessation program and/or use a quit line service • How well: # of mothers complete smoking cessation program and/or engage in the quit line services • Difference made: % and # of mothers who stop smoking
Health clinics	Tobacco replacement therapy, support groups	Smoking cessation	• Difference made: % and # of mothers who stop smoking

259

program populations; and how to track progress effecting change in the whole population.

Results leaders are using the data from performance measures, reach, and impact of strategies to answer the question: *Are these set of strategies likely to achieve the set targets? If not, what is the gap that needs to be addressed?* What needs to change? The answers to these questions are the basis on which leaders engage in quality improvement work, moving quickly to identify the changes they must implement in order to hit their targets.

It should now be clear how shared performance measures, documented and shared via strategy work plans, matrices, and timelines, help results leaders sustain progress toward a population-level result—and yes—even "achieve the scope that makes a difference by strategically integrating potentially synergistic programs and activities."

Rapid-cycle Quality Improvement: Making Adjustments as You Go!

Before closing this discussion of how leaders, partners, and stakeholders work together, it's worth noting that being agile is key. Results leaders must pay attention to the data they have at hand—specifically the performance measures they are using to assess the impact of their work. As we've seen, performance measure data is used at a strategy level, a program level, an activity level, and a role level. The discipline of performance measure data allows results leaders to know if they are on track. If the data is not trending positively, leaders may not know if this is because the strategies are the wrong ones; those strategies are ill-executed; if there may be deeper systems dynamics at play; or if there are other, perhaps overlooked, barriers that need to be explored.

Executing toward a population-level result is often experimental and steeped in learning and reflecting. Rapid-cycle quality improvement processes are an important part of a results leader's ability to effectively engage in results work. The discipline imposed by the targets, timelines, and performance measures allows results leaders to be learners and make changes as they go. With performance measures in place, they can evaluate their work over time, determine if targets are being met, and make course corrections where needed.

Mid-course corrections: As the work progresses, leaders use data to see if they are making the desired progress towards the targets established by the strategies and programs that they have developed and aligned. By establishing and monitoring data, leaders can track whether a strategy or program is achieving the intended results. Even more importantly, good data guides leaders in how to change or improve strategies and/or programs to get better results. These course corrections, which can be painful as they require acknowledging failure, are a critical part of the process. They lead to more rapid and agile change in strategies and programs to increase their efficacy.

Program-level course correction: Some key questions results leaders can ask to evaluate what might need to change about a program include:

- **Population served:** Are we reaching those most in need, and/or with the greatest disparities?
- **Program practices:** Are our practices producing the expected level of "difference made" results?
- **Program changes:** What can we do to strengthen, align, or adjust programs so they get better results?
- **Course correction assessments:** Have our program changes worked as intended to get better results? Are there additional changes we need to make?
- **Cost effectiveness:** What is the return on investment of the work?
- **Capacity and competence:** Do we have the right set of skills to do the work effectively?
- **Targets:** Are our targets too ambitious or not ambitious enough—if so why and what has happened to lead to this assessment?
- **Scope and scale:** Are there ways to leverage this program and take the work to scope and scale so it can have even more impact?

Population-level course correction: Course corrections also can be based on an intentional evaluation of a program's impact on meeting the population-level result. *There should be a correlation (even if not statistically verifiable) between achievement of a program's performance measure targets and population-level indicators.* For example, if leaders find that they are meeting all of their performance measure targets but there is no impact on the population-level indicator, it might be time to examine the various elements of the Results Playbook, including the work of the programs and/or overarching strategies. To illustrate further,

Dreama Gentry and Partners for Education (see Chapter 6) held chronic absenteeism as one indicator of academic success in middle and high schools. They developed a set of strategies—primarily focused on student accountability, family engagement, and school culture—that they felt would reduce the rates of chronic absenteeism in the counties in which they were working. After a few months of implementing these strategies they were not seeing the rate of absenteeism drop in a significant way. They went back and examined their assumptions around absenteeism and were willing to test them. They realized they needed to include strategies that addressed healthcare (opioid addition was impacting their communities), homelessness and unstable housing, and transportation. This population-level course correction allowed the team to bring in new partners and create new strategies in order to make progress toward their result.

Some questions to ask in this assessment process include:

- Is this the right program-level work to be doing in order to make a contribution to overarching strategies we embraced to get to the population-level result?
- Have we selected the right overarching strategies to make progress on the population-level indicator?
- Have we selected the right indicators to measure the quantity, quality, and impact of our program work? Are we missing important indicators that might help us understand why we are not seeing correlation between the program and the population-level result?

Rapid-cycle quality improvement (RCQI): Having used data and performance measures to assess the need for course correction, results leaders will reveal their orientation towards action by igniting a rapid-cycle quality improvement process. These leaders know that they will have to learn as they go—that no matter how well they plan and execute, their efforts will not go completely as planned. Instead of floundering, results leaders engage in rapid-cycle quality improvement to quickly learn what has worked and what hasn't. Engaging in improvement cycles helps leaders identify challenges, solve problems, improve practices, and create productive environments for new ways of work. Each attempt to implement an innovation leads to new learning—whether or not the outcome is completely successful.

Chapter 7: "Us in the World"—Working Toward Scope and Scale

The foundation of improvement cycles is the **Plan, Do, Study, Act Cycle** or **PDSA Cycle**. PDSA is a process derived from industrial quality control research.[7] The PDSA Cycle is used to test small incremental improvements that can lead to significant progress and change by helping define and refine new innovations and ways of working. Results leaders use the PDSA cycles as part of their work to achieve given performance measures.

PDSA Cycle:

PLAN phase: Identifying barriers or challenges and developing processes to move programs forward.

DO phase: Using those processes as intended.

STUDY phase: Monitoring the process. How did it go? What does the data say?

ACT phase: Applying what was learned to improve the process and outcomes as well as the next cycle.

PDSA Used to Address Racial and Ethnic Disparities

For example, one team I worked with was addressing the issue of racial and ethnic disparities that exist in their juvenile justice system. Their programmatic focus was to decrease re-offense rates for youth of color.

One factor the team sought to address was the fact that community resources were not being accessed by or made available to youth of color and their families. These resources were there either to support these youth and their families so as to avoid entering into the juvenile justice system or were court-ordered as part of a sentencing requirement.

One strategy this team implemented was to hire a case manager whose sole focus was to work with this issue regarding access to community resources by youth and their families. However, they discovered that just hiring a case manager was not enough. They chose to implement a PDSA to test ways to increase referrals from the court and raise awareness of the work of the new case manager. Table 7.8 shows their PDSA worksheet.

> See PDSA worksheet in the apps/tools section at the end of this chapter. It is offered to help results leaders to engage in rapid-cycle quality improvement. A blank template for this PDSA Worksheet is also included.

Part 2: Executing to Scope and Scale

Table 7.8 **PSDA Worksheet**

CASE MANAGER PDSA WORKSHEET

BACKGROUND:

The lack of number of referrals to this new grant-funded position, Racial and Ethnic Fairness (REF) Case Manager led us to this project. This project is relevant because the role of the REF Case Manager is to work with youth of color (YoC) and their families to help them access the community resources that they need or are court-ordered to receive and to make it to upcoming court hearings as scheduled.

If YoC access the services that they need or are court-ordered to seek such services as chemical dependency evaluations, outpatient therapy, etc, they are more likely to increase their stability and decrease the likelihood of having further justice system involvement. They will also not be in violation of a court order and at risk of going deeper into the justice system. In addition, if they attend their scheduled court hearing, they will not be charged with failure to appear and have a warrant out for their arrest, which also deepens their involvement in the justice system.

There is no baseline data for this position as it is a new position in County A. However, we do have baseline data for a similar position in County B. County B's FTA (failure to appear) rate is 5.6% and re-offense rate is 7.7%. County A's FTA rate is 7.9% and re-offense rate is 16.1% (for the first half of 2016).

Round 1

PLAN:

Aim/Objective Statement for this cycle:
What do you hope to learn? What are you trying to improve (aim), by how much (goal) and by when (timeframe)?

- We are trying to increase the caseload for the REF Case Manager by 100%—from 5 cases to 10.
- We are trying to increase the number of court reminder calls for those on the docket from 0 to 100% - from 0 calls per week to approximately 50; however, we

Used and adapted with permission of source

need a court order authorizing us to have access to the docket in order to begin making reminder calls based on who is on the docket.

Specific questions to address in this cycle:

1. How do we increase referrals from the court?
2. How do we increase awareness of the REF case manager position?

Predictions/Hypotheses (What do you think will happen?)

- A clearly outlined referral form will help referral sources understand whom the REF case manager can serve.

- A meeting tour to share the referral form and do a face-to-face meet and greet with REF Case Manager will help people know the resource is available and put a face with a name.

- Email reminders to the county coordinator on a routine basis should increase the likelihood of the court order getting completed.

Plan for change/test/intervention

- Who (target population): Juvenile justice youth and their referral sources
- What (change/test): Disseminate referral form
- When (dates of test): 3/20
- Where (location): Email and on-site at court house
- How (description of plan):

  1. REF Case Manager Supervisor and REF Case Manager will email out the approved referral form with a description of the services and set up face-to-face meetings

  2. REF Case Manager along with Supervisor or the agency's Diversion Case Manager will meet with all potential referral sources to discuss services and the referral process

  3. REF Case Manager will email the county coordinator regarding the court order needed and the status of the order on a weekly basis

Part 2: Executing to Scope and Scale

Measures
(What will you measure in order to meet your aims? How will know that a change is an improvement? Will you use outcome or process measures?)

Number of cases on REF Case Manager caseload and number of calls made to remind of upcoming court hearings.

Plan for <u>data collection</u>

- Who (will collect): Vice President
- What (measures): Caseload data and call data
- When (time period): 3/20-4/3
- Where (location): County A program area
- How (method): REF Case Manager Excel Spreadsheet

<u>DO</u>:
We observed that success and positive word of mouth is increasing awareness of the services available within the court system. The court system has witnessed youth, who historically would not have made it to court, attend court following reminder calls and a ride from the case manager. The court system has seen youth who have been struggling to complete court ordered CD evaluations, with the assistance of the REF Case Manager, schedule and attend those evaluation. Word of mouth is quickly spreading of these success stories and there is a reputation growing of how "great" this service is and how "helpful" the REF Case Manager is. As word of mouth has been increasing, we are seeing an increase in referrals. We have also witnessed some misconceptions of what the REF Case Manager can do and the timeline within which they can do it; therefore, in addition to educating people on how to make a referral, there will need to be ongoing communication about what is realistic and within what timeframes certain actions can be completed.

<u>STUDY</u>:
The caseload target was met: REF Case Manager caseload increased by 5 cases to a total of 10 cases.

However, court order still not completed so unable to do court docket reminder calls yet, so that number did not increase for the current level of 0.

- We have agreement from the State's Attorney's offices and the Judge involved.
- Judge on the juvenile court bench will draft a new court order to allow for the docket calls.
- That order will need to be reviewed by and signed by the presiding Circuit Court Judge.

100% increase to REF Case Manager Caseload. 0% increase to docket court reminder calls. 15 youth total served so far since start of grant.

ACT:

1. Need to continue to encourage court referrals for REF Case Manager but there are more juveniles who can be reached. Need to find alternate referral sources to maximize the time we have available to offer services. There is still free time available given that the court docket calls cannot be made yet.

2. Getting the new court order will be a process and we will need to vigilantly remind them we are in need of this on a weekly basis so that it doesn't fall off the radar.

3. There are juveniles within our internal agency services who are justice involved and who could benefit from the REF Case Manager's services and attention on a daily basis. Think about what we can do to offer services to these youth.

Next steps:

1. Vigilantly remind county coordinator and State's Attorney's office about the court order needed to do the docket court reminder calls.

2. Identify ways to educate internal service providers about the services available and ways to collaborate to meet the needs of the youth and their families to help them achieve successful outcomes. Bring this topic to the internal work group of agency services that work with justice involved youth and their families and include REF Case Management services in the next factor analysis exercise in that group.

Making adjustments as you go is simply what we do as we encounter changing conditions while en route to a destination. Within collaborative work cycles, we make corrections mid-course. We do this even at the program and population level if we judge our original destination has changed or that reaching our basic goal might require a different strategy. Rapid-cycle quality improvement, using the PDSA Cycle, keeps us from going too far in any direction before checking its validity.

Chapter 7 Summary

Our focus in this chapter has been the factors that, together, allow a group of leaders to execute to scope and scale: Executing at a systems level, using performance measures (both within a work group and across collaborating work groups), and making timely adjustments through rapid-cycle quality improvement. Without all of this, results leaders may find their days spent in "sound and fury, signifying nothing."[8]

Chapter 7 Applications: Tools and Worksheets

1. System Leverage Points 270
2. Strategy Work Plan Template 272
3. Strategy Matrix 273
4. Shared Performance Measure Worksheet 274
5. PDSA Worksheet 276

To download these apps, visit the book's online resources:
http://ChooseResultsBook.com/resources.html

Systems Leverage Points[1]
Raj Chawla

Areas for Leverage	Analysis to Create Focused Action
Norms and Practices	• What are the current assumptions, hypotheses and theories (i.e., their mental models) that partners use to explain why the problem exists? • What are the "stated" values guiding current programs, policies, and practices of current partners? How are they expressed in their theory of change? • What are the "lived" values of current partners? Is there a gap between "stated" and "lived"? If so, in what ways does this impact the systems change work? • What losses might a stakeholder have to endure if systems change is successful?
Resources	*Human Resources* • How will partners be expected to engage if the systems change effort is successful? Will their contribution change or be the same? Do partners have needed skillsets, practices, and knowledge to make their contribution if systems change is successful? • Are there "internal" champions for the change? Do they know how to support the change within their organization? What is needed to support system partners during this change? *Social Resources* • In what ways are relationships among the various stakeholders a contributing factor to the issue? • What aspects of the system might support or hinder relationship development? Are policies/procedures put into place to guide, support and encourage collaborative relationships and aligned contributions? *Economic Resources* • Will resource allocation need to change as a result of this systems initiative? Who might perceive this reallocation as a loss? What can be done to support that stakeholder or partner?
Policies, Rules and Regulations	• What existing policies, practices and procedures impede progress towards the shared result and/or contribute to the existing problem at hand? Which ones are rooted in maintaining legacy relationships

[1] Building on the work of Pennie, Nowell and Yang (2007). Putting the system back into systems change: a framework for understanding and changing organizational and community systems

	or long established "status quo"?
• What current policies, practices and procedures are incompatible with the new or planned change? Which ones might get in the way of the systems change effort succeeding?
• Is there a gap between the stated policy or policies and the implementation of the policy? If so, why?
• What policies are not in place but are needed to fully support the goals and philosophies of the results work?
• What current practices or procedures are incompatible with the new or planned strategies? Which ones might get in the way of the systems change effort succeeding?
• What daily routines will support and encourage the desired changes? Which ones might get in the way of this change being fully enacted?
Decision-Making	• What types of information and resources are most important to the system and who controls access to these resources?
• Where does the power and decision making of the system exist? Do these individuals support the systems change and results effort?
• How does the systems change effort challenge the existing power and decision-making structures? What resistance can be expected?
Relationships between system partners	• How do current systems partners and their actions (e.g., policies, attitudes, relationships) currently interact with each other?
• Where is the longest delay moving from one part of the system to the other? What do these characteristics mean for systems change effort? Is there a current feedback mechanism between system partners?
• Will strengthening, deleting or changing existing interdependent relationships accelerate the achievement of the desired change? What resistance can be expected with this change?
• Where can interdependencies within the system be leveraged strategically to promote sustainability of the desired change over time?
• In what ways do existing feedback processes support or impede the results work? What additional feedback mechanisms could be added to facilitate systems change (consider the tops, middles, frontline and/or customers in feedback loop)?

Part 2: Executing to Scope and Scale

Strategy Work Plan Template

Strategy Name:				
Strategy Result: *Key members of strategy:*				
Activities	Who	When	Impact	Performance Measures

Strategy Matrix

Strategy Matrix				
Strategy:	Strategy (Name)	Strategy (Name)	Strategy (Name)	Strategy (Name)
Strategy Result:				
Strategy Target:				
Strategy Performance Measure:				
Strategy Partners:				

Part 2: Executing to Scope and Scale

Shared Performance Measures Work Sheet
Synthesized by Jolie Bain Pillsbury

Note: Ideally, this is to be done with the stakeholders and partners working towards a shared result

1. Review your "result in the center chart" and your results action plan.
    a. Identify those partners (internal and external, current and desired) who are critical to achieving the results and where stronger aligned contributions are needed to achieve results more rapidly.
    b. For those desired critical partners hypothesize why they may not be engaged in the collaborative work already.

2. For the current partners and stakeholders identify the key performance measures that are used to "drive" their work. Note: If the performance measures have not been identified, hypothesize what they might be.
    a. Identify the aligned contributions for each partner
    b. Identify the performance measures that align with other partners
    c. Develop a work plan that will support the partners developing and sharing performance measures in the execution of their work
    d. Use timelines and targets to create shared execution of the work
    e. Make next steps as to who will do what, with whom, and by when.

3. For the critical partners and stakeholders who have not yet joined, hypothesize the performance measures that "drive their work.
    a. Hypothesize the aligned contributions for these partners
    b. Hypothesize the performance measures that align with other partners
    c. Create a plan to engage or enroll these critical partners and stakeholders
    d. Make next steps as to who will do what, with whom, and by when.

Shared Performance Measure Template

Who can contribute?	What is their contribution? Their performance measures	What strategy will leverage their contribution?	What performance measures can be shared to create aligned action?

Reflection:
As the work is being executed, pay attention to the challenges that may occur within and among the partners and stakeholders who share performance measures.
- Are these challenges systems related? Role related?
- What are the conversations that might be needed to help support high action and high alignment?
- Notice where there might be competition. Notice the pull towards fragmentation.
- In what ways can the results culture that has been created support this work?

Part 2: Executing to Scope and Scale

PDSA worksheet

BACKGROUND: What led you to start this project? Is this cycle a continuation of another cycle? Why is this topic relevant? Include any baseline data that has already been collected. Include relevant information from literature.

PLAN:
Aim/Objective Statement for this cycle: What do you hope to learn? What are you trying to improve (aim), by how much (goal) and by when (timeframe)?

Specific questions to address in this cycle:
1.
2.
3.

Predictions/Hypotheses (What do you think will happen?)

Plan for change/test/intervention
Who (target population):
What (change/test):
When (dates of test):
Where (location):
How (description of plan):

Measures (What will you measure in order to meet your aims? How will know that a change is an improvement? Will you use outcome or process measures?)

Plan for data collection
Who (will collect):
What (measures):
When (time period):
Where (location):
How (method):

PDSA worksheet

DO: Carry out the change/test. Collect data.
Note when completed, observations, problems encountered, and special circumstances. Include names and details.

STUDY: Summarize and Analyze data (quantitative and qualitative). Include charts, graphs.

ACT: Document/summarize what was learned. Did you meet your aims and goals? Did you answer the questions you wanted to address? List major conclusions from this cycle.
1.
2.
3.

Define next steps. Are you confident that you should expand size/scope of test or implement? What changes are needed for the next cycle?
1.
2.
3.

CALL TO ACTION

Choose Results

*Another world is not only possible,
she is on her way.
On a quiet day, I can hear her breathing.*

– Arundhati Roy

I've had the great fortune to work with a variety of passionate and courageous results leaders. These are leaders who are not afraid to call out what is happening in their community and urge partners and stakeholders to do something different, to do something revolutionary—to put results in the center of all of their work.

Several years ago I was in Minneapolis working with partners and stakeholders of the Northside Achievement Zone (NAZ), an organization focused on education outcomes from early learning through college and career. The work with NAZ was part of the Promise Neighborhoods results program—convened by the Annie E Casey Foundation and partners.[1] NAZ's primary population focus was on 1000 families living within a defined zone in that part of the city. On this particular day, a group of 30 partners and stakeholders—representing the school system, early learning centers, family engagement networks, and the housing, healthcare, and a variety of other sectors—were to come together for a daylong planning session. They were going to do the work that any group of results leaders would do—review their performance measures, targets, and strategies, and then implement any needed quality improvement measures.

Prior to listening to the call to action, this group of leaders engaged in a data walk and could see the fruits of the hard work that the NAZ team and their partners had produced in this community. The data showed that the NAZ kids consistently outperformed the children who lived outside the NAZ-defined boundary. Everyone had a right to be proud of that. Yet, there was another conversation these leaders were having as part of their data walk. While things seemed to be getting better for those who lived or went to school in the NAZ "footprint," there was a murmur about what was happening in the wider Northside region.

After the data walk, Sondra Samuels, the President and CEO of NAZ, delivered a passionate call to action to all present that named what was alive in the room that day. The Northside community had experienced a police shooting a few days earlier, and all were still in shock. Sondra spoke to the pain and the fear of community residents, and how that pain and fear manifested itself in a demonstration in front of the police department. She spoke to the urgency that everyone—including the police—felt as they acknowledged the need to work and engage in a different way. She concluded with a challenge to the leaders in the room to engage in a way that produced tangible results and created a sense of a better future for these residents of the north side of Minneapolis.

The work that day, as it is everyday for results leaders, was to take that passion and energy and convert it into meaningful action. These leaders could take pride in the intensive and powerful work that had happened for the 1000 families NAZ supported. They could also see the need to impact the greater Northside community of approximately 40,000 people. That day in Minneapolis, after Sondra's call to action and the authentic and emergent conversation about the circumstances that were alive in the Northside, I felt the need to bring the people of the community into the room, (metaphorically speaking), so I asked the leaders about them: Who were they? What were their lives like? People in the room started shouting out responses. Northsiders were diverse, creative, artistic, under-appreciated, misunderstood. They were also predominantly black or African American; many were poor with poverty that stretched across generations. Northsiders represented many successful people, too. Underlining it all, I heard, "A lot of us are Northsiders!"

I asked the group to explore why things were the way they were for the residents of the Northside. I asked them to drill down just a bit and identify what was contributing to the multi-generational poverty. Again the responses poured forth, and I recorded them on a whiteboard as quickly as they came: Disinvestment. Family mobility ("People are leaving"). No small business loans. No home loans. No new investments in any of their corridors. "We need to build out those businesses and invest in education and jobs." You could see disinvestment in the smallest things, like the lack of heated bus stops. "We are like Minnesota's stepchild."

Someone in the room wanted to talk about education and asked about outcomes for all the kids in the Northside. A grim set of statistics emerged. Maybe 30 percent of its kids were entering school ready to learn. Just 30 percent were at reading level by third grade. Only 64 percent graduated from high school. Many families were displaced, moving twice a year on average. Unemployment was between 10 and 15 percent, nearly twice the national average.

It was during this conversation that Sondra leaned over to talk to her Chief Operating Officer, Michelle Martin. They knew that to make a measurable difference for all the residents in Northside Minneapolis, there would need to big changes. They wondered if they and others were up to the task. They knew that one reason they had been successful in their NAZ neighborhood was the ability to use that funding to create structures and partnerships to support their own families, making their stakes somehow more personal and relevant.

In order to move to scale in the whole of the Northside, they would need to engage with partners and stakeholders with the result in the center and a commitment to aligned action. They wondered what it would take to make the needed changes to go to scale: the policy changes, the systems reform, the cross-sector organizational alignment, the community engagement, and the individual accountability in order to make progress.

Sometime during that meeting Sondra and Michelle stood up and reminded everyone in the room that no one agency, politician, or leader could create the result we all wanted to achieve. They said, "All of us have to be aligned to make a measurable difference. Are we willing to move together—to put the result in the center, to use the discipline of data, to engage in the collaborative work cycle—to see what we can create together?"

That day relationships were tested, trust was discussed, accountability was highlighted, and commitments were made. Not every partner in the room chose to engage with the others. Those who did identified the need to have a shared results action plan and do the heavy lifting to bring their organizations on board to create both High Action and High Alignment. Their journey to scope and scale for the whole of the Northside of Minneapolis, not just the 1000 families of NAZ, began.

I am reminded of that experience as I think about the work results leaders are engaged in all over the country. Now is the time for all leaders who are interested in confronting the complex public problems that concern them to take action. And it is not truly not a trivial pursuit to put results in the center of the work and engage in a space of High Action and High Alignment. Egos, turf, power, control, differing mental models and points of view—all of these conspire against us.

As I say to the results leaders who are my colleagues in this labor: Identify the ways this work connects to your values and purpose. Then do the hard work to engage differently with others and create a culture that intentionally supports results work and moves forward toward scope and scale. My friend and colleague, Kathy White, would often challenge the leaders with a particular quote: "Everyone has privilege. The question is, what are you doing with yours?" My challenge to leaders is to use their privilege to choose results!

ACKNOWLEDGEMENTS

Leadership is not a solitary act. Instead, as the saying goes, it is done with other consenting adults. So too, has been the work that provided the platform for me to write this book. The primary platform was provided by The Annie E Casey Foundation, with whom I have had a long partnership that provided a place from which to develop, test, experiment with, and implement many of the concepts you will find in this book. Donna Stark was an early champion of the Leadership In Action Programs (LAP) sponsored by Casey and instrumental in building on the successes of LAP to create a foundation for results-based leadership to emerge. Barbara Squires built upon the earlier results-based leadership programs to lead the effort to create Casey's current Results Count™ program. Most of my learning about results leadership stems from my work with Casey under the leadership of Donna and Barbara, and for that, I am truly grateful.

Jennifer Gross and Ashley Stewart provided great leadership in their roles at Casey, and helped test many of the concepts found in this book. Katie Norris, Maureen Pritchard, and Ann Jackson also worked as part of teams implementing Casey's programs and I deeply appreciate their work as project support. I've also had the benefit of working with great co-faculty in many of the leadership programs led by Casey, including, Angela Hendrix-Terry, Bill Shepardson, Marian Urquilla, Phyllis Rozanski, Kathy White, and Tom Gilmore—who are all thought leaders in their own right and great partners with whom to learn and practice. It would be difficult to name all the results leaders I worked with through the Casey Foundation without leaving out someone. Instead, I'll list the programs as a proxy: The Children and Family Fellowship, Atlanta Leaders for Results, Leadership Institute for State-Based Advocates, Skills to Accelerate Results (in partnership with the Department of Education's Promise Neighborhoods initiative), Child Health Leadership Network, and the JDAI Applied Leadership Network.

I appreciate my work with many other organizations and networks also and want to highlight one in particular: The John T. Gorman Foundation. Under the leadership of Tony Cipollone and Lauralee Raymond, the Foundation has led the efforts to bring results leadership to Maine. Thank you also to all the results leaders who have participated in the John T. Gorman Fellowship in order to practice these tools and methods and make a measurable difference in the lives of Mainers.

I must acknowledge two amazing individuals here also who had the scholarship and patience to instill inside me the discipline that was needed to produce results. First, Vicki Goddard-Truitt was instrumental in my learning how to hold results (and in the writing of this book). She provided coaching, lifted my spirits, and gave the needed feedback so I could get this book done. Thank you Vicki for your help and guidance.

Second, Jolie Bain Pillsbury needs special acknowledgement from me. She plays multiple roles in my life: teacher, mentor, coach, partner, friend, and guide. In many ways this book is co-authored with Jolie. It was Jolie who first challenged me to do the hard work required to make a measurable difference, supported me in my learning, and advocated for me so that I could become the results leader I wanted to be. I have never met anyone as powerful and gifted as Jolie. A thank-you and acknowledgment seems insufficient but is what I offer on these pages.

I also want to acknowledge the results leaders who are highlighted in this book and thank them for their direct contribution to making the book possible and bringing the concepts to life: Michael McAfee, Terri Clark, Carter Friend, Josh Davis, Deborah Moore, Carolyn Willis, Karin Scott, Jim Czarniak, Paola Maranan, JaNay Queen, Austin Dickson, Dave Newell, Dreama Gentry, Erica King, Sheila Weber, Rebecca Knudsen, Sondra Samuels, and Michelle Martin.

This book would not have been possible without the team that helped put it together. Sarah White, the book developer, helped me find my voice and navigate my shortcomings in order to get this book written and served as editor, coach, sage, and supporter. Will Fay was instrumental in getting the stories of the results leaders into the book, and Justin Frank helped me in the inner journey that was needed during the writing of this book.

Finally, I want to thank my wife and business partner, Patton Stephens. Patton had to endure the starts and stops of the writing, the endless complaining, and the time away from family in order to write. She was often the first reader and editor of the work, the chief supporter during the numerous times of doubt, and finally the lead mobilizer of action when it was most needed. As always, she is the person in the family who gets things done. As I often say, thank goodness Patton is in my life!

NEXT STEPS

Congratulations on reading *Choose Results!* As noted many places in the book, the best and only way to integrate results leadership skills and competencies in your work is to practice them day-to-day and over time. To support that learning, visit our book website to register and download all the application tools and worksheets referenced in the book. Please use them in real-life applications and as reference tools along the way:

http://ChooseResultsBook.com/resources.html

Two other websites may be of interest also as you integrate results leadership skills:

- The RBF Network website (www.rbfnetwork.com) provides information about Results Based Facilitation, a key set of competencies that support groups in implementing a results leadership framework and moving from talk to action.
- The Annie E Casey Foundation's Results Count™ website is nicely positioned to support emerging results leaders: (www.aecf.org/work/leadership-development/results-count/)

BIBLIOGRAPHY

Argyris, Chris. "Teaching Smart People How to Learn" (PDF). *Harvard Business* Review 4, no. 2 (1991). pds8.egloos.com/pds/200805/20/87/chris_argyris_learning.pdf

Austin, J. L. *How to Do Things with Words.* Cambridge: Harvard University Press, 1962.

Behn, Robert, D. "Innovative Governance in the 21st Century," The PerformanceStat Potential: A Leadership Strategy for Producing Results. Brookings/Ash Center Series, "Innovative Governance in the 21st Century," Brookings Institution Press, Washington, DC, 2014.

Brothers, Chalmers. *Language and the Pursuit of Happiness.* Naples, FL: New Possibilities Press, 2004. Kindle.

Conklin, E. Jeffrey, and William Weil. "Wicked Problems: Naming the Pain in Organizations." Group Decision Support Systems, 1997.

Conklin, Jeff. *Dialogue Mapping: Building Shared Understanding of Wicked Problems.* Chichester, UK: John Wiley & Sons, 2005.

Flores, Fernando. *Conversations for Action and Collected Essays: Instilling a Culture of Commitment in Working Relationships.* San Francisco: Printed by CreateSpace, 2012. Kindle.

Forman, John P., and Laurel A. Ross. "Integral Leadership: The Next Half-Step." SUNY series in Integral Theory/2013-04-18, Albany, NY, 2013. Kindle.

Friedman, Mark. *Results Based Accountability.* Santa Fe, New Mexico: Parse Publishing, 2009.

Friedman, Mark. *Trying Hard Is Not Good Enough: 10th Anniversary Edition: How to Produce Measurable Improvements in Customers and Communities.* 3rd ed., Santa Fe, NM: Printed by CreateSpace, 2015.

Goodman, M. "The Iceberg Model." Hopkinton, MA: Innovation Associates Organizational Learning. 2002. PDF.

Green, Zachary Gabriel, and René J. Molenkamp. "The BART System of Group and Organizational Analysis Boundary, Authority, Role and Task." Unpublished paper, 2005. Available at www.it.uu.se/edu/course/homepage/projektDV/ht09/BART_Green_Molenkamp.pdf

Haselton, M. G., Nettle, D., & Andrews, P. W. *The Handbook of Evolutionary Psychology,* Hoboken, D. M. Buss (Ed.). NJ: John Wiley & Sons Inc, 2005.

Hayden, Charla and Rene Molenkamp. "Tavistock Primer II," AK Rice Institute for Study of Social Systems, 2002. PDF

Hayes, Christopher. *Twilight of the Elites: America after Meritocracy.* New York: Broadway Books, 2013.

Heath, Chip and Dan. *Made to Stick.* NY: Random House, 2007.

Heifetz, Ronald, Alexander Grashow, and Marty Linsky. *The Practice of Adaptive Leadership: Tools and Tactics for Changing Your Organization and the World.* Cambridge: Harvard Business School. 2009.

Heifetz, Ronald A.; Linsky, Marty. *Leadership on the Line: Staying Alive Through the Dangers of Leading.* Perseus Books Group. Kindle. 2002.

Kahneman, Daniel. *Thinking, Fast and Slow.* New York: Farrar, Straus and Giroux, 2011.

Kirwan Institute for the Study of Race and Ethnicity, "Understanding Implicit Bias," Ohio State University. PDF.

Kling, Arnold. *The Three Languages of Politics: Talking across the Political Divides.* Washington, DC: Cato Institute, 2017. Kindle.

Luke, Jeffrey S. *Catalytic Leadership: Strategies for an Interconnected World.* San Francisco: Jossey-Bass, 1998. Kindle.

McLeod, Saul on the website: Simply Psychology, simplypsychology.org/qualitative-quantitative.html. Originally published 2008; updated 2017.

Meadows, Donella. "Leverage Points: Places to Intervene in a System." The Donella Meadows Archives, Norwich, VT, 1999. donellameadows.org/archives/leverage-points-places-to-intervene-in-a-system/

National Scientific Council on the Developing Child. *Supportive Relationships and Active Skill-Building Strengthen the Foundations of Resilience: Working Paper 13*. Cambridge, MA. 2015. www.developingchild.harvard.edu

O'Brien, J., Littlefield, J. & Goddard-Truitt . "A Matter of Leadership: Connecting a Grantmaker's Investments in Collaborative Leadership Development to Community Results." *The Foundation Review,* Vol. 5: Iss. 1, Article 4. Grand Valley State University, Allendale, MI. 2013.

Olalla, Julio and Ralph Echeverria. *Learning to Learn.* Newfield Network, 2004.

Oyserman, Daphna. "Psychology of Values," *International Encyclopedia of the Social & Behavioral Sciences,* Second Edition, Vol. 25. Oxford: Elsevier. 2015.

Panzar, John, C. and Robert D. Willig, "Economies of Scope," *American Economic Review,* May 1981.

Peschl, M.F. "Triple-loop learning as foundation for profound change, individual cultivation, and radical innovation." Construction processes beyond scientific and rational knowledge. *Constructivist Foundations* 2(2-3). 2007. Available at www.univie.ac.at/constructivism/journal/.

Pillsbury, Jolie Bain, PhD, *Results Based Facilitation Book Two: Advanced Skills—2nd Edition: Moving from Talk to Action.* Sherbrooke Consulting Inc. 2016.

Pillsbury, Jolie Bain, PhD, *Results Based Facilitation: Book One: Foundation Skills.* Sherbrooke Consulting Inc. 2015.

Pillsbury, Jolie Bain, PhD; edited by Vicki Goddard-Truitt, Ph.D. *The Theory of Aligned Contributions: An Emerging Theory of Change Primer.* Sherbrooke Consulting, Inc. 2016.

Pizlo, Zygmunt, Joshi, Anupam, and Graham, Scott, M. "Problem Solving in Human Beings and Computers", (formerly "Heuristic Problem Solving)", Computer Science Technical Reports: Paper 1174. Purdue University. 1994.

Roser, Max. "Our World in Data," ourworldindata.org

Roy, Arundhati, *War Talk*. South End Press: First edition, 2003.

Ruiz, Don Miguel. *The Four Agreements*. Amber-Allen Publishing, Inc., 2010. Kindle.

Senge, Peter. *The Fifth Discipline: The Art and Practice of the Learning Organization,* 1st Ed. NY: Doubleday. 2006.

Solomon, Robert C.; Flores, Fernando. *Building Trust: In Business, Politics, Relationships, and Life.* Oxford University Press. Kindle. 2001.

Stephens, Patton. *Creating a Container to Achieve Results: A Guide for Leaders, Teams, Project Managers, and More!.* Printed by CreateSpace. 2014.

Thaler, Richard H., and Cass R. Sunstein. *Nudge*. New Haven, CT: Yale University Press, 2008.

Ward, Kate. "Mental Models: The Key to Making Reality-Based Decisions." West Chester, PA: HRDQ Skills Development. Kindle.

West, Geoffrey. Scale: *The Universal Laws of Life and Death in Organisms, Cities, and Companies.* Penguin Press; First Edition. 2017.

Wilber, Ken. "Introduction to Integral Theory and Practice: IOS Basic and the AQAL Map." *AQAL Journal of Integral Theory and Practice* 1, no. 3 Spring 2005 PDF

Zachariah, Ellis. "Shared Leadership and the Creation and Maintenance of a Holding Environment," presentation at Academy of Religions Leadership, Chicago, IL. Undated. PDF

NOTES

Preface

1. Luke, Jeffrey S. *Catalytic Leadership: Strategies for an Interconnected World.* San Francisco: Jossey-Bass, 1998. Kindle.
2. Pizlo, Zygmunt, Anupam Joshi, and Scott M. Graham. "Problem Solving in Human Beings and Computers (formerly: Heuristic Problem Solving)." Department of Computer Science Technical Reports: Paper 1174, Purdue University, West Lafayette, IN, 1994. docs.lib.purdue.edu/cstech/1174.

Introduction

1. Pillsbury, Jolie Bain. *Results Based Facilitation: Book One – Foundation Skills.* Arlington, VA: Sherbrooke Consulting, 2008, and Pillsbury, Jolie Bain. *Results Based Facilitation: Book Two – Advanced Skills.* 2nd ed. Arlington, VA: Sherbrooke Consulting, 2008.
2. To read more about Mark Friedman's work, see Results Based Accountability. Santa Fe, NM: PARSE Publishing, 2009.
3. Wilber, Ken. "Introduction to Integral Theory and Practice: IOS Basic and the *AQAL Map.*" *AQAL Journal of Integral Theory and Practice* 1, no. 3 (Spring 2005): pp. 25–27.
4. To read more about Julio Olalla's work, visit the Newfield Network website: newfieldnetwork.com
5. Austin, J. L. *How to Do Things with Words.* Cambridge: Harvard University Press, 1962.
6. Results Count™ is an official trademark of the Annie E. Casey Foundation, www.aecf.org/work/leadership-development/results-count/

Chapter 1: The Kinds of Problems Results Leaders Face

1. Hayes, Christopher. *Twilight of the Elites: America after Meritocracy.* New York: Broadway Paperbacks, 2013. p. 102.

2. The Promise Neighborhoods program is authorized under the Elementary and Secondary Education Act of 1965 (ESEA) as amended by the Every Student Succeeds Act (ESSA). See innovation.ed.gov/what-we-do/parental-options/promise-neighborhoods-pn/
3. "Indianola, Mississippi (MS) Poverty Rate Data." City-Data.com. www.city-data.com/poverty/poverty-Indianola-Mississippi.html, and Semega, Jessica L., Kayla R. Fontenot, and Melissa A. Kollar. "Income and Poverty in the United States: 2016," Report Number: P60-259, United States Census Bureau, U.S. Department of Commerce, Washington, DC, 2017. www.census.gov/library/publications/2017/demo/p60-259.html
4. Luke, Jeffrey S. *Catalytic Leadership: Strategies for an Interconnected World.* San Francisco: Jossey-Bass, 1998. Kindle.
5. Ibid.
6. Denning, Peter J., "Resolving Wicked Problems through Collaboration." Chap. 11 in *Handbook of Research on Socio-Technical Design and Social Networking Systems.* Hershey, PA: Information Science Reference, 2009.
7. Conklin, E. Jeffrey, and William Weil. "Wicked Problems: Naming the Pain in Organizations." Group Decision Support Systems, 1997. www.leanconstruction.dk/media/17537/Wicked_Problems__Naming_the_Pain_in_Organizations_.pdf
8. Heifetz, Ronald A., and Marty Linsky. *Leadership on the Line: Staying Alive through the Dangers of Leading.* Perseus Books Group, New York, 2002. Kindle edition, location 14.
9. The Campaign is a national collaborative effort focused on ensuring that more children from low-income families succeed in school and graduate prepared for college, a career, and active citizenship. The Campaign focuses on an important predictor of school success and high school graduation: grade-level reading by the end of third grade. For more information, visit gradelevelreading.net
10. Conklin, Jeff. *Dialogue Mapping: Building Shared Understanding of Wicked Problems.* Chichester, UK: John Wiley & Sons, 2005. Kindle edition, location 220.
11. Ibid.

Chapter 2: Aligned Contributions—From Fragmentation to Shared Accountability

1. Pillsbury, Jolie Bain. *Theory of Aligned Contributions: An Emerging Theory of Change* Primer. Arlington, VA: Sherbrooke Consulting, 2008. www.sherbrookeconsulting.com/products/TOAC.pdf
2. Ibid.
3. The Juvenile Detention Alternatives Initiative is designed to reduce reliance on local confinement of court-involved youth. www.aecf.org/work/juvenile-justice/jdai/
4. Luke, Jeffrey S. *Catalytic Leadership: Strategies for an Interconnected World.* San Francisco: Jossey-Bass, 1998. Kindle edition.
5. Ibid.
6. Friedman, Mark. *Trying Hard Is Not Good Enough: 10th Anniversary Edition: How to Produce Measurable Improvements in Customers and Communities.* 3rd ed. Santa Fe, NM: Printed by CreateSpace, 2015. p. 19
7. Friedman, Mark. *Trying Hard Is Not Good Enough.* Santa Fe, NM: Printed by CreateSpace, 2015. Kindle edition, location 19.
8. Friedman, Mark. *Trying Hard Is Not Good Enough: 10th Anniversary Edition: How to Produce Measurable Improvements in Customers and Communities.* 3rd ed. Santa Fe, NM: Printed by CreateSpace, 2015. pp. 19–20.
9. Ibid. Kindle edition, location 20.
10. Pillsbury in conversation with the author.
11. Pillsbury, *Theory of Aligned Contributions: An Emerging Theory of Change Primer.* Arlington, VA: Sherbrooke Consulting, 2008. www.sherbrookeconsulting.com/products/TOAC.pdf

Chapter 3: Moving Toward Execution—The Results Action Plan

1. For more information on qualitative and quantitative data (updated in 2017), see Saul McLeod's work on the Simply Psychology website: simplypsychology.org/qualitative-quantitative.html
2. Ibid.
3. Mark Friedman's book offers a step-by-step process to engage in a factor analysis. Friedman, Mark. *Trying Hard Is Not Good Enough.* Appendix E., Santa Fe, NM: Printed by BookSurge Publishing, 2009. Kindle edition, location 156.
4. Ibid.

5. Friedman, Mark. *Trying Hard is Not Good Enough.* Santa Fe, NM: Printed by BookSurge Publishing, 2009. Kindle edition, location 20.
6. Members of the Promise Neighborhood implementation team included representatives from the Annie E. Casey Foundation, the U.S. Department of Education, the Center for Study of Social Policy, and the Promise Neighborhood Institute.

Chapter 4: "Me"—Leader Readiness and Working on the Self

1. Oyserman, Daphna. "Psychology of Values." In *International Encyclopedia of the Social & Behavioral Sciences,* edited by James Wright. 2nd ed. Amsterdam, Netherlands: Elsevier, 2015. pp. 36–40.
2. Ibid.
3. Forman, John P., and Laurel A. Ross. "Integral Leadership: The Next Half-Step." SUNY series in Integral Theory/2013-04-18, Albany, NY, 2013. Kindle edition, locations 515–20.
4. Senge, Peter M. *The Fifth Discipline: The Art and Practice of the Learning Organization.* pp. 174–75. New York: Doubleday, 2006.
5. Ward, Kate. "Mental Models: The Key to Making Reality-Based Decisions." West Chester, PA: HRDQ Skills Development. Kindle edition, locations 85–88.
6. For more information, see Kahneman, Daniel. *Thinking, Fast and Slow.* New York: Farrar, Straus and Giroux, 2011. See also Thaler, Richard H., and Cass R. Sunstein. Nudge. New Haven, CT: Yale University Press, 2008.
7. Haselton, M. G., D. Nettle, & P. W. Andrews. "The Evolution of Cognitive Bias." In *The Handbook of Evolutionary Psychology,* edited by D. M. Buss. Hoboken, NJ: John Wiley & Sons, 2005. pp. 724–46.
8. "Understanding Implicit Bias." Kirwan Institute for the Study of Race and Ethnicity, Ohio State University, Columbus, OH, 2015. kirwaninstitute.osu.edu/research/understanding-implicit-bias/
9. "Study: Teachers' 'Implicit Bias' Starts in Preschool," USA Today (New York), September 28, 2016. www.usatoday.com/story/news/2016/09/28/study-teachers-implicit-bias-starts-preschool/91179538/
10. Kling, Arnold. *The Three Languages of Politics: Talking across the Political Divides.* Washington, DC: Cato Institute, 2017. Kindle edition, locations 51–57.
11. Ibid.

12. See learning cycles developed by Kurt Lewin, David Kolb, and Peter Honey/Alan Mumford as examples.
13. Peschl, M. F. "Triple-loop Learning as Foundation for Profound Change, Individual Cultivation, and Radical Innovation. Construction Processes beyond Scientific and Rational Knowledge." *Constructivist Foundations* 2, no. 2–3 (2007): pp. 136–45.
14. Argyris, Chris. (1991). "Teaching Smart People How to Learn" (PDF). *Harvard Business Review* 4, no. 2 (1991): pp. 99–109.
15. Adapted from the article: Olalla, Julio, and Rafael Echeverria. "Learning to Learn." Niwot, CO: Newfield Network, 2004. www.newfieldnetwork.com

Chapter 5: "Me with You"—Work Group Readiness

1. The Annie E. Casey Foundation's Leadership in Action Program (LAP) is a results-based leadership development project designed to build the capacity of high- and midlevel public agency leaders and their community partners.
2. Ruiz, Don Miguel. *The Four Agreements: A Practical Guide to Personal Freedom.* San Rafael, CA: Amber-Allen Publishing, 2010. Kindle edition, locations 349–50, 392–94.
3. Material on Requests and Offers comes from the frame of Speech Acts. I draw on the work of John Searle, J. L Austin, Fernando Flores, and Julio Olalla, among others.
4. Newfield Network. Adapted from Speech Acts II: Declarations, Requests, Promises And Offers. Unpublished article, 2000.
5. Brothers, Chalmers. *Language and the Pursuit of Happiness: A New Foundation for Designing Your Life, Your Relationships and Your Results.* Naples, FL: New Possibilities Press, 2004. Kindle edition, location 246.
6. "Achieving Results with Collaboratives: Strategies for Helping Collaborative Leaders Hold Themselves and Each Other Accountable for Action." A Research Brief, The Results Based Leadership Collaborative at The University of Maryland School of Public Policy, College Park, MD, 2011. www.alaeditions.org/files/Stoltz_Inspired_WE/Stoltz_WebExtraC.pdf
7. O'Brien, Julia D., Jennifer N. Littlefield, and Victoria Goddard-Truitt. "A Matter of Leadership: Connecting a Grantmaker's Investments in Collaborative Leadership Development to

Community Results." *The Foundation Review*, 5, no. 1 (2013): pp. 26–42.
8. Flores, Fernando. *Conversations for Action and Collected Essays: Instilling a Culture of Commitment in Working Relationships.* San Francisco: Printed by CreateSpace, 2012. Kindle edition, location 4.
9. L. J. Austin developed Speech Act Theory. Many thinkers, including John Searle and Fernando Flores, have enhanced this theory.
10. Green, Zachary Gabriel, and René J. Molenkamp. "The BART System of Group and Organizational Analysis: Boundary, Authority, Role and Task." Unpublished paper, December 2005.
11. Ibid., p. 6.
12. "Supportive Relationships and Active Skill-Building Strengthen the Foundations of Resilience." Working Paper No. 13. Center on the Developing Child, Harvard University, Cambridge, MA, 2015. developingchild.harvard.edu
13. This work on trust comes from the important distinctions offered by Fernando Flores and added to by Julio Olalla. See Bibliography.
14. Flores, Fernando. *Conversations for Action and Collected Essays: Instilling a Culture of Commitment in Working Relationships.* San Francisco: Printed by CreateSpace, 2012. Kindle edition, location 70.

Chapter 6: "Us"—Creating a Results Culture

1. Pillsbury, Jolie Bain. *Results Based Facilitation: Book Two – Advanced Skills – 2nd Edition: Moving from Talk to Action.* Arlington, VA: Sherbrooke Consulting, 2016. Kindle edition, locations 2336–37.
2. Ibid, 662–63.
3. Hayden, Charla, and René J. Molenkamp. *Tavistock Primer II.* Portland, OR: A. K. Rice Institute for the Study of Social Systems, 2002. p. 7.
4. McRae, Mary B., and Ellen L. Short. *Racial and Cultural Dynamics in Group and Organizational Life: Crossing Boundaries.* p. 133. Thousand Oaks, CA: SAGE Publications, 2009.
5. Heifetz, Ronald, Alexander Grashow, and Marty Linsky. *The Practice of Adaptive Leadership: Tools and Tactics for Changing Your Organization and the World.* Boston: Harvard Business School, 2009. Kindle edition, locations 1530–31.

6. Modified from the work of Behn, Robert D. "The PerformanceStat Potential: A Leadership Strategy for Producing Results." Brookings/Ash Center Series, "Innovative Governance in the 21st Century," Brookings Institution Press, Washington, DC, 2014. pp. 261–81.
7. Heifetz, Ronald, Alexander Grashow, and Marty Linsky. *The Practice of Adaptive Leadership: Tools and Tactics for Changing Your Organization and the World.* Boston: Harvard Business School. 2009. Kindle edition, locations 1543–55.
8. For more on a holding environment, see the work of Winnicott, Donald W. *The Child, the Family, and the Outside World.* New York: Perseus Books, 1992.
9. Patton Stephens. *Creating the Container to Achieve Results: A Guide for Leaders, Teams, Project Managers, and More!* Silver Springs, MD: Printed by CreateSpace, 2014. p. 2.
10. *Poetry Behind the Walls (PBW)* is the only ongoing journal in the world dedicated to writings from incarcerated youth. PBW is a collaborative project of Save the Kids, Le Moyne College's Center for Urban and Regional Applied Research, SUNY Cortland's Criminology Department, the journal Social Advocacy and Systems Change, and Hillbrook Youth Detention Center. "Ronny." Poetry Behind the Walls 3, no. 1 (Winter 2010).
11. For more on a holding environment, see the work of Winnicott, Donald W. *The Child, the Family, and the Outside World.* 2nd edition. New York: Perseus Books, 1992.
12. Heifetz, Ronald A., and Marty Linsky. *Leadership on the Line: Staying Alive through the Dangers of Leading.* New York: Perseus Books, 2002. Kindle location 102.
13. Ellis, Zachariah. "Shared Leadership and the Creation and Maintenance of a Holding Environment." *Journal Discernment: Theology and the Practice of Ministry* 3, no. 2 (2017): p. 6.
14. Excerpts reprinted with permission from Pillsbury, Jolie Bain. *Results Based Facilitation: Book Two – Advanced Skills – 2nd Edition: Moving from Talk to Action, An Introduction,* Arlington, VA: Sherbrooke Consulting, 2013.
15. Pillsbury, Jolie Bain. *Results Based Facilitation: An Introduction: 2nd Edition: Moving from Talk to Action.* Arlington, VA: Sherbrooke Consulting, 2015. Kindle locations 140–43.
16. Pillsbury, Jolie Bain. *Results Based Facilitation: Book Two - Advanced Skills - 2nd Edition: Moving from talk to action.* Arlington, VA: Sherbrooke Consulting, 2015 (Kindle Locations 2328-2331).
17. Children and Family Fellowship: http://www.aecf.org/work/leadership-development/children-and-family-fellowship/

18. Heath, Chip, and Heath, Dan. *Made to Stick: Why Some Ideas Survive and Others Die.* New York: Random House, 2007. pp. 253–56.
19. Members of the Promise Neighborhoods implementation team included representatives from the Annie E. Casey Foundation, the U.S. Department of Education, the Center for Study of Social Policy, and the Promise Neighborhoods Institute.

Chapter 7: "Us in the World"—Working Toward Scope and Scale

1. Annie E. Casey Foundation, The. "Indiana Results-Based Leadership: Helping Ex-Offenders Turn Their Lives Around in Marion County, Indiana." The Annie E. Casey Foundation, Baltimore, MD, 2010. http://www.aecf.org/resources/indiana-results-based-leadership/
2. Panzar, John C., and Robert D. Willig. "Economies of Scope." *American Economic Review* 71, no. 2 (May 1981): pp. 268–72.
3. West, Geoffrey. Scale: *The Universal Laws of Life, Growth and Death in Organisms, Cities and Companies.* New York: Penguin Press, 2017.
4. This quote is attributed to W. Edwards Deming, American professor and management consultant.
5. Goodman, M. "Systems Thinking: What, Why, When, Where, And How?" *The Systems Thinker* 8, no. 2 (March 1997): p. 2.
6. Meadows, Donella. "Leverage Points: Places to Intervene in a System." The Donella Meadows Archives, Norwich, VT, 1999. p. 1. donellameadows.org/archives/leverage-points-places-to-intervene-in-a-system/.
7. For more information see The National Implementation Research Network's Active Implementation Hub, http://implementation.fpg.unc.edu/module-1
8. Shakespeare, William. Macbeth, Act V, Scene 5. shakespeare.mit.edu/macbeth/full.html

Call to Action

1. Members of the Promise Neighborhoods implementation team included representatives from the Annie E. Casey Foundation, the U.S. Department of Education, the Center for Study of Social Policy, and the Promise Neighborhood Institute.